T0280993

Pro Vagrant

Włodzimierz Gajda

Apress®

Pro Vagrant

Copyright © 2015 by Włodzimierz Gajda

This work is subject to copyright. All rights are reserved by the Publisher, whether the whole or part of the material is concerned, specifically the rights of translation, reprinting, reuse of illustrations, recitation, broadcasting, reproduction on microfilms or in any other physical way, and transmission or information storage and retrieval, electronic adaptation, computer software, or by similar or dissimilar methodology now known or hereafter developed. Exempted from this legal reservation are brief excerpts in connection with reviews or scholarly analysis or material supplied specifically for the purpose of being entered and executed on a computer system, for exclusive use by the purchaser of the work. Duplication of this publication or parts thereof is permitted only under the provisions of the Copyright Law of the Publisher's location, in its current version, and permission for use must always be obtained from Springer. Permissions for use may be obtained through RightsLink at the Copyright Clearance Center. Violations are liable to prosecution under the respective Copyright Law.

ISBN-13 (pbk): 978-1-4842-0074-2

ISBN-13 (electronic): 978-1-4842-0073-5

Trademarked names, logos, and images may appear in this book. Rather than use a trademark symbol with every occurrence of a trademarked name, logo, or image we use the names, logos, and images only in an editorial fashion and to the benefit of the trademark owner, with no intention of infringement of the trademark.

The use in this publication of trade names, trademarks, service marks, and similar terms, even if they are not identified as such, is not to be taken as an expression of opinion as to whether or not they are subject to proprietary rights.

While the advice and information in this book are believed to be true and accurate at the date of publication, neither the authors nor the editors nor the publisher can accept any legal responsibility for any errors or omissions that may be made. The publisher makes no warranty, express or implied, with respect to the material contained herein.

Managing Director: Welmoed Spahr
Lead Editor: Louise Corrigan
Technical Reviewer: Tyler Merry
Editorial Board: Steve Anglin, Mark Beckner, Gary Cornell, Louise Corrigan, Jim DeWolf,
    Jonathan Gennick, Robert Hutchinson, Michelle Lowman, James Markham, Susan McDermott,
    Matthew Moodie, Jeffrey Pepper, Douglas Pundick, Ben Renow-Clarke, Gwenan Spearing,
    Matt Wade, Steve Weis
Coordinating Editor: Christine Ricketts
Copy Editor: Nancy Sixsmith
Compositor: SPi Global
Indexer: SPi Globa
Artist: SPi Global

Distributed to the book trade worldwide by Springer Science+Business Media New York, 233 Spring Street, 6th Floor, New York, NY 10013. Phone 1-800-SPRINGER, fax (201) 348-4505, e-mail orders-ny@springer-sbm.com, or visit www.springeronline.com. Apress Media, LLC is a California LLC and the sole member (owner) is Springer Science + Business Media Finance Inc (SSBM Finance Inc). SSBM Finance Inc is a Delaware corporation.

For information on translations, please e-mail rights@apress.com, or visit www.apress.com.

Apress and friends of ED books may be purchased in bulk for academic, corporate, or promotional use. eBook versions and licenses are also available for most titles. For more information, reference our Special Bulk Sales–eBook Licensing web page at www.apress.com/bulk-sales.

Any source code or other supplementary material referenced by the author in this text is available to readers at www.apress.com. For detailed information about how to locate your book's source code, go to www.apress.com/source-code/.

For Beata

Contents at a Glance

Contents

About the Author

Włodzimierz Gajda is an experienced trainer and a highly passionate teacher. During the last 20 years, he has conducted numerous courses on various subjects, ranging from programming in C language and TCP/IP networking to building LEGO robots and developing web applications with PHP. Włodzimierz is currently employed at the Institute of Mathematics and Computer Science, John Paul II Catholic University of Lublin. His preferred leisure activities are trekking in the Tatra Mountains and playing the blues (http://www.youtube.com/user/gajdaw). He lives with his wife and three children in Lublin, Poland.

Włodzimierz provides training all over Europe on various topics, including Vagrant, git, PHP, Symfony, TDD, and BDD. You can contact him by e-mail at: gajdaw@gajdaw.pl.

About the Technical Reviewer

Tyler Merry is a UX Technologist for Universal Mind, where his focus is on bridging the gap between idea and implementation. Tyler approaches all problems through the filter of experimentation. He believes that the fastest and most accurate solution is working provocatively through multiple experiments and informal testing.

Through past work experiences with Coke, Sony, Pfizer, P&G, Ford, and Vail Resorts, Tyler has learned the value of accuracy and communication. His work with early startups helped to reinforce the value of iteration, speed, and efficiency.

When not keeping uptodate with web and UX trends, Tyler spends his time on his fewer-than-four-wheeled-vehicles (bicycle, motorcycle, unicycle) or learning whatever skill catches his fancy for the day: knitting, photography, or juggling, for example.

Acknowledgments

First and foremost, I want to thank all the authors of the software this book describes. My sincere thanks go to Mr. Mitchell Hashimoto and all the contributors at Vagrant and Packer. I am also very indebted to Oracle for its VM VirtualBox product; and to Puppet Labs, Chef Software, and Ansible for their provisioners.

Thanks to Ubuntu, Chef Software, and HashiCorp for their boxes available at `atlas.hashicorp.com`; and to Chef Software, Mischa Taylor, and Anna Moujan for their `chef/bento` and `boxcutter/ubuntu` products.

Because git plays an important role in the way I handle my boxes, I also want to express my gratitude to git authors Linus Torvalds and Junio Hamano, and to the whole git community.

The staff of Apress has done an outstanding job during the production of this book. I want to thank

- Michelle Lowman and James Markham for their confidence
- Christine Ricketts for her constant support and patience
- Louise Corrigan for handing the initial stage of the project
- Nancy Sixsmith for copy editing
- And Kumar Dhaneesh for his work on my manuscript

My special thanks go to technical reviewer Tyler Merry who helped me get the book into its final shape. Thanks, Tyler!

—Włodzimierz Gajda
Lublin, Poland
April 28, 2015

■ ■ ■

## CHAPTER 1

Getting Started with Vagrant

This chapter introduces Vagrant, the tool you want to master. We start with a short description of Vagrant: its role and why you should learn it in the first place. To fully appreciate its benefits, we will analyze the current approaches to set up a development environment for a web application. After summarizing the problems with traditional methods, we will discuss how virtualization can help resolve various issues. With a clear image of the virtual approach, we will demonstrate the simplicity offered by Vagrant. Then we will proceed with the installation of the software; finally, you will take a look at the built-in manual and the Vagrant documentation. The pros of using Vagrant that you will learn here should convince you to give Vagrant a try.

What Is Vagrant?

Vagrant is a tool that simplifies the workflow and reduces the workload necessary to run and operate virtual machines (VMs) on your computer. It also does the following:

- Offers a very simple command-line interface to manage VMs

- Supports all major virtual solutions: VirtualBox, VMWare, and Hyper-V

- Supports most popular software configuration tools, including Ansible, Chef, Puppet, and Salt

- Facilitates procedures to distribute and share virtual environments

Vagrant shines when it is used for web applications but is not restricted to this particular task. It should be considered a general-purpose tool to work with VMs. If you have any previous experience with virtualization, you will be amazed by the simplified workflow offered by Vagrant. If virtual solutions are something that you have not tried yet, you will be surprised by the opportunities Vagrant offers.

Vagrant provides a simple and uniform command-line interface. You can think of it as the way to standardize the workflow when using VMs. No matter which virtualization solution you use or how intricate your virtual environment might be, Vagrant will boot your VM (or VMs) with just one command:

```
$ vagrant up
```

This single command is the most fundamental and important feature of Vagrant and it is all your team members need to know to proceed with their work. You might be working with VirtualBox, VMWare, Hyper-V, or any other virtual platform. Your application can be written in arbitrary languages and frameworks, such as Ruby/Ruby on Rails, Python/Django or PHP/Symfony. You might use arbitrary operating systems (OSs) to deploy your application: Linux, FreeBSD, or Windows. All these details are of no importance because (thanks to Vagrant) the complete virtual environment can be brought to life with just one command:

```
$ vagrant up
```

If you were to run the virtual development environment manually — without Vagrant's help, that is — you would have to follow these steps:

1. Download the VM image.

2. Start the VM.

3. Configure the VM's shared directories and network interfaces.

4. Maybe install some software within the VM.

With Vagrant, all these tasks (and many more) are automated. The command $ vagrant up can do the following (depending on the configuration file):

- Automatically download and install a VM, if necessary

- Boot the VM

- Configure various resources: RAM, CPUs, network connections, and shared folders

- Install additional software within the VM by using tools such as Puppet, Chef, Ansible, and Salt

---

■ **Note**   Vagrant is a tool that provides a simple and unified command-line interface to work with VMs managed by well-known virtualization solutions such as VirtualBox, VMWare, and Hyper-V.

Although Vagrant is a general-purpose tool and can be used in many different ways, the easiest way to learn about its features is to adopt it for web development (because of the nature of web applications, which have front ends and back ends).

The next three sections discuss the background knowledge you need about the following:

- The nature of web applications and the problems that accompany setting up a development environment for a web application

- Traditional methods for setting up development environments for web applications

- Virtualization

Client/Server Paradigm and its Aftermath

The dual nature of web applications imposes difficulties that can turn the task of setting up a development environment into a chore. Web applications work on the basis of the client/server paradigm, using the HTTP protocol for communication purposes. When you run the application, it consists of two communicating parties: the client, which is the process that sends requests; and the server, which is the process responsible for responding.

The very nature of the application is to enable the client and server to be run on different machines, usually equipped with different hardware and OSs. The client is the process that is being executed on your laptop, and the server is the process that runs on a remote machine accessible through the network. This setting is depicted in Figure 1-1.

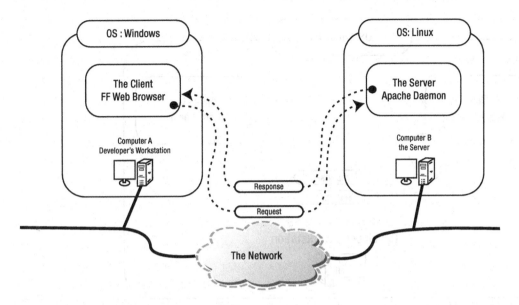

Figure 1-1. *A web application in action*

Figure 1-1 shows two different computers using two different OSs: Windows and Linux. The client is the Firefox web browser running on Windows; the server is the Apache daemon executed on the Linux machine. The consequence of the client/server paradigm is that the application consists of two different pieces of code: the code that runs on the client and the code that runs on the server. A developer who works on the application needs (at least sometimes) to run and access the client-side code as well as the server-side code.

■ **Note**   The two ingredients of a web application are commonly referred to as the *front end* and *back end*. The front end is executed within a web browser on the client side; the back end runs on the server side.

Traditional Approach to Setting up a Developer Environment

There are two ways to set up a development environment. In the first, both the client and server processes are run on the same machine; in the second, the client and server run on different computers.

The first solution is shown in Figure 1-2. The developer installs all the software on the workstation, and the front and back ends run locally. The source code of the application is stored on the developer machine's hard drive.

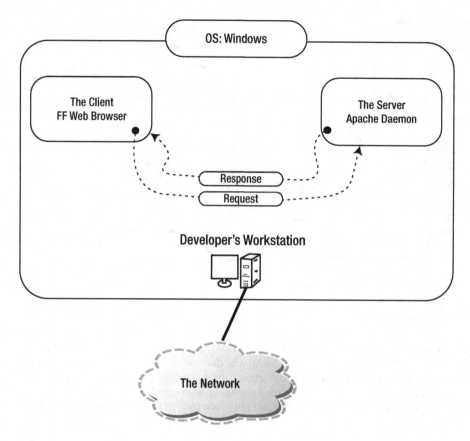

Figure 1-2. *Development environment: the client and the server run on the same machine as the processes of the same OSs*

The second approach, the one in which the client and the server run on different machines, imitates the way the deployed application is executed by end users. The client-side software runs on the developer's workstation, and the server-side software runs on a remote machine. The source code of the application is stored on remote machine and, depending on preferences, the developer can do the following:

- Synchronize the files from within the integrated development environment (IDE), as shown in Figure 1-3.

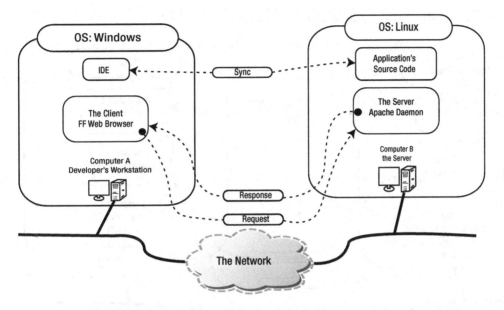

Figure 1-3. *Development environment: the client and the server run on different machines; the application's source code is synchronized within the IDE*

- Access the source with the terminal (e.g., SSH/vi), as shown in Figure 1-4.

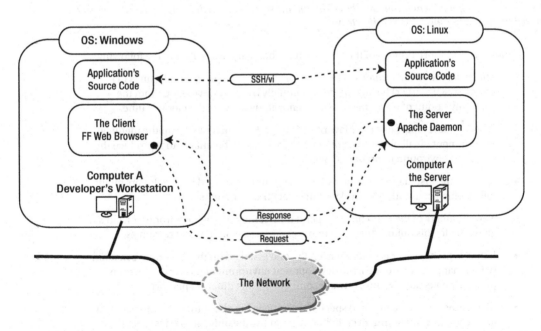

Figure 1-4. *Development environment: the client and the server run on different machines; the source code is accessed via a terminal session SSH/vi*

- Emulate local access with drive mapping (see Figure 1-5)

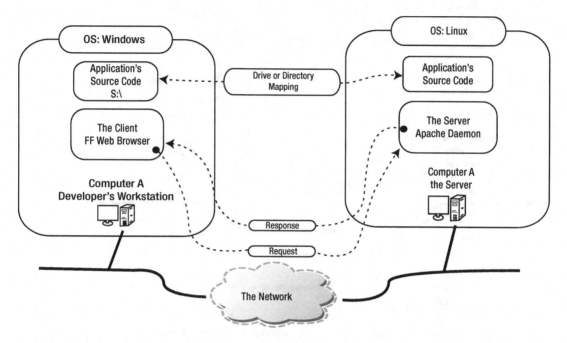

Figure 1-5. *Development environment: the client and the server run on different machines; the source code is accessed through a mapped drive or directory*

The most evident shortcomings of the first solution shown in Figure 1-2 are the following:

- The installation and updates of the server-side software (for example, an HTTP server or SQL Server) have to be done manually by every developer. From the company's point of view, this can be an enormous waste of developers' time.

- When all developers use their favorite OS, it can be difficult to set up the identical environment on all platforms. Some developers might be unable to reproduce the complete environment on their machines.

- Because the installation is done by hand, environments used by developers might differ, which can lead to "it works on my machine" problems.

- New members of the team have to spend time setting up their environment. On a global scale, this onboarding is an unnecessary waste of time and resources.

- If the OS of the server is different from the one installed on the developer's machine (which happens very often), the development environment always differs from production because it runs software compiled for the different platform.

- All members of the team need specialized knowledge about the software necessary for the application to run. Even if they are responsible only for the design of the application and don't take part in development, they still have to know how to install and configure everything. So it can be difficult for designers to install all packages required by the back end.

- Developers who work on multiple projects at the same time can have problems because one development environment is shared by different projects. For example, one project might be designed to work under settings (e.g., PHP 5.3) different from other project (e.g., PHP 5.5). The projects are not separated from each other: they share compilers, interpreters, and tools installed on the host system.

- With multiple projects, the procedures to start or shut down necessary daemons and services are usually project-dependent. For every project, you might need to run different commands or start different services to run the application.

The scenarios shown in Figures 1-3, 1-4, and 1-5 have the following disadvantages:

- They all require a network connection to work on an application; the performance of the server-side software influences the work of every developer. When the network is down, all the developers are idle.

- Some companies can apply restrictive security policies and forbid access to the servers from the outside world. Thus, development environments can't be accessed by collaborators working remotely;

Now that you understand the possible drawbacks that accompany the traditional approach, let's look at some virtual solutions.

Virtualization to the Rescue

Virtualization helps to exploit the best features of both previous solutions while eliminating drawbacks at the same time. When working with VMs, we install both front end and back end components of the application on the same machine: the developer's computer. The client's processes are managed exactly as before: as regular processes in the native OS of the developer's workstation. The server-side software, however, runs within a VM. Both the front and back ends run at the same machine, but the solution closely imitates the production settings, thanks to virtualization (see Figure 1-6).

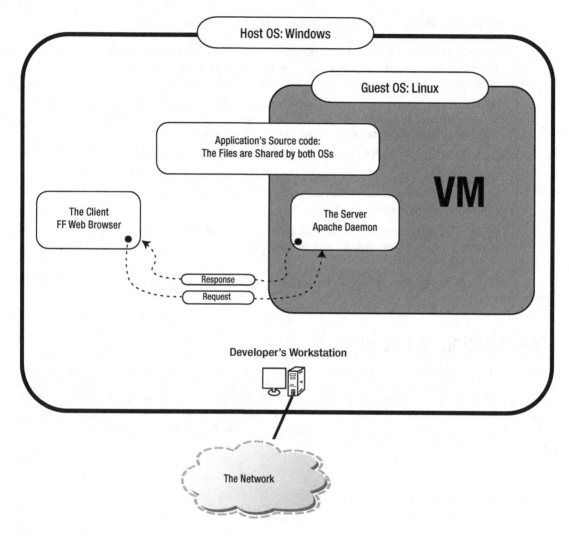

Figure 1-6. *Development environment using a VM*

When you work in the system shown in Figure 1-6, you are dealing with two (usually different) OSs labelled as *host* and *guest*. The original OS of the developer's machine will hereafter be referred to as *host OS* and the VM's OS will be called the *guest OS*. In Figure 1-6, the host OS is Windows and the guest OS is Linux.

■ **Note** The host OS is the system that boots when you power on your computer. If you work on Mac OS X, your host OS is OS X. When you work on a laptop running Windows 7, your host OS is Windows 7. It should also be obvious that there is only one host OS.

The guest OS is the system used by the VM. Because you can boot many VMs at the same time, you can have more than one guest at the same time.

To be sure, the settings shown in Figure 1-6 can be achieved with various virtualization platforms: VirtualBox, VMWare, and Hyper-V, to name the most popular. But the procedure to install, distribute, start, stop, and configure VMs is manual, so it differs depending on the solution you use. This is where Vagrant can help; it provides a very simple and uniform interface to manage VMs, regardless of the virtualization solution you use.

Enter the Vagrant

Vagrant is open source software distributed under an MIT license. It was originally authored by Mitchell Hashimoto, and as of February 2015, almost 500 programmers have contributed to it. The source code of Vagrant is available at `https://github.com/mitchellh/vagrant`.

Vagrant sits on top of existing and well-known virtualization solutions such as VirtualBox, VMWare Workstation, VMWare Fusion, and Hyper-V; and provides a unified and simple command-line interface to manage VMs. This architecture is shown in Figure 1-7.

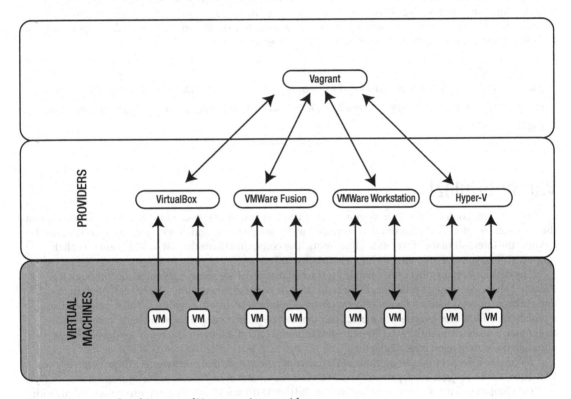

Figure 1-7. *Layered architecture of Vagrant using providers*

To quote its home page, Vagrant is a tool that helps to "create and configure lightweight, reproducible, and portable development environments."[1]

---

[1]The quote comes from the Vagrant home page: `http://vagrantup.com`.

In Vagrant's terminology, the underlying virtualization solutions are called *providers*. To work with Vagrant, you have to install at least one provider. The official list of providers includes the following:

- VirtualBox

- VMWare (Fusion and Workstation)

- Docker

- Hyper-V

■ **Note** In Vagrant terminology, a *provider* is a software virtualization solution such as VirtualBox, VMWare Fusion, or VMWare Workstation.

Although it is technically possible to work with virtual development environments without using Vagrant, doing so requires a fair share of manual labor. Vagrant automates lots of things and exposes the magic $ `vagrant up` command to developers. In many cases, this single command is all developers need to boot the application, no matter how complicated the server-side settings are.

■ **Note** Vagrant sits on top of providers and exposes a very simple, consistent, and powerful command-line interface to all of them. This interface consists of commands such as $ `vagrant up`, $ `vagrant halt`, and $ `vagrant destroy`.

Vagrant Rulez!

How does Vagrant outclass traditional approaches? The first and most eye-catching feature of Vagrant is that the complete development environment is created with a single command: $ `vagrant up`. You don't need to know the internals of the server-side ingredients. The command boots the VM or VMs, and sets all the properties: RAM size, shared directories, networking, and so on.

The developer is no longer responsible for the installation of the server-side software; although it is executed on the developer's machine, there is no struggle with the installation. The burden of preparing and configuring server-side software is moved from developers to system engineers. The developers use a prefabricated VM they may treat as a black box that can be turned on and off with Vagrant commands. In general, it takes a minute or two to get the development environment up and ready for development, although that can depend on many factors.

As you look deeper into the internals of Vagrant operation, note that every project runs within its own VM. Thus, all the projects are separated, and each can use whatever software stack is appropriate.

One project can use a Linux/Apache/MySQL/PHP (LAMP) stack; the other can use Ruby on Rails with Nginx and PostgreSQL (Postgres), all running on FreeBSD. At the same time, even though VMs are truly isolated, you still use only one and the same interface to control (to boot or shut down) the environment. This process simplifies the workflow enormously, and the workflow is no longer project-dependent.

Project isolation can be seen as breaking the ties between your workstation and the project. When working with Vagrant, you can replace your computer or its OS without worrying about the software necessary to run the project. Once you install the provider and Vagrant, the project should run exactly as it did before the changes took place. You don't have to search for and install all the libraries used in any of the projects on which you are collaborating.

Yet another aspect of using virtualization is that developers do not have to install software that expose resources, such as network ports, to the outside world. With Vagrant, you are using a sandboxed solution that by default is not accessible by the outside world. You can ease those restrictions, of course, but it is done explicitly and in a consistent way for all the resources. And, of course, the configuration of exposed resources is done by your sysadmin — the person who can be relied on when it comes to security. Thus, the overall security of your workstation is improved.

From a company perspective, problems with different versions of server-side software used by different developers will vanish. Everyone in the organization uses exactly the same virtual environment prepared by a system engineer. This not only leaves no place for "works on my machine" issues but also facilitates the creation of development environments that are identical to production settings — the system engineer can use the same recipes to prepare the development and production configuration. Moreover, the procedure of updating the server-side software on all the machines used by developers is also painless — all that has to be done is to distribute a new boxed VM. (In fact, it is the main reason I loved Vagrant right from the very moment I learned how to use it.) More on this in the following "Vagrant for Trainers, Instructors, and Teachers" section.

When you combine all the features discussed above with the fact that Vagrant is an open source, free software that works seamlessly across many platforms (including Windows, Linux, and OS X), you will see that the advantages of Vagrant over the traditional approach are overwhelming.

To summarize, let's enumerate Vagrant's most important features:

- Vagrant has an easy workflow: one command (`$ vagrant up`) gets the development environment ready.

- The time needed to bring the development environment to life, even though it depends on many factors, is only a minute or two.

- The developer can change the workstation or replace the OS without having to install software. There are only two packages to be reinstalled: a provider (e.g., VirtualBox) and Vagrant.

- The developer is no longer responsible for installing server-side software.

- The VMs used by all developers are prepared by system engineers.

- Everyone uses exactly the same server-side software.

- Every developer can create, destroy, and re-create virtual environments within a couple of minutes.

- Vagrant facilitates easy updates of server-side software on developers' machines.

- Access to all the resources, such as network ports, is restricted by default.

- The explicit rules that expose a workstation's resources are defined by a sysadmin who is responsible for preparing the sandboxed VM. Thus, the security of all the machines used by developers can be managed globally in a consistent way.

- You can quite easily get 1:1 (or nearly 1:1) mapping across development, testing, and production environments.

- Virtual development environments are created on a per-project basis (all the projects run in isolated cocoons).

- Every project can use arbitrary packages (e.g., one project can use Linux/PHP 5.3; another can use CentOS/Rails).

- One workflow is used for all projects, no matter what virtualization platform, guest OS, language, framework, or server-side software is used.

- Developers don't need a network connection to proceed with their work.

- Vagrant works on all major platforms, including Windows, Linux, and Mac OS X.

- Vagrant is open source and free.

- Vagrant has detailed, well-organized, and clear documentation.

- If you find it necessary, you can extend Vagrant's features with plug-ins.

- The popularity of Vagrant is growing exponentially; it is quickly becoming the tool of choice in many companies.

Disadvantages of Vagrant

The most important disadvantage of using Vagrant is efficiency; the workstations used by developers have to be powerful enough to work with the chosen provider. Moreover, the workstation used by the sysadmin to prepare boxed VMs needs to be even more superior; otherwise, the process of preparing and testing the boxed VMs will be nerve-wracking. When I started preparing boxed VMs, I had to upgrade my laptop to Mac Book Pro.

These constraints don't constitute the complete list. Some combinations of host OSs and providers are known to yield ineffective outcomes. For example, the access time to the shared directory of VMs created with the VirtualBox provider is quite slow. When your host OS is Linux or Mac OS X, you can bypass this issue using a network file system (NFS), but there is no universal solution if you use Windows. Although a workaround is to avoid using shared folders and to use deployment procedures to access the storage in VM instead, it requires additional effort from developers.

Vagrant for Trainers, Instructors, and Teachers

I have loved Vagrant from the very first day I learned how to use it during my classes. It has really changed the way I work. I am the only one who bears the responsibility for creating development environments, so I am the only one who has to deal with installing software, updating system libraries, and so on. I don't have to explain how to install the software any more. Last year, when I introduced Vagrant on a mass scale (for all my classes), I finally stopped spending hours dealing with the installation of all the server-side stuff.

Right now, no matter what platform is used in the computer laboratory or what OS is installed on students' laptops, all I have to do is distribute boxed VMs and tell the students how to use them, which can take as little as five minutes. And, of course, the procedure doesn't change when we change language or framework; once learned, it can't be forgotten.

Exactly the same arguments apply for the training I provide for commercial companies. To proceed with training without any hassle, I need a boxed solution available on the desktop computer of every participant. When that is done and verified, everything goes smoothly. Before Vagrant, there were always problems that could be classified as "doesn't work on my machine" issues.

I also find Vagrant indispensable when I want to take a look at applications or solutions. Gerrit, Gitlab, or Jenkins — you don't have to mess with your desktop any more just to try them. (This is exactly what I suggest to my readers in my book *Git Recipes*.)[2] To recompile git or experiment with gitolite, you can use VM managed by Vagrant/VirtualBox. Working this way, I can provide a single tutorial to be followed by all readers, no matter what platform they work on. Were the readers to install the software on their computers, the instructions would be OS-specific, and it would be much more time-consuming to uninstall everything because the process would be manual.

---

[2]Gajda, Włodzimierz. *Git Recipes: A Problem-Solution Approach*. Apress, 2013.

Installing the Software

During this course you will need three packages (all are free and open source):

- Git
- VirtualBox
- Vagrant

Git

Git is a distributed version control system that has gained enormous popularity since its birth ten years ago and is the *de facto* standard for open source projects. You have probably already had some experience with git; if not, don't worry — I will provide you with all git-related information you may need.

To install git, visit `http://git-scm.com` and download the release for your platform. During the installation, leave all the available options with their default values. Then run the command line and type this command, which should output the version of git:

```
$ git --version
```

■ **Note** If you work on Windows, don't use the standard Windows command line shipped with the system. Run the `git bash` shell instead. Working this way, you can use the commands exactly as they appear in the book without any modifications.

VirtualBox

The home page of VirtualBox is `https://www.virtualbox.org`. Go to the Downloads section and fetch the latest version available for your platform. (During the writing of this book, I used VirtualBox 4.3.22, but that is not mandatory.) Proceed with the typical procedure you use to install software on your platform. The main screen of the installation program on OS X is shown in Figure 1-8.

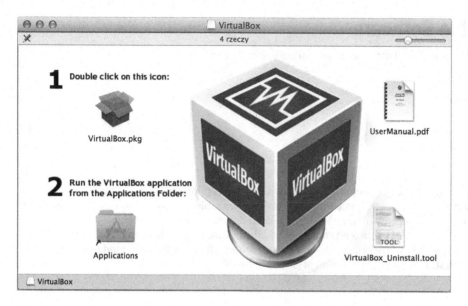

Figure 1-8. *Main screen of VirtualBox installator on OS X*

Recent VirtualBox distributions are known to be quite easy to install, but in case of any problems, the VirtualBox manual can come in handy: www.virtualbox.org/manual/ch02.html.

If you have an older version of VirtualBox on your workstation, remove it prior to installing a newer version. And because VirtualBox installs low-level drivers, you might have to restart the system after the installation or removal of VirtualBox (at least on Windows).

Vagrant

To install Vagrant go to www.vagrantup.com/downloads.html and download the distribution for your system. Then proceed with the installation of the downloaded package. The main window of the Vagrant installator is shown in Figure 1-9.

Figure 1-9. *Main screen of the Vagrant installator*

Check the Installation

How do you verify that Vagrant is ready to work? Just open your command line[3] and execute one of the commands shown here:

```
$ vagrant --version
$ vagrant -v
```

The command should produce output similar to the following:

```
Vagrant 1.7.2
```

I used Vagrant 1.7.2 during the work on this book. I usually prefer to work with the latest software version and suggest that you to do the same (although it isn't obligatory).

■ **Caution** If you work on Windows and your account contains non-Latin letters with diacritical marks, such as óąśż, Vagrant doesn't work. You have to create and use a new account that consists only of Latin characters.

---

[3]If you work on Windows. I strongly advise you to use the `git bash` prompt that is shipped with git.

Basic Vagrant Configuration

By default, Vagrant stores boxed VMs in a current user's home directory in the `~/.vagrant.d/` folder. Because boxed VMs are images of the complete guest OS, they are quite large. It is not uncommon to have a box consuming 1 – 2 GB. And because the boxes are used only as templates, they can be shared by all users who work on the given computer without any negative consequences. By sharing installed Vagrant boxes, users save hard disk drive (HDD) space and gain immediate access to all boxes without having to download them again. This can be important when workstations are used by many people, as in a computer laboratory, for example.

The location of the Vagrant home directory can be redefined with the `VAGRANT_HOME` environment variable. You can change its value by executing the following command in bash:

```
$ export VAGRANT_HOME=/some/shared/directory
```

When working on Windows, you can set a new environment variable using System/Properties/ Advanced System Settings/Environment Variables dialog box.

■ **Note** The list of other environment variables used by Vagrant can be found at `https://docs.vagrantup.com/v2/other/environmental-variables.html`.

Documentation

Sooner or later, you'll need other sources of information. You can use the Vagrant built-in manual, which comes very handy, indeed. Access it with the following commands:

```
$ vagrant
$ vagrant -h
$ vagrant --help
```

When you run one of them, the output is similar to the one shown in Figure 1-10.

```
~$ vagrant
Usage: vagrant [options] <command> [<args>]

    -v, --version                    Print the version and exit.
    -h, --help                       Print this help.

Common commands:
    box             manages boxes: installation, removal, etc.
    connect         connect to a remotely shared Vagrant environment
    destroy         stops and deletes all traces of the vagrant machine
    global-status   outputs status Vagrant environments for this user
    halt            stops the vagrant machine
    help            shows the help for a subcommand
    init            initializes a new Vagrant environment by creating a Vagrantfile
    list
    login           log in to HashiCorp's Atlas
    package         packages a running vagrant environment into a box
    plugin          manages plugins: install, uninstall, update, etc.
    provision       provisions the vagrant machine
    push            deploys code in this environment to a configured destination
    rdp             connects to machine via RDP
    rebuild
    reload          restarts vagrant machine, loads new Vagrantfile configuration
    resume          resume a suspended vagrant machine
    share           share your Vagrant environment with anyone in the world
    ssh             connects to machine via SSH
    ssh-config      outputs OpenSSH valid configuration to connect to the machine
    status          outputs status of the vagrant machine
    suspend         suspends the machine
    up              starts and provisions the vagrant environment
    version         prints current and latest Vagrant version

For help on any individual command run `vagrant COMMAND -h`

Additional subcommands are available, but are either more advanced
or not commonly used. To see all subcommands, run the command
`vagrant list-commands`.
```

Figure 1-10. *The output of the $ vagrant command describes basic usage and lists all the subcommands*

The Vagrant interface consists of commands such as these:

```
$ vagrant box
$ vagrant package
$ vagrant up
```

During the course, we will discuss all these commands. Some of them have subcommands such as the following:

```
$ vagrant box add
$ vagrant box list
$ vagrant box remove
```

These subcommands will also be explained in the following chapters. Right now, remember that to print the syntax of any of the commands and subcommands, you have to use the --help or -h switch, as shown in these examples:

```
$ vagrant box -h
$ vagrant box --help
$ vagrant box add -h
$ vagrant box add --help
```

When the manual is not enough, you can access Vagrant documentation online: https://docs.vagrantup.com/v2/getting-started/. The documentation is very clear and includes in-depth descriptions of all Vagrant features.

Summary

In this chapter, I wanted to give you a clear picture of the advantages that Vagrant offers. When working with Vagrant, you move the responsibility for setting development environment from developers to one central point — a sysadmin, for example. Developers run both client-side and server-side software of the application on their workstations. Server-side services such as a database server or HTTP server are executed within a virtual system that can mimic the system used on a production server. The VM can be seen by developers as a black box. All developers need to know about server-side software is reduced to a couple of commands that turn the environment on and off, such as the following:

```
$ vagrant up
$ vagrant halt
```

Moreover, all projects that developers might be working on are separated, and each can use arbitrary server-side solutions. The projects do not overlap nor do they collide with each other.

The Vagrant's workflow not only facilitates easier onboarding of new developers but also simplifies the task of updating the environment used by all developers. This is especially attractive for training and teaching purposes.

Because Vagrant really changed the way I work, I sincerely recommend it and promote it to everyone.

In the Next Chapter, You'll Learn . . .

There's nothing better than hands-on experience. All the discussions from this chapter will be more understandable after you run the examples awaiting you in Chapter 2. In just a few minutes, you will run four web applications, each written in different language:

- JavaScript/AngularJS
- Python/Django
- Ruby/Ruby on Rails
- PHP/Symfony

Even without any knowledge of these languages and frameworks, with Vagrant you can still run them all on your computer.

Reading List

If you're interested in reading more about Vagrant, the first source of information should be its documentation: https://docs.vagrantup.com/v2/getting-started/.

For a more detailed, extensive, and thorough introduction, I strongly recommend *Vagrant: Up and Running*, by Mitchell Hashimoto.[4] Hashimoto is Vagrant's author and project leader, and his book is an excellent source of information for novices and advanced Vagrant users alike.

---

[4]Hashimoto, Mitchell. *Vagrant: Up and Running*. O'Reilly, 2013.

You might also need more information about your provider. For VirtualBox, see www.virtualbox.org/manual/.

For Vagrant's untypical behavior, the list of current issues can be helpful: https://github.com/mitchellh/vagrant/issues.

For basic introduction to web applications and the client/server model, see the following Wikipedia entries:

- http://en.wikipedia.org/wiki/Web_application
- http://en.wikipedia.org/wiki/Client-server_model

Test Yourself

1. What is Vagrant? Define it in one sentence.

2. What is the most important Vagrant command?

3. What is the URL of the Vagrant home page?

4. What difficulties are caused by the client/server paradigm for developers?

5. What traditional approaches to setting development environments do you know?

6. Explain the Vagrant approach to setting up the development environment.

7. Define the terms *host* and *guest*.

8. Define the term *provider*.

9. Name the providers supported by Vagrant.

10. What is the command to print the Vagrant version?

11. What is the command to print the Vagrant built-in manual?

12. How do you list Vagrant commands?

13. How do you print the manual for one of the subcommands?

14. Where does Vagrant store boxes? Why should you want to change this location? How can you do it?

CHAPTER 2

■ ■ ■

Four Web Frameworks in Four Minutes

Chapter 1 discussed some of the amazing advantages of Vagrant: how it can change the workflow of a company and how every member of the team can benefit from using it. I specifically underlined the advantages of running a web application in a virtualized environment with just one command: $ vagrant up.

Because the best way to understand Vagrant is to see it in action, this chapter will act as a guided tour to running four simple web applications written in four popular web frameworks:

- AngularJS (JavaScript)

- Django (Python)

- Rails (Ruby)

- Symfony (PHP)

Of course, this discussion can't be a complete tour of AngularJS, Django, Ruby on Rails, or Symfony. I will not dive into details concerning any of the frameworks because that is not the purpose of this book. I aim to prove to you that even if you are new to these frameworks and languages (and even if you don't have Python, Ruby, or PHP on your laptop), you can still run the examples with just one command. And the procedure to run each of them is almost identical.

Each of the four projects presents exactly the same web pages; each is set up and brought to life in a couple of minutes (maybe not exactly at the speed of an example per minute, as promised in the title, but much faster than can be done manually). And most importantly, the booting of the applications is completely automated. It leaves no place for mistyped commands, misconfigured services, incorrect configuration settings, and similar typos and other human errors.

Just one more notice before we proceed. Every example uses one TCP port on your host computer:

- *AngularJS project*: port 8800

- *Django project*: port 8000

- *Ruby on Rails project*: port 3000

- *Symfony project*: port 8880

If any of these ports is not available on your computer, the project will not run. (This problem will be addressed and solved in the next chapter.) Right now, let's assume that at least some of the listed ports are available. And if security is a concern, you might want to postpone the practical exercises described in this chapter until you have fully understood the implications of running the $ vagrant up command. This topic is described in great detail in Chapter 4.

■ **Tip** The source code for all the projects discussed in this chapter and in the entire book is stored on GitHub at `http://github.com/pro-vagrant`.

Project 1: "Songs for kids" Written in AngularJS

The first project is the application titled "Songs for kids," which is written in AngularJS framework. It consists of three web pages, each of which displays the text of one song for kids. To run the project, execute the commands shown in Listing 2-1.

Listing 2-1. Commands to Run "Songs for kids" in AngularJS

```
$ cd folder/with/examples
$ git clone https://github.com/pro-vagrant/songs-app-angularjs.git
$ cd songs-app-angularjs
$ vagrant up
# Run webbrowser and visit http://localhost:8800/
```

■ **Note** AngularJS is a web framework written in JavaScript. Its home page is `https://angularjs.org/`.

Depending on your connection, the complete procedure to get this first example running can take up to several minutes. My timing was about 2 minutes and 10 seconds.

Here is the explanation for the commands in Listing 2-1. Start by entering a directory in which you want to keep the examples:

```
$ cd folder/with/examples
```

You might have to create this folder, of course. It can be located anywhere on your hard drive (it really doesn't matter where).

The source code of the AngularJS "Songs for kids" project is available at `https://github.com/pro-vagrant/songs-app-angularjs.git`. To copy the sources from the GitHub server to the hard drive, use the `$ git clone` command:

```
$ git clone https://github.com/pro-vagrant/songs-app-angularjs.git
```

You now have the complete source code of the application inside the `songs-app-angularjs/` directory. Enter the project's folder:

```
$ cd songs-app-angularjs
```

You can boot the VM required to run the application with this command:

```
$ vagrant up
```

Although this command prints a lot of output, at this point I want to skip it. I prefer to postpone the in-depth discussion concerning the messages printed by Vagrant during booting until Chapter 3. Right now, I intend to convince you how simple Vagrant really is. With that goal in mind, wait until the command has finished running and proceed with the next step of this example.

■ **Note** An in-depth analysis of the internals behind vagrant commands such as $ `vagrant up`, $ `vagrant ssh`, and $ `vagrant destroy` is in Chapter 3. Chapter 2 is meant to be the bait that gets you hooked; no matter what the server-side solution is, you can get the project running in a couple of minutes without any specific knowledge about the back end.

Start your web browser and visit `http://localhost:8800/`. The web page that displays is shown in Figure 2-1.

Figure 2-1. *"Songs for kids" application written in Angular JS*

At this point your computer runs two OSs:

- Host: primary OS
- Guest: virtual OS started by $ `vagrant up`

To verify, start VirtualBox and take a look at its main window. It should contain a VM with a name that starts with songs-app-angularjs_default. The state of this VM should be denoted as Running (see Figure 2-2).

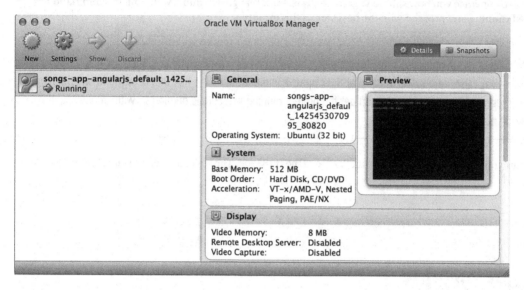

Figure 2-2. *VM started for the project written in Angular JS*

You can also list all the VMs started by Vagrant with the following command:

```
$ vagrant global-status
```

Right now, it should output just one item:

```
id       name     provider    state    directory
--------------------------------------------------------------------
17b0c01  default  virtualbox  running  /examples/songs-app-angularjs
```

The application shown in Figure 2-2 is being served by an HTTP server running inside the guest OS: Ubuntu 14.04.

The application consists of:

- The front end which runs in a web browser executed in the host OS.

- The back end which runs in Ubuntu 14.04 guest OS (see Figure 2-3).

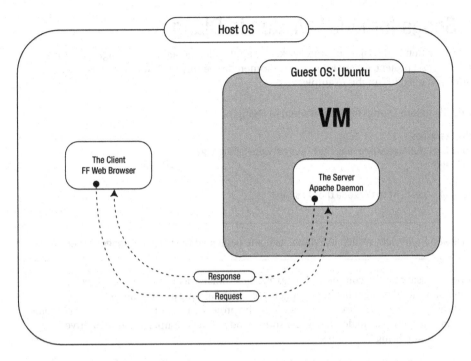

Figure 2-3. *Communication between the web browser and HTTP Apache daemon*

Before proceeding with another example, let's modify one of the pages, which will clarify the notion of file sharing between host and guest OSs. The source code of the application is available in both the host OS and VM. Moreover, the changes you make to files in one OS are instantly reflected in the other OS.

Open the file songs-app-angularjs/web/data/song/1.json with any text editor (vi is used here):

```
$ vi songs-angularjs-app/web/data/song/1.json
```

Change the title of the song. The third line of the file looks like this:

```
"title": "Baa, baa, black sheep",
```

Change it into this:

```
"title": "ABC... ",
```

Note that this is an ordinary file available in your host OS. Even though it is being served by an HTTP daemon that runs within the guest VM, you can still access it with your favorite text editor (running on the host OS).

After you change and save the file, refresh the page displayed in the browser:

```
http://localhost:8800/
```

You will see the page containing the title "ABC" instead of "Baa, baa black sheep". The source code of the application is available on the host OS, which is very convenient.

The first example is running, so let's move forward to the second project.

Project 2: "Songs for kids" Written in Django

The second example is written in the Django framework. The application generates web pages that look exactly as they did in the first project, except for a small comment to identify the framework. Listing 2-2 shows the commands you need to run this example.

Listing 2-2. Commands to Run "Songs for kids" written in Django

```
$ cd folder/with/examples
$ git clone https://github.com/pro-vagrant/songs-app-django.git
$ cd songs-app-django
$ vagrant up
# Run webbrowser and visit http://localhost:8000/
```

■ **Note** Django is a web framework written in Python. Its home page is `https://www.djangoproject.com/`.

For me, the time necessary for the command $ `vagrant up` to finish was 1 minute and 40 seconds. Yours, depending on many factors, might be much longer (it can take as long as 10 minutes).

Start the procedure by entering the directory created for the projects. The purpose of the $ `git clone` command stays the same: it is the way to download the source code of the example to the hard drive. Enter the folder with the sources and bring VM to life:

```
$ cd songs-app-django
$ vagrant up
```

Wait until the command finishes and use your browser to visit `http://localhost:8000/`. You should see the web page shown in Figure 2-4.

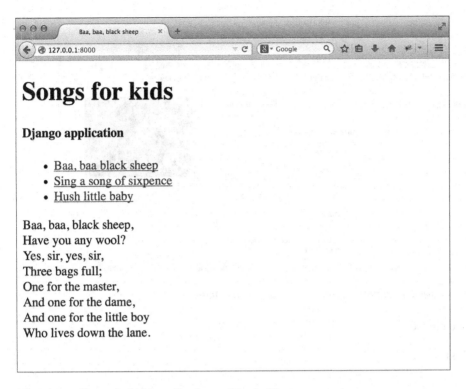

Figure 2-4. *"Songs for kids" application written in Django*

Now your computer runs three OSs:

- Host OS

- First VM for the first project

- Second VM for the second project

To verify this, go to the VirtualBox main window. It should contain two VMs, which are shown in Figure 2-5.

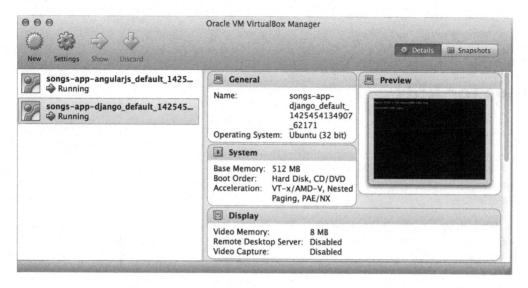

Figure 2-5. *Two VMs started in examples written in AngularJS and Django*

The following command:

```
$ vagrant global-status
```

now produces two items:

```
id        name      provider    state    directory
--------------------------------------------------------------------
17b0c01   default   virtualbox  running  /examples/songs-app-angularjs
82dcf84   default   virtualbox  running  /examples/songs-app-django
```

This time, the overall picture of your system is more complicated as shown in Figure 2-6. Your host contains two guest VMs: one for the AngularJS application and the other for the example written in Django. Both guests run Ubuntu 14.04.

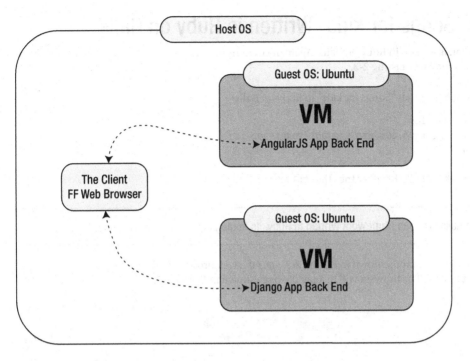

Figure 2-6. *Host OS with two guest VMs*

Let's change one of the pages. Use vi to open the first baa.html file:

```
$ vi songs-app-django/songs/songs/templates/baa.html
```

The file contains the block named content that begins with the following code:

```
{% block content %}
    <h2>Baa, baa, black sheep</h2>
    <p>
```

Change the preceding lines to these:

```
{% block content %}
    <h2>ABC </h2>
    <p>
```

Refresh the page shown in Figure 2-5. You should see the new title "ABC" in your browser.

Project 3: "Songs for kids" Written in Ruby on Rails

The third application is written in Ruby on Rails. Again, it contains the same three web pages. The procedure to run this project is shown in Listing 2-3.

Listing 2-3. Commands to Run "Songs for kids" in Ruby on Rails

```
$ cd folder/with/examples
$ git clone https://github.com/pro-vagrant/songs-app-rails.git
$ cd songs-app-rails
$ vagrant up
# Run webbrowser and visit http://localhost:3000/
```

■ **Note**   Ruby on Rails is a web framework written in Ruby. Its home page is `http://rubyonrails.org/`.

After running the commands shown in Listing 2-3, start the web browser and visit `http://localhost:3000/`. The browser will display the page shown in Figure 2-7.

Figure 2-7. *"Songs for kids" application written in Ruby on Rails*

The purpose of each command is almost identical to the previous projects. The following command creates a local copy of the project's source on the hard drive:

```
$ git clone https://github.com/pro-vagrant/songs-app-rails.git
```

Enter the project's directory with this:

```
$ cd songs-app-rails
```

Finally, the virtual system is brought up:

```
$ vagrant up
```

Right now, the host is running three VMs:

- VM for AngularJS example
- VM for Django example
- VM for Rails example

This situation is depicted on Figure 2-8.

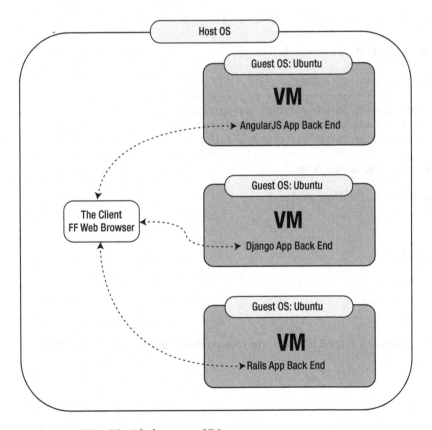

Figure 2-8. *Host OS with three guest VMs*

All three guests are displayed in the VirtualBox main window, as shown in Figure 2-9.

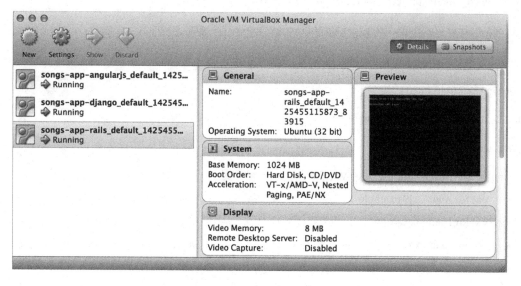

Figure 2-9. *Three running guest VMs displayed by VirtualBox*

The output of $ vagrant global-status now looks like this:

```
id        name      provider     state    directory
----------------------------------------------------------------------
17b0c01   default   virtualbox   running  /examples/songs-app-angularjs
82dcf84   default   virtualbox   running  /examples/songs-app-django
68d0c57   default   virtualbox   running  /examples/songs-app-rails
```

To change the title of the first song, open this file:

```
$ vi songs-app-rails/app/views/lyrics/baa.html.erb
```

Replace this line:

```
<h2>Baa, baa, black sheep</h2>
```

with this one:

```
<h2>ABC</h2>
```

Go to the web page shown in Figure 2-7 and refresh it. The browser should display the new title "ABC".

Project 4: "Songs for kids" Written in Symfony

I have created the final project in PHP using the Symfony framework. To run it, execute the commands shown in Listing 2-4.

Listing 2-4. Commands to Run "Songs for kids" in Symfony

```
$ cd folder/with/examples
$ git clone https://github.com/pro-vagrant/songs-app-symfony.git
$ cd songs-app-symfony
$ vagrant up
# Run webbrowser and visit http://localhost:8880/
```

■ **Note**   Symfony is a web framework written in PHP. Its home page is `http://symfony.com/`.

Again, do the following:

- Clone the source code with `$ git clone`.
- Enter the `projects` directory with `$ cd`.
- Boot the VM with `$ vagrant up`.

When these commands finish, you can visit the web page of the project by running the web browser and visiting `http://localhost:8880/`. You should see the web page shown in Figure 2-10.

Figure 2-10. "Songs for kids" application written in Symfony

As you can guess, the VirtualBox will now display four VMs running, as shown in Figure 2-11.

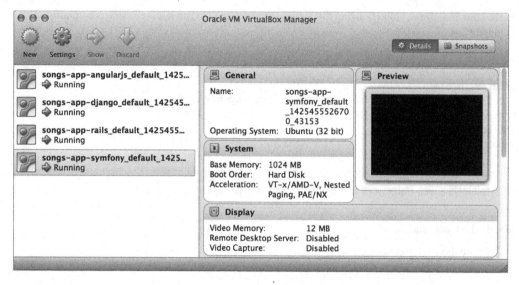

Figure 2-11. *VirtualBox with four VMs running: one VM for each example project*

The same four VMs are included in the output of the $ `vagrant global-status` command:

```
id       name     provider    state    directory
------------------------------------------------------------------
17b0c01  default  virtualbox  running  /examples/songs-app-angularjs
82dcf84  default  virtualbox  running  /examples/songs-app-django
68d0c57  default  virtualbox  running  /examples/songs-app-rails
913bbce  default  virtualbox  running  /examples/songs-app-symfony
```

Your computer now runs five OSs:

- Host OS of your machine

- Four guest VMs

Your web browser sends requests to four back ends (see Figure 2-12).

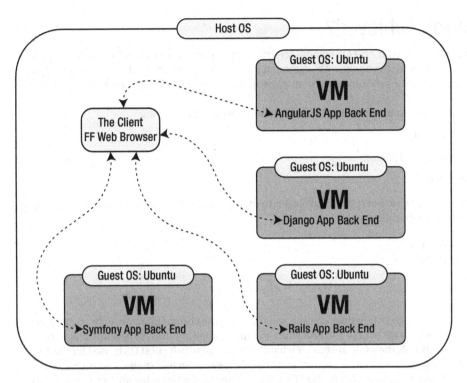

Figure 2-12. *Communication within the host running four examples*

To modify one of the pages, open this file:

```
$ vi songs-app-symfony/src/AppBundle/Resources/views/Default/baa.html.twig
```

Change the block body. Replace these lines:

```
{% block body %}
    <h2>Baa, baa, black sheep</h2>
    <p>
```

with the following contents:

```
{% block body %}
    <h2>ABC</h2>
    <p>
```

To display the new contents in a browser, visit `http://localhost:8880/app_dev.php/`.

■ **Note** The Symfony framework doesn't refresh cached templates when you use `http://localhost:8880` URL. The easiest way to force template reloading is to use the `app_dev.php` front controller. That's why the URL to use is `http://localhost:8880/app_dev.php`.

What Have You Achieved?

To run the first example within your host OS without referring to virtualization, you would have to install and configure the Apache web server in your host OS. Although it is not a very complicated task, it requires some amount of manual work, and the procedure is system-dependent. It is slightly different for Windows, Linux, and OS X hosts.

To run the other three example projects, you would have to install the following:

- *Project 2*: Python

- *Project 3*: Ruby and NodeJS

- *Project 4*: PHP

Again, it is not a difficult task, but it is manual and system-dependent. By using Vagrant, you can reduce the procedure to start any application to this:

```
$ cd folder/with/examples
$ git clone APPLICATION
$ cd APPLICATION
$ vagrant up
```

Refer to Listings 2-1 through 2-4. Besides cloning and changing the current directory with cd, they all contain just one command: $ vagrant up. The procedure to run the applications is very simple; there is nothing manual and it is exactly the same, no matter what the OS is and which guest OS is used for the back end. All the examples are also completely isolated from each other; each can use arbitrary software, and there is no interference between them. Finally, the TCP ports opened by the following are not accessible to anyone but you; they cannot be accessed remotely:

- *AngularJS application*: http://localhost:8800

- *Django application*: http://localhost:8000

- *Rails application*: http://localhost:3000

- *Symfony application*: http://localhost:8880

I hope that the pros of using Vagrant have become clearer to you. As for the cons, well, the time necessary to run each example is definitely much longer than one minute. In the sequel, you will learn how to minimize the time necessary to boot a VM, but I can't promise that you'll get below the one-minute threshold.

Shared Folders

The instructions to modify the title of a song aim to convince you of the simplicity offered by Vagrant. Even though the application is being served by the guest OS, the source code is available in your host OS.

You can edit the files with your favorite IDE. By default, the directory in which you run the $ vagrant up command is available inside the guest OS. The two OSs, host and guest, share the project's directory.

Stopping VMs

As you already know, the following command displays information about all VMs started by Vagrant:

```
$vagrant global-status
```

Its output is similar to the one shown in Listing 2-5.

Listing 2-5. Output of $ vagrant global-status

```
id        name     provider    state    directory
------------------------------------------------------------------
17b0c01  default  virtualbox  running  /examples/songs-app-angularjs
82dcf84  default  virtualbox  running  /examples/songs-app-django
68d0c57  default  virtualbox  running  /examples/songs-app-rails
913bbce  default  virtualbox  running  /examples/songs-app-symfony
```

To stop each of the applications, go to its directory and run the $ vagrant destroy command. Here is the procedure to stop AngularJS:

```
$ cd folder/with/examples
$ cd songs-app-angularjs
$ vagrant destroy
```

If you now visit http://localhost:8800/, you can see the message about the unavailable web page. And, of course, the VM will vanish from the VirtualBox main window. Now the command $ vagrant global-status should print information about the three VMs still running.

You can also stop VMs without changing the current directory. The ID displayed in the first column in Listing 2-5 can be passed to the $ vagrant destroy command. The following command stops the third VM visible in Listing 2-5, no matter what the current directory is:

```
$ vagrant destroy 68d0c57
```

You can also stop the VM by doing the following on the VirtualBox main menu:

1. First, use Machine/Close/Power Off for a selected machine.

2. Then use Machine/Remove/Delete All Files for the same machine.

■ **Caution**   If you turn off your computer without destroying the VMs with $ vagrant destroy, the output of $ vagrant global-status might contain stale entries. To remove them, run $ vagrant global-status --prune.

Summary

Now that you have seen Vagrant in action, its features should become more understandable. I have purposefully provided you with four projects written in different languages and frameworks. If you were able to run the examples with the commands displayed in Listings 2-1 through 2-4, it proves that your fluency in PHP, Ruby, Python, and JavaScript is of no importance at all. Even if you have no experience with a given language, say PHP/Symfony2, you can still run the application with a couple of commands: $ vagrant up being the most important.

The advantages of Vagrant are these:

- To run each of the examples you need to run $ vagrant up.

- Exactly the same command is used no matter which

  - host OS you work on

  - guest OS is used

  - language and framework used for the application

- You don't need any specialized knowledge of how to install software because everything is baked into the guest VM.

- All the examples run in isolation and don't interfere with each other or with your host OS.

- Every example can closely imitate the production settings.

- All the resources allocated for guest VMs (such as TCP ports 8800, 8000, 3000, and 8880) are available only to your host OS; they are not accessible remotely.

- The source code of every example is available in the host OS; you can change the files (e.g., song titles) with your favorite editor running on the host OS.

The most obvious disadvantage of using Vagrant is its time inefficiency. The procedures shown in Listings 2-1 through 2-4 can last for many minutes. Don't let this discourage you, however; the whole process of running applications is automatic, and that's what really matters. Once you know how Vagrant works, you can keep the time necessary to boot and reboot the applications at a reasonable level.

■ **Tip** As a teacher and instructor, I just couldn't believe that a course of developing a web application in any language could be started without any hassle. In less than five minutes, every student can get the examples running on their laptops, no matter which host OS is used. And, what is extremely appealing, students can take the working solution home with them. For me, that was a complete revelation!

In the Next Chapter, You'll Learn . . .

When misused, Vagrant can quickly cause confusion and dissatisfaction. The way to avoid this is to learn the actions performed in the background when you run $ vagrant up. The analysis of the various stages of booting provide a detailed characterization of all the states that VM can possibly enter. I will specifically focus attention on timing, which will act as the basis of the search of the most effective workflow.

Reading List

For more information about the four frameworks from this chapter, see their documentation:

- *AngularJS*: https://angularjs.org/
- *Django*: https://www.djangoproject.com/
- *Ruby on Rails*: http://rubyonrails.org/
- *Symfony2*: http://symfony.com/

The Vagrant command `$ vagrant global-status` is documented at https://docs.vagrantup.com/v2/cli/global-status.html

To learn about its syntax, use its build-in manual: `$ vagrant global-status --help`

Test Yourself

1. How do you boot a VM in one of the example applications?

2. What software do you need to install to run Projects 1 through 4?

3. How do you stop a VM using the command line?

4. How do you stop a VM using the VirtualBox main window?

5. How can you list all guest VMs started by Vagrant using the command line?

6. How can you check all guest VMs using the VirtualBox main window?

7. What are the advantages of using virtual development environments for Projects 1 through 4?

8. What does it mean that the projects are isolated and do not interfere with each other?

9. What does it mean that the Vagrant workflow is not project-dependent?

10. Can you explain a scenario in which one or all of the projects would not run?

11. What are the exact commands to run the first example?

12. What does the term *file sharing* mean?

Exercises

1. Run the first project written in AngularJS and change the title of "Sing a song of sixpence" to "Second song." Verify the new title in your web browser.

2. Run the second project written in Django and change the title of "Sing a song of sixpence" to "Second song." Verify the new title in your web browser.

3. Run the third project written in Ruby on Rails and change the title of "Sing a song of sixpence" to "Second song." Verify the new title in your web browser.

4. Run the fourth project written in Symfony and change the title of "Sing a song of sixpence" to "Second song." Verify the new title in your web browser.

5. Add one new song to the application "Songs for kids" written in AngularJS.

6. Add one new song to the application "Songs for kids" written in Django.

7. Add one new song to the application "Songs for kids" written in Ruby on Rails.

8. Add one new song to the application "Songs for kids" written in Symfony.

CHAPTER 3

■ ■ ■

The States of VM

Now that you know how to run applications within a Vagrant-controlled environment, it's time to learn more about Vagrant internals and get acquainted with the operations behind the $ vagrant up command. In this chapter, you will learn about the following:

- Vagrantfile

- Versioning strategy for the Vagrantfile format

- Base boxes (where they come from and how, and when they get installed on your computer)

- Starting and stopping a VM

- States that a VM can enter

- Vagrant commands to manage a VM state

- Resolving the problem of colliding ports

To simplify this analysis of $ vagrant up, Vagrant's actions will be divided into three stages. I will draw your attention to various files and directories that are involved during booting as well as the timing of the three stages. It will help you understand how Vagrant can be used in the most efficient way.

Then I will analyze the five different states that the guest OS can enter. This part of the chapter, together with explanation of all Vagrant commands to change states, will ultimately provide you with precise descriptions for all the methods to do the following:

- Boot the guest OS

- Shut down the guest OS

The example used in this chapter is quite similar to the ones used in Chapter 2. This time, the application "Songs for kids" will be written in the Sinatra web framework. Similar to the examples presented in the previous chapter, you don't need any knowledge of Sinatra to run the application. But in order to get a deeper insight into the way various resources such as files and processes are handled by VM, you will start the HTTP server manually within the guest VM.

Before You Begin

Let's start by making sure there are no VMs running on our hosts. Run this command:

```
$ vagrant global-status
```

If the list of VMs is not empty, use the following command to destroy the VM:

```
$ vagrant destroy ID
```

The ID parameter stands for the ID displayed by $ vagrant global-status. You might have to run this command:

```
$ vagrant global-status --prune
```

The previous command removes stale VMs. The $ vagrant global-status command caches the data about VMs and it could print outdated results. This problem can be resolved with the --prune option, which clears the cache used by the $ vagrant global-status command.

When there are no VMs running on your host, you are ready to go.

Getting the Source Code of the Example Application

To work with the project, you have to download its source code. For this chapter, I prepared the example project "Songs for kids" written in Sinatra. It is hosted on GitHub at https://github.com/pro-vagrant/songs-app-sinatra/. The following command will clone the project from GitHub to your local drive:

```
$ cd folder/with/examples
$ git clone https://github.com/pro-vagrant/songs-app-sinatra.git
```

Enter the newly created project's directory:

```
$ cd songs-app-sinatra
```

Vagrantfile

The configuration of a VM used within a project is stored on a per-project basis inside the Vagrantfile file. Every project has its own Vagrantfile that governs the properties of the VM used. This file is written in the Ruby language and contains the name of the so-called base box for the guest OS (among other things).

The Vagrantfile is supposed to be shared by all developers, so it should go into the version control. If all the developers have the same Vagrantfile, they will have identical development environments.

Although Vagrant is pretty stable right now, it is still being actively developed, so its format might change. The strategy used by Vagrant's author to denote the version of the Vagrantfile format relies on stable releases, which have the second number equal to 0. Thus, the following facts are true:

- Vagrant 1.0.* was the first stable release (published on March 6, 2012).

- Vagrant 2.0.* will be the second stable release.

- Vagrant 3.0.* will most probably be the third stable release, and so on.

The Vagrantfile format for the first stable release was denoted as format number 1. It was developed in Vagrant from 0.1.0 up to 1.0.0, and fixed in Vagrant up to 1.0.7. Since version 1.0.0, this format has been frozen — it won't change any more. Because Vagrant guarantees backward-compatibility, you can use this format safely in all future versions of Vagrant.

The next format, the one denoted as version 2, is being developed in versions up to 2.0.0. Once the Vagrant reaches version 2.0.0, format 2 will become stable and it won't change (except for some bug fixes in versions 2.0.*). Because Vagrant has not reached the 2.0.0 release yet, this format is still under development (so it still might change).

■ **Note** All the examples in the book use Vagrantfile format 2, even though there is a slight risk of publishing outdated information.

The Vagrantfile for the project "Songs for kids" written in Sinatra is shown in Listing 3-1.

Listing 3-1. Vagrantfile for "Songs for kids" written in Sinatra

```
Vagrant.configure(2) do |config|
  config.vm.box = "http://boxes.gajdaw.pl/sinatra/sinatra-v1.0.0.box"
  config.vm.network :forwarded_port, guest: 4567, host: 45670, host_ip: "127.0.0.1"
end
```

As shown in Listing 3-1, this Vagrantfile uses version 2, which can also be done with the variable VAGRANTFILE_API_VERSION:

```
VAGRANTFILE_API_VERSION = "2"
```

passed ass a parameter to Vagrant.configure():

```
Vagrant.configure(VAGRANTFILE_API_VERSION) do |config|
  ...
end
```

The VM used in this project is configured with two instructions:

```
config.vm.box = "http://boxes.gajdaw.pl/sinatra/sinatra-v1.0.0.box"
config.vm.network :forwarded_port, guest: 4567, host: 45670, host_ip: "127.0.0.1"
```

The first instruction sets the base box used in the project to the one available at http://boxes.gajdaw.pl/sinatra/sinatra-v1.0.0.box; the second defines port forwarding. Requests sent to port 45670 on the host OS will be forwarded to port 4567 in the guest OS. Thanks to the host_ip parameter, the guest OS will accept only connections originating at the host with the IP address set to 127.0.0.1 (this is the host, of course). This is the way to restrict remote access to a VM.

Where Does the VM Image Come From?

The complete VM used by Vagrant to create and run the guest OS is stored in a single file. This file, often referred to as a *box file* or an *image file*, is usually quite large: from a few hundred megabytes to a few gigabytes. That's not surprising because the file contains a complete preinstalled OS such as Linux, CentOS, or FreeBSD, for example. The extension used by Vagrant for the base boxes is usually .box, but it is not mandatory.

■ **Tip**   To avoid inadvertent commits of .box files, consider adding this rule to your global gitignore file: *.box.

The file that I prepared for this example is named sinatra-v1.0.0.box, which consumes 700 MB of hard drive space. The time necessary to download this file depends on the bandwidth of your Internet connection. It usually takes a couple of minutes to download the base box, but it might take much longer. The file is uploaded onto my server and is available at http://boxes.gajdaw.pl/sinatra/sinatra-v1.0.0.box.

To run the example, you have to download this file and install it into your system. Vagrant is smart enough to perform these operations during the execution of $ vagrant up, which is why this command takes so much time when you run it for the first time.

■ **Note**   Of course, you can set the config.vm.box to an arbitrary URL; for example, config.vm.box = "http://example.net/some/other.box". You can also use the Vagrant Cloud service to use names such as gajdaw/sinatra or ubuntu/precise32. Vagrant Cloud services will be discussed in Chapter 10.

Booting the VM

When you run the command $ vagrant for the first time, you will see output similar to the one shown in Listing 3-2.

Listing 3-2. Output of $ vagrant up Run for the First Time

```
❶Bringing machine 'default' up with 'virtualbox' provider...
❶==> default: Box 'http://boxes.gajdaw.pl/sinatra/sinatra-v1.0.0.box' could not be found.
Attempting to find and install...
❶      default: Box Provider: virtualbox
❶      default: Box Version: >= 0
❶==> default: Adding box 'http://boxes.gajdaw.pl/sinatra/sinatra-v1.0.0.box' (v0) for
provider: virtualbox
❶      default: Downloading: http://boxes.gajdaw.pl/sinatra/sinatra-v1.0.0.box
❶==> default: Box download is resuming from prior download progress
❶==> default: Successfully added box 'http://boxes.gajdaw.pl/sinatra/sinatra-v1.0.0.box'
(v0) for 'virtualbox'!
❷==> default: Importing base box 'http://boxes.gajdaw.pl/sinatra/sinatra-v1.0.0.box'...
❸==> default: Matching MAC address for NAT networking...
❸==> default: Setting the name of the VM: songs-app-sinatra_default_1425397277271_42545
❸==> default: Clearing any previously set network interfaces...
❸==> default: Preparing network interfaces based on configuration...
❸      default: Adapter 1: nat
❸==> default: Forwarding ports...
```

```
③    default: 4567 => 45670 (adapter 1)
③    default: 22 => 2222 (adapter 1)
③==> default: Booting VM...
③==> default: Waiting for machine to boot. This may take a few minutes...
③    default: SSH address: 127.0.0.1:2222
③    default: SSH username: vagrant
③    default: SSH auth method: private key
③    default: Warning: Connection timeout. Retrying...
③    default:
③    default: Vagrant insecure key detected. Vagrant will automatically replace
③    default: this with a newly generated keypair for better security.
③    default:
③    default: Inserting generated public key within guest...
③    default: Removing insecure key from the guest if its present...
③    default: Key inserted! Disconnecting and reconnecting using new SSH key...
③==> default: Machine booted and ready!
③==> default: Checking for guest additions in VM...
③==> default: Mounting shared folders...
③    default: /vagrant => /examples/songs-app-sinatra
③==> default: Running provisioner: shell...
③    default: Running: inline script
③==> default: stdin: is not a tty
```

The process of booting the machine consists of three main stages:

- Stage I: downloading and installing the box in the system (denoted in Listing 3-2 with ❶)

- Stage II: importing the base box into the project (denoted in Listing 3-2 with ❷)

- Stage III: booting the system (denoted in Listing 3-2 with ❸)

Before the analysis of the above three states, take a look at the timing shown in Table 3-1 and the space consumption summarized in Table 3-2. Although the data I present are taken from my system and will probably be different in your situation, the tables will give you the basic understanding of the time and space necessary to work with a VM created by Vagrant.

Table 3-1. *Timing of the Initial $ vagrant up Command*

Stage	Time
Stage I: Download and install the box	3 minutes
Stage II: Import the box	15 seconds
Stage III: Boot the system	20 seconds
Total	3 minutes, 35 seconds

Table 3-2. *Space Occupied After the First Two Stages*

Stage	Directory	Space
Stage I: Download and install the base box	~/.vagrant.d/boxes/	800 MB
Stage II: Import the box	~/VirtualBox VMs/	2.2 GB
Total (after Stages I and II)		2.8 GB

Stage I: Downloading and Installing the Box in the System

In Listing 3-2, the first stage starts with this message:

```
❶==> default: Box 'http://boxes.gajdaw.pl/sinatra/sinatra-v1.0.0.box' could not be found.
Attempting to find and install...
```

It ends with this message:

```
❶==> default: Successfully added box 'http://boxes.gajdaw.pl/sinatra/sinatra-v1.0.0.box'
(v0) for 'virtualbox'!
```

During this Stage I, Vagrant checks to see whether the box is available on your computer. If not, which is the case during the first run, Vagrant downloads the box and installs it in the system. Because the file consumes about 800 MB, the operation can last a couple of minutes. In my case, it took about 3 minutes. (This process is one of the most time-consuming parts of booting the VM.) But, as you will see in Chapter 6 on provisioning, not necessarily the longest one.

Once downloaded, the box is installed in your home directory; you'll find it inside ~/.vagrant.d/boxes/. If you have changed the VAGRANT_HOME environment variable, you'll find it in the

```
$VAGRANT_HOME/.vagrant.d/boxes/
```

directory. To verify, run one of these commands:

```
$ ls -l ~/.vagrant.d/boxes/
$ ls -l $VAGRANT_HOME/.vagrant.d/boxes/
```

The name of the directory in which Vagrant stores the downloaded VM is the same as the URL, but each slash (/) is replaced with -VAGRANTSLASH-. The image downloaded from http://boxes.gajdaw.pl/sinatra/sinatra-v1.0.0.box will be stored in this folder: http:-VAGRANTSLASH--VAGRANTSLASH-boxes.gajdaw.pl-VAGRANTSLASH-sinatra-VAGRANTSLASH-sinatra-v1.0.0.box.

Note that the boxes stored in the .vagrant.d/boxes/ directory are used as templates by your projects. No matter how many projects using a particular base box you have on your computer, you need only one entry for this box inside the .vagrant.d/boxes/ directory.

■ **Note** Downloading and installing the box can be done manually (see Chapter 5).

Stage II: Importing the Base Box into the Project

The second stage, importing the base box into the project, is shown in Listing 3-2 with just one line:

```
❷==> default: Importing base box 'http://boxes.gajdaw.pl/sinatra/sinatra-v1.0.0.box'...
```

During this stage, the template box stored in the .vagrant.d/boxes/ directory is copied into the Virtual Box directory: ~/VirtualBox VMs/. You can verify it with the following command:

```
$ ls -l ~/VirtualBox\ VMs/
```

Think of this step as creating the VM instance in ~/VirtualBox VMs/ using the template from .vagrant.d/boxes/. The name of the directory for this instance is the name of your project's directory with a timestamp, similar to this: ~/VirtualBox\ VMs/songs-app-sinatra-123456-9876/.

Note that the box stored in .vagrant.d/boxes/ is compressed and consumes about 800 MB. However, the imported box, the one stored within the ~/VirtualBox VMs/ directory, is decompressed and thus much larger. (In the case of a VM for Sinatra, it is about 2.2 GB.)

This operation is a local one, so it usually takes much less time than downloading. In my case, it took about 15 seconds.

Stage III: Booting the System

The third stage, the actual process of booting the guest OS, starts right after the import and lasts until the end. In Listing 3-2, this stage is denoted with ❸:

```
❸ ==> default: Matching MAC address for NAT networking...
...
❸     default: /vagrant => /examples/songs-app-sinatra
```

In this stage, Vagrant boots the guest OS — the one stored as a subdirectory of ~/VirtualBox\ VMs/ — and sets the configuration for networking and shared hosts.

The networking that is defined in Vagrantfile with the following directive:
config.vm.network :forwarded_port, guest: 4567, host: 45670, host_ip: "127.0.0.1"
results in the following message (refer to Listing 3-2):

```
❸ ==> default: Forwarding ports...
❸     default: 4567 => 45670 (adapter 1)
```

When the booting is finished, you might be surprised that nothing happens. Well, not exactly nothing. Vagrant brought up the guest OS that you can work with. The system works in headless mode, which means that it has no GUI interface. You can verify it with the following command:

```
$ vagrant status
```

This command prints the information about the status of the guest OS in the current project. After a successful $ vagrant up operation, the guest OS is running in the background and its state is denoted as follows:

```
default          running (virtualbox)
```

The main window of VirtualBox now contains a VM labeled Running (see Figure 3-1).

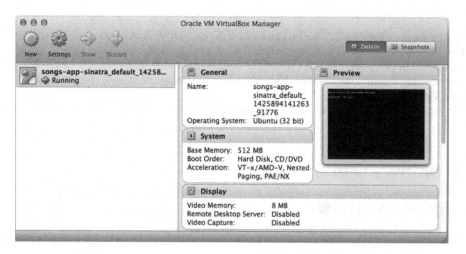

Figure 3-1. *The main window of VirtualBox with songs-app-sinatra running*

If you list the contents of the project's directory with $ `ls -la`, you'll see this item among others:

```
drwxr-xr-x  3 gajdaw  staff  102 12 lis 08:18 .vagrant
```

This directory is the place in which Vagrant stores the ID and some other information about the guest OS. The size of this directory might be neglected; it is only a couple of kilobytes. The following command prints the output of approximately 20 KB:

```
$ du -hs .vagrant/
```

This directory should not be shared with other developers. What's more, it also can't be copied. It is designed to be created and destroyed only by Vagrant commands such as $ `vagrant up` and $ `vagrant destroy`.

To avoid sharing `.vagrant/` directory, remember to add the following entry to your `.gitignore` file:

```
/.vagrant/
```

You can also add this entry to your global `.gitignore` configuration.

■ **Warning** What happens if you inadvertently remove the `.vagrant/` directory in a project? You'll lose the information about the VM, but if the machine was already started before the removal, it won't be automatically stopped. To stop or remove the machine, use the VirtualBox main window shown in Figure 3-1. After selecting the VM, use `Machine/Close` option/`Power off`. You can also use the $ `vagrant global-status` command. In general, you should avoid performing any filesystem operations on Vagrant directories, such as `.vagrant/` or `.vagrant.d/`; rely on Vagrant commands instead.

Files and Directories: Summary

Figure 3-2 presents a summary of files and directories that are relevant to $ vagrant up. It will help you better understand the process of bringing up a new guest OS to life.

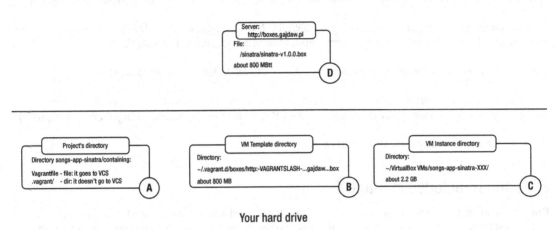

Figure 3-2. *Files and directories relevant to the $ vagrant up command*

■ **Note**   From now on, I'll refer to the directories shown in Figure 3-2 as the project's directory as A, the VM template directory as B, and the VM instance directory as C.

The directory labelled A is where the source code of the project resides (for an existing project, this directory is created with the $ git clone command). This is the place where you should run all Vagrant commands such as $ vagrant up or $ vagrant status. Inside this directory, you can find the Vagrantfile file and the directory .vagrant/.

■ **Notice**   To start the work on a new project from scratch, you need the $ vagrant init command, which will be discussed in Chapter 4.

Please note that right after the $ git clone command, the project's directory A does not contain .vagrant/ subdirectory; it is created only after the $ vagrant up command. Keep in mind the following:

- Vagrantfile should always go into the version control.
- .vagrant/ should always be ignored by the version control. You can't copy this directory to some other location on your hard drive.

Now let's dive into the actions performed by Vagrant during each of the three stages of $ vagrant up.

Files and Directories in Stage I

During Stage I, Vagrant downloads the box file (about 800 MB) from the server and installs the box in the system inside the VM template directory denoted as B in Figure 3-2. This template can be reused by many projects. In other words, the directory denoted as B is created (if it does not already exist) during Stage I of $ vagrant up.

The directory ~/vagrant.d/boxes/http:-VAGRANTSLASH-...gajdaw...boxsinatra consumes about as much as the file downloaded from the server — about 800 MB. You can verify it with this:

```
$ du -hs ~/.vagrant.d/boxes/http:-VAGRANTSLASH--VAGRANTSLASH-boxes.gajdaw.pl*
```

Because this file is not user- or project-dependent, it is a very reasonable solution to install it on your system only once for all users. You can do this with the VAGRANT_HOME environment settings (refer to Chapter 1):

```
$ export VAGRANT_HOME=/some/shared/directory
```

Files and Directories in Stage II

During this stage, the VM template stored in directory B is copied and uncompressed into directory C. This is the guest OS that will be used only by this particular project. Every project that you run uses its own VM instance.

At this stage, the VM instance directory shown in Figure 3-2 as C is created. The subdirectory C contains uncompressed version of the VM, so it can consume much more space. In the case of my sinatra-v0.2.0 box, it is about 2.2 GB, as you can verify with the following command:

```
$ du -hs ~/VirtualBox\ VMs/songs-app-sinatra*
```

Files and Directories in Stage III

During this step, the guest OS is started. This step is the most complicated one. It will be discussed in more detail in following chapters. Now, I want to focus on the VM state and the directories and files that take part during $ vagrant up.

At this stage, the .vagrant/ directory is created inside the project's folder and consumes only a couple of kilobytes. You'll find only some text files that identify the VM instance to be used inside this directory. You have to remember to ignore it from VCS (Version Control System).

Guest OS States

The guest OS is up and running. To verify this, you can use the $ vagrant status command, which prints the information about the state of the VM.

In all, there are five different states that your machine can enter. They are denoted by $ vagrant status as follows:

- running
- poweroff
- saved
- not created
- aborted

running State

When the command $ vagrant status prints:

```
Current machine states:

default              running (virtualbox)
```

the guest OS is running, and you can access it using ssh and other protocols (such as HTTP) that were made available in the VM and Vagrantfile configuration.

When you access the guest OS with ssh, you can create files and directories inside virtual filesystems, and you can start processes. These files, directories, and processes remain in the system as long as the system is working (i.e., as long as you do not halt, reboot, or destroy it).

For the project in this state, your hard drive contains both directories B and C shown in Figure 3-2. VirtualBox uses the Running label to denote this VM state (refer to Figure 3-1).

poweroff State

If the output of the $ vagrant status is the following, the guest OS was halted:

```
Current machine states:

default              poweroff (virtualbox)
```

You cannot access the VM with ssh any more, of course. When the VM enters this step, it halts all the processes that were running. As a consequence, when you bring the machine back to life, some of the processes might not be available. But the files that you have created inside the guest VM are not removed. If you reboot the system, it will contain the files created during the previous run.

In this state, your hard drive contains both directories B and C shown in Figure 3-2. When a VM enters this state, the VirtualBox main window labels the state as Powered Off (see Figure 3-3).

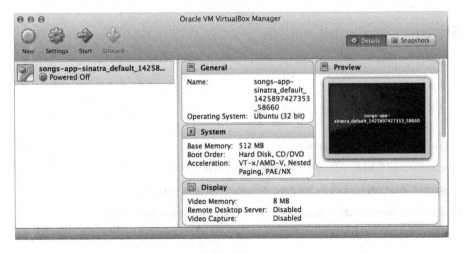

Figure 3-3. *Virtual machine in poweroff state*

saved State

The next state is described as follows by the $ vagrant status command:

Current machine states:

default   saved (virtualbox)

In this state, the VM is frozen. The exact state of the guest OS, with all the processes still running with the contents of RAM and so on, is saved into directory C. This means that when you resume the system, you'll get all the files, processes, and RAM back.

In this state, the C directory can consume much more space than in the other states because the VM RAM is dumped to a file. VirtualBox uses the Saved label, as shown in Figure 3-4.

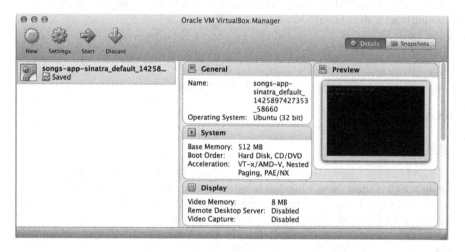

Figure 3-4. *VM in a saved state*

not created State

The fourth state is described as follows:

Current machine states:

default   not created (virtualbox)

The VM is in this state in these two situations:

- Before the first run of $ vagrant up (directories B and C don't exist)

- After $ vagrant destroy (directory B exists; directory C doesn't exist)

There is a slight difference between these two cases. In the first one, the box file hasn't been downloaded yet, so directory B doesn't exist. In the second case, directory B exists. In both cases, directory C doesn't exist.

When the VM is in this state, the main window of VirtualBox is empty — the state is not listed at all by VirtualBox because the VM doesn't exist.

aborted State

The last state is described by $ vagrant status as follows:

```
default          aborted (virtualbox)
```

The VM can enter this state in these two situations:

- Your host OS goes to sleep
- You interrupt $ vagrant up by pressing Control+C

The VirtualBox main window with a guest OS in this state is shown in Figure 3-5.

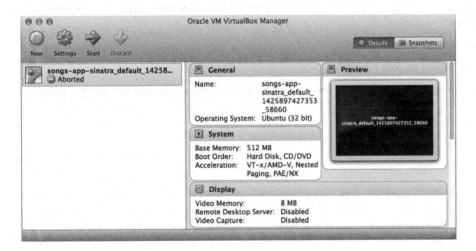

Figure 3-5. *VM in the aborted state*

Vagrant Commands

Vagrant offers a number of commands that deal with a machine's state:

```
$ vagrant status
$ vagrant global-status
$ vagrant up
$ vagrant halt
$ vagrant suspend
$ vagrant destroy
$ vagrant reload
```

The first command reports the state of a machine in the current directory. When you try to run it outside the project's directory, as follows:

```
$ cd ~
$ vagrant status
```

you'll see only the following notice:

```
A Vagrant environment or target machine is required to run this
command. Run `vagrant init` to create a new Vagrant environment. Or,
get an ID of a target machine from `vagrant global-status` to run
this command on. A final option is to change to a directory with a
Vagrantfile and to try again.
```

The second command, $ vagrant global-status, prints a system-wide report that informs you about all VMs controlled by Vagrant.

For other commands that manage the VM state, see Figure 3-6. The commands to manage the VM state differ with two aspects:

- Time necessary to boot the VM

- Space occupied on your hard drive

As you might expect, the larger the space occupied on a drive, the shorter the time necessary to bring the VM to life.

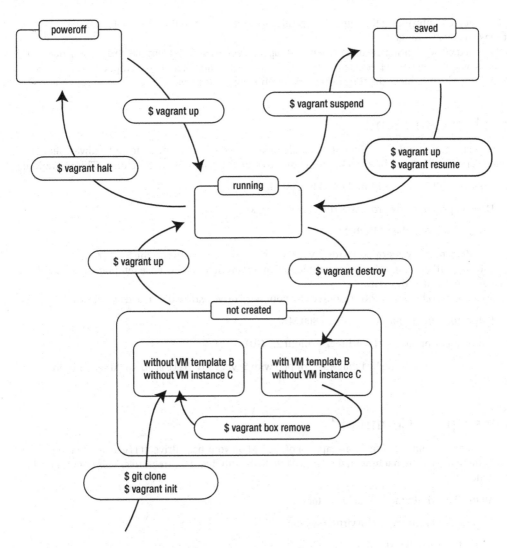

Figure 3-6. *How Vagrant commands modify the state of the guest VM*

$ vagrant up Command

When you run the $ vagrant up command, the actual actions performed by Vagrant can include the following:

- Stage I, if necessary (the box was not downloaded and installed; in other words, when the VM template directory B shown in Figure 3-2 does not exist, it will be created)

- Stage II, if necessary (if the VM instance directory C shown in Figure 3-2 does not exist, it will be created)

- Stage III, depending on the state, it boots or resumes the VM

No matter what the previous state was, you always end in the running state, in which the directories for VM template (B) and for VM instance (C) always exist.

Stage I is executed only during the initial $ vagrant up (or if you manually remove the box with $ vagrant box remove command).

Stage II is executed only during the initial $ vagrant up (or if you used $ vagrant destroy to stop the VM).

If you use $ vagrant halt or $ vagrant suspend, both Stage I and Stage II are skipped during the next $ vagrant up run, which reduces the time necessary to reboot the guest VM.

$ vagrant halt Command

The $ vagrant halt command stops the VM. It should be executed in a running state and it always leaves the machine in a poweroff state with both VM template (B) and VM instance (C) directories. This operation:

- Preserves all the files within the VM filesystem

- Doesn't preserve any processes running in the VM

- Doesn't preserve the VM's RAM

To boot the VM when it was stopped with $ vagrant halt, you'll have to run the $ vagrant up command. Only Stage III is executed in this case. Stages I and II are skipped because template directory B and instance directory C already exist.

The space consumed by the various resources on your hard drive can be described as follows:

- B directory (for a sinatra box, about 800 MB)

- C directory (for songs-app-sinatra, about 2.2 GB)

The time necessary to boot the VM that was stopped with $ vagrant halt is about 30 seconds on my system.

$ vagrant suspend Command

The $ vagrant suspend command saves a snapshot of the VM on your hard drive. It is executed in the running state, and it leaves the machine in the saved state with both B and C directories. This operation will preserve the following:

- All the files within the virtual filesystem

- All processes running in the virtual system

- RAM of the virtual system

A VM in a suspended state can consume much more space on your hard drive (about 2.2 GB for songs-app-sinatra). The time necessary to resume the VM from the saved state is the shortest; no other method brings a VM to life more quickly. On my system, it takes about 20 seconds.

$ vagrant destroy Command

The $ vagrant destroy command stops the guest OS and removes the VM instance from the drive. It removes the VM instance directory C shown in Figure 3-2. Keep in mind that the directory labelled as template directory B is not removed, so after the following two commands, you'll still have the box installed during $ vagrant up in your system:

```
$ vagrant up
$ vagrant destroy
```

$ vagrant reload Command

The $ `vagrant reload` command restarts the VM. It is equivalent to the following:

```
$ vagrant halt
$ vagrant up
```

You can use this command to reload changes in Vagrantfile, such as port forwarding or shared folder configuration.

How to Start and Stop a VM

The three aspects of starting and stopping VM are these:

- Time necessary to boot the system (during $ `vagrant up` or $ `vagrant resume`)

- Space on the hard drive necessary for storage (after $ `vagrant halt`, $ `vagrant suspend`, or $ `vagrant destroy`)

- Which resources — such as files, processes, or RAM contents — are preserved in the guest OS and which are lost

To start the guest OS, you need only one command: $ `vagrant up`. It brings the VM to life, no matter what the current state of your project is. The time necessary to complete this operation depends on your previous actions.

When you run $ `vagrant up` for the first time for a given box, it will take quite a while to complete. Depending on your hardware and the bandwidth of the network, it can be a nerve-wracking operation, so make sure that it is executed only once.

When the guest OS is running on your machine, things will work much better. If you need to stop the machine, use either $ `vagrant halt` or $ `vagrant suspend`. Then, the next time you boot the machine with $ `vagrant up`, the operation will be finished quite quickly. Of course, when you stop the system, the guest doesn't consume the RAM or processor of your host machine. A stopped or suspended guest consumes only your hard drive space.

The summary of starting and stopping VMs is shown in Tables 3-3 and 3-4.

Table 3-3. *Timing of Starting VMs from Different States*

Boot VM from the State	Stage I Download	Stage II Import	Stage III Boot/Resume	Total Time
not created (after $ `vagrant init`, when the box is not installed)	3 minutes	15 seconds	boot: 20 seconds	3 minutes, 35 seconds
poweroff (after $ `vagrant halt`)	-	-	boot: 20 seconds	20 seconds
saved (after $ `vagrant suspend`)	-	-	resume: 10 seconds	10 seconds
not created (after $ `vagrant destroy`)	-	15 seconds	boot: 20 seconds	35 seconds

Table 3-4. *Properties of Three Different Methods of Shutting Down VMs*

	VM Processes and RAM	VM Filesystem	VM Template in ~/.vagrant.d/boxes/	VM Instance in ~/VirtualBox VMs/	Space
`$ vagrant destroy`	not preserved	not preserved	preserved — 700 MB	not preserved	700 MB
`$ vagrant halt`	not preserved	preserved	preserved — 700 MB	preserved — 2.1 GB	2.8 GB
`$ vagrant suspend`	preserved	preserved	preserved — 700 MB	preserved — 2.2 GB	2.9 GB

■ **Warning**   Timing and space estimates are for my computer and for `songs-app-sinatra` using the box version v1.0.0. They are not universal; you will probably get other results.

Running "Songs for kids" in Sinatra

Let's take a look at Vagrant commands and VM states in practice by using the example application. If you have not already completed the execution of `$ vagrant up`, do it right now:

```
$ vagrant up
```

When the command finishes, the guest system should be in the `running` state. To verify it, use this command:

```
$ vagrant status
```

To access the application through your browser, start the HTTP server with the following commands:

```
$ vagrant ssh
$ ruby app.rb -o 0.0.0.0 &
$ logout
```

The `ruby` command starts the process to serve the application over the HTTP protocol. Using the IP 0.0.0.0 enables connections to the guest OS from an arbitrary IP, which is how you allow the connections incoming from the host OS. When this process is running, you can visit the application using the web browser running on your host OS. If you use your browser to visit `http://127.0.0.1:45670`, you'll see a web page identical to the one shown in Figure 3-7.

Figure 3-7. *"Songs for kids" written in Sinatra*

Killing and Preserving Processes in a Guest OS During Shutdown

Suppose that you have finished coding for today and you want to finish dealing with the application. You can use the halt subcommand to stop the guest machine:

```
$ vagrant halt
```

The guest OS is no longer present in your computer's RAM. It has just entered the poweroff state. When you are eager to start coding again, first bring the guest OS to life by using this command:

```
$ vagrant up
```

This time, the command should be completed in much shorter time because it consists only of Stage III. As I have already mentioned, it takes about 30 seconds, which I consider to be reasonable. Wait for the command to finish and try to use your web browser to visit http://127.0.0.1:45670.

The page is not available because all processes running in the guest OS are killed during
$ vagrant halt. When you reboot the VM, the system runs only the processes that are started up at boot time.

To visit http://127.0.0.1:45670, you have to start the process again using the following commands:

```
$ vagrant ssh
$ ruby app.rb -o 0.0.0.0 &
$ logout
```

Again, the process to serve the pages is running, and the URL http://127.0.0.1:45670 works just fine in your browser. Now, try to stop the system using the $ vagrant suspend command:

```
$ vagrant suspend
```

At this point, the VM is in the saved state; it doesn't consume the host's RAM or CPU. Of course, the URL http://127.0.0.1:45670 is inaccessible.

To wake the system up, you can now use either of two commands:

```
$ vagrant up
$ vagrant resume
```

Whichever command you choose, Vagrant will resume the suspended VM. When one of these two commands is executed, the system will run again; this time, you can access http://127.0.0.1:45670 at once with your browser. The process to serve the application (the one started before $ vagrant suspend) is present in the guest OS:

```
$ ruby app.rb -o 0.0.0.0 &
```

As you can see, the $ vagrant suspend command preserves the processes within the guest OS.

You can also try to stop the VM with the $ vagrant destroy command and wake the VM again with $ vagrant up. But when you stop the guest OS with $ vagrant destroy, all its processes are killed, so when you reboot the VM with $ vagrant up, you have to start the HTTP server by hand.

Here's a summary to remember:

- *$ vagrant suspend followed by $ vagrant up*: The HTTP server started by hand is preserved

- *$ vagrant halt followed by $ vagrant up*: The HTTP server started by hand is killed and has to be started again manually

- *$ vagrant destroy followed by $ vagrant up*: The HTTP server started by hand is killed and needs to be started again manually

Preserving and Losing Files in a Guest OS During Shutdown

Finally, I want to discuss what happens to files when the guest VM is rebooted. The answer is quite simple:

- When you use $ vagrant destroy followed by $ vagrant up, all the files that you may have created within the guest OS are removed.

- When you use $ vagrant halt followed by $ vagrant up, the files within the guest OS are preserved.

The files within the project's directory are always preserved. Even if you stop the guest VM with $ vagrant destroy, all the files within a project's directory will be preserved.

Colliding Ports

If port 45670 on your host system is already in use, the command $ vagrant up will fail. You can resolve this issue in two ways:

- Close the application that allocated the port 45670

- Change the port defined in the Vagrantfile

To change the port used in Listing 3-1 from 45670 to 9090, open the Vagrantfile and change the fourth line to this:

```
config.vm.network :forwarded_port, guest: 4567, host: 9090, host_ip: "127.0.0.1"
```

Reboot the system with this:

```
$ vagrant reload
```

Start the web server:

```
$ vagrant ssh
$ ruby app.rb -o 0.0.0.0 &
$ logout
```

Use your web browser to access http://127.0.0.1:9090. You should see the web page shown in Figure 3-8.

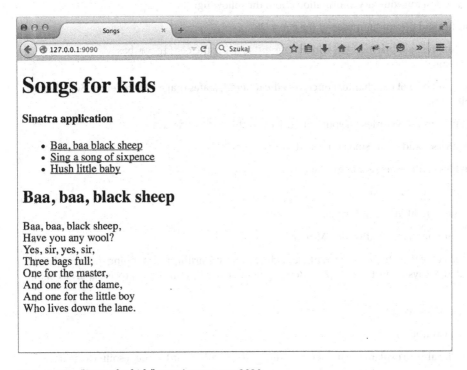

Figure 3-8. *"Songs for kids" running on port 9090*

Removing the Box

To list the boxes installed during the $ `vagrant up` command, use this command:

$ `vagrant box list`

The output of the command contains the names of all installed boxes. Every box can be removed from the system with this command:

$ `vagrant box remove NAME`

The `NAME` has to be replaced with the name of the box that you want to remove. The command removes the VM template directory for the box (this directory is labeled B in Figure 3-3). If you remove the box the next $ `vagrant up` command will download the box again.

Summary

Although the contents of this chapter might seem too complicated at first glance (at least for beginners), they serve a very important purpose. If you want to avoid the pitfall of spending endless minutes waiting for Vagrant to boot your development environment, you need to master all the different methods to start and stop VMs. I was struggling with Vagrant for quite a long time, and it was not until I learned the three ways of stopping the guest OS that I made progress in reducing the time necessary for each boot. That's not all that you need to know to work with Vagrant efficiently, but it's a sound starting point.

This chapter gave you introductory information about the following:

- Vagrantfile and the configuration of the guest OS

- How to set the base box for a VM within Vagrantfile using the `config.vm.box` instructions

The most important part of the chapter concerned the different states that a VM can enter. Specifically, you learned the following:

- Which files and directories on your hard drive are affected by Vagrant

- Which files should be version controlled

- Which files can't be version controlled

- Different states that a VM can enter

- Three stages behind $ `vagrant up`

- All the commands to modify the VM state

The practical aspect of this chapter is in-depth knowledge about starting and stopping VM. You should be able to explain all the ways to start and stop the development environment, giving precise analysis of the following:

- Time necessary to run

- Space consumption

You should also be able to explain the influence of the method with regard to the resources inside a guest OS.

In the Next Chapter You Will Learn . . .

Chapter 4 is devoted to security. You will get a thorough explanation of all the risks that accompany using Vagrant and VMs.

Reading List

The most important source for information about Vagrant commands is (not surprisingly) the manual. Access `https://docs.vagrantup.com/v2/cli/index.html` to get detailed documentation for all Vagrant commands, including the ones discussed in this chapter.

Test Yourself

1. What is the versioning strategy for the Vagrantfile format?

2. What Vagrantfile entries do you use to define the base box to be used?

3. What are the three stages behind `$ vagrant up` executed for the first time for a given box?

4. What happens during Stage I: downloading and installing the base box? How long does the stage take? What directories and files are affected?

5. What happens during Stage II: importing the base box? How long does the stage take? What directories and files are affected?

6. What happens during Stage III: booting? How long does the stage take? What directories and files are affected?

7. Which files and directories on your hard drive are affected by Vagrant?

8. Where does Vagrant store base boxes (i.e., templates to run a guest OS)?

9. When should you change Vagrant's configuration concerning the directory in which the base boxes (templates) are stored? How can you do it?

10. Where does Vagrant store running/halted/suspended guest OSs? Can you change the location? How?

11. Which Vagrant-related directories and files should always be committed into version control?

12. Which Vagrant-related directories and files should never be version controlled?

13. How does `$ vagrant destroy` affect processes and files of VMs?

14. How does `$ vagrant destroy` affect the directories on your host's hard drive?

15. How does `$ vagrant halt` affect processes and files of VMs?

16. How does `$ vagrant halt` affect the directories on your host's hard drive?

17. How does `$ vagrant suspend` affect processes and files of VMs?

18. How does `$ vagrant suspend` affect the directories on your host's hard drive?

19. What is the purpose of $ vagrant reload? How does it affect files and directories inside a VM? How does it affect processes inside a VM?

20. Can you run $ vagrant status in an arbitrary directory? Why would you do so?

21. Can you run $ vagrant global-status in an arbitrary directory? Why would you do so?

22. Suppose that you have inadvertently removed .vagrant/ directory for a currently running VM. What can you do?

Exercises

1. Run the first example from Chapter 2 ("Songs for kids" written in AngularJS) using port 7878.

2. Run the second example from Chapter 2 ("Songs for kids" written in Django) using port 9100.

3. Remove the box installed for the "Songs for kids" written in Sinatra from your host.

4. Measure the time required for the up, halt, suspend, reload, and destroy commands for the "Songs for kids" Sinatra example.

■ ■ ■

## CHAPTER 4

Default Configuration and Security Settings of the Guest VM

In Chapter 2, you had the opportunity to take a look at Vagrant in action; and thanks to Chapter 3, you now understand the actions performed by Vagrant when you boot or halt the guest OS. Now it's time to get acquainted with the default configuration of a VM.

In this chapter, you will find the answers to the following questions:

- How does the guest OS communicate with the outside world?

- What aspects of communication can be defined?

- What default settings are used by Vagrant?

- How can these settings be changed?

In particular, the chapter will cover the following:

- Port forwarding

- Directory sharing between the host and guest OS

- Working with SSH

All these topics are crucial because they give you insight into the security of your workstation. With the knowledge gained from this chapter, you will be aware of the most common security pitfalls and know how to avoid them.

■ **Note**   To proceed with the examples, stop all VMs that may be running on your host. You don't have to destroy them; you can just halt or suspend them.

Atlas

To start a new project that will use a guest OS, you need an image of the preinstalled OS. This image, which is called a *base box* in Vagrant terminology, can be either created from scratch (using installation CD ROM, for example) or downloaded from the network.

■ **Note** The topic of creating base boxes from scratch isn't covered here because it will be discussed thoroughly in Chapter 7. This chapter will use a base box that comes from the network, as in the previous two chapters.

The Vagrantfile included in all the examples in Chapters 2 and 3 contains a line similar to the one shown here:

```
config.vm.box = "http://boxes.gajdaw.pl/sinatra/sinatra-v1.0.0.box"
```

When you boot the VM, Vagrant downloads the file using the URL assigned to `config.vm.box`. Starting with version 1.6, Vagrant can also use a cloud service named Atlas to download base boxes. This service, which is available at `https://atlas.hashicorp.com`, acts as a huge catalog of boxes. Each box is identified by a name that consists of two parts: the vendor's name and the name of the box.

For example, the name `hashicorp/precise64` refers to the box authored by Hashicorp and named `precise64`. It is an Ubuntu release with the code name `Precise` built for 64-bit hardware. The details about this box are available at `https://atlas.hashicorp.com/hashicorp/boxes/precise64`. To search for other boxes, visit `https://atlas.hashicorp.com/boxes/search` and type the name of the system or framework that you are interested in.

Among the huge collection of boxes, the most important, in my opinion, are the ones produced by well-known companies such as Hashicorp, Puppet, Chef, and Ubuntu (to name a few). Their boxes are available here:

- Hashicorp

  - `https://atlas.hashicorp.com/hashicorp`

- Puppetlabs

  - `https://atlas.hashicorp.com/puppetlabs`

  - `http://puppet-vagrant-boxes.puppetlabs.com/`

  - `https://github.com/puppetlabs/puppet-vagrant-boxes`

- Chef

  - `https://atlas.hashicorp.com/chef`

  - `http://chef.github.io/bento/`

  - `https://github.com/chef/bento`

- Ubuntu

  - `https://atlas.hashicorp.com/ubuntu`

  - `https://cloud-images.ubuntu.com/vagrant/`

Although there are lots of OSs, I will stick to the 32-bit Ubuntu 14.04 box published by Ubuntu. This box is available in Atlas under the name `ubuntu/trusty32`.

To create a development environment that imitates your production settings, use the box with the same OS as is used by the server in which you deploy your application. For example, if your production server is CentOS 7.0, this box might be useful: `puppetlabs/centos-7.0-64-nocm`. And if you deploy your applications on a machine running Fedora 21, this box might be appropriate: `chef/fedora-21`.

The complete procedure to deploy one of the examples will be discussed in Chapter 10.

> ■ **Tip**　I prefer to use 32-bit versions of base boxes because they can be run on a large assortment of hardware. If you're sure that your hardware supports a 64-bit OS, you can try `ubuntu/trusty64`.

Initializing a New Project

The Vagrant command to start a new project is $ `vagrant init`. To create a new project using the ubuntu/trusty32 box, run the commands shown in Listing 4-1.

Listing 4-1.　Starting a Project Using the ubuntu/trusty32 Base Box

```
$ cd folder/with/examples
$ mkdir new-project-chapter-04
$ cd new-project-chapter-04
$ vagrant init -m ubuntu/trusty32
```

The sole purpose of the $ `vagrant init` command is to create a configuration file named Vagrantfile. The file created by the following command is shown in Listing 4-2:

```
$ vagrant init -m ubuntu/trusty32
```

Listing 4-2.　Vagrantfile Created with $ vagrant init -m ubuntu/trusty32

```
Vagrant.configure(2) do |config|
  config.vm.box = "ubuntu/trusty32"
end
```

As you already know, the file is written in the Ruby language. The file shown in Listing 4-2 is equivalent to the following:

```
VAGRANTFILE_API_VERSION = "2"
Vagrant.configure(VAGRANTFILE_API_VERSION) do |config|
  config.vm.box = "ubuntu/trusty32"
end
```

At this point, you should understand that the Vagrantfile shown in Listing 4-2 is written using version 2 for Vagrantfile syntax, and the VM will use a box named ubuntu/trusty32 that comes from the Atlas service. The parameter you pass to $ `vagrant init` is used as the value for the config.vm.box configuration entry.

The -m flag used in Listing 4-1 forces Vagrant to create a minimal Vagrantfile. If you skip this flag, you will get a Vagrantfile with a lot of comments explaining diverse configuration options. I will stick with a minimal Vagrantfile, but you can experiment with $ `vagrant init` without an -m flag.

Another $ `vagrant init` flag of that you will find useful is -f. By default, $ `vagrant init` will not create a new Vagrantfile if one is already present in the current directory. Using the -f flag can force Vagrant to overwrite an existing Vagrantfile with new contents.

Keep in mind that the sole purpose of $ `vagrant init` is to create a Vagrantfile. If you prefer, you can create a Vagrantfile by hand using your favorite text editor and skip using $ `vagrant init` at all.

At this point, I assume that your new-project-chapter-04/ directory contains the Vagrantfile shown in Listing 4-1.

Security Concern #1

Using a base box downloaded from the network is the first potential security risk. Using a base box means downloading a packed file that contains a complete OS and then booting this system on a laptop. When you run $ `vagrant up`, you actually boot up the guest OS prepared by someone else. Of course, a guest OS can contain malicious software, just like any other binary executable. Before you bring a VM up, you have to ask yourself whether the author of the base box can be trusted.

That's where the security begins. If you download and boot the system that has been created with bad intentions or has been tampered with by attackers, you might compromise the security of your machine or even your network.

I recommend several VMs available on Vagrant Cloud, including the following:

- `hashicorp/precise64`
- `ubuntu/trusty32`
- `chef/centos-6.5`

More generally speaking, I have confidence in all the boxes available from `Hashicorp`, `Ubuntu`, or `Chef`, but I don't use boxes by vendors that I am not familiar with.

All the boxes that I have prepared for this book are open source. The source code is hosted at GitHub, and the binary versions are hosted at `http://boxes.gajdaw.pl`. You can download the source code and build the boxes yourself, which will require some additional work (but you'll avoid running binaries that come from external sources). You can also run the examples with a simple $ `vagrant up`, but it will entail downloading and using my binary boxes. The choice is yours. I'll give you the complete and in-depth explanation of how to build my boxes and run the examples using your binaries in Chapter 9.

■ **Warning** Running $ `vagrant up` for a base box that you know nothing about can be compared to running a binary application that comes from an unknown source. It can compromise your workstation or even the whole network.

Booting the Guest OS

If you have used the `ubuntu/trusty32` box in some of your projects, please remove the box from your system. You can use this command to do so:

```
$ vagrant box remove ubuntu/trusty32
```

You can verify that the box is not present in your system with these commands:

```
$ vagrant box list
$ vagrant box list | grep ubuntu
```

Now that the Vagrantfile is ready, and the `ubuntu/trusty32` box is not present in your system, you can boot the guest OS with this:

```
$ vagrant up
```

The output produced by this command is shown in Listing 4-3. This time, you'll concentrate on the code marked with ❶, ❷, and ❸.

Listing 4-3. Output of $ vagrant up Executed for the First Time for the Vagrantfile Shown in Listing 4-2

```
new-project-chapter-04$ vagrant up
Bringing machine 'default' up with 'virtualbox' provider...
❶ ==> default: Box 'ubuntu/trusty32' could not be found. Attempting to find and install...
❶     default: Box Provider: virtualbox
❶     default: Box Version: >= 0
❶ ==> default: Loading metadata for box 'ubuntu/trusty32'
❶     default: URL: https://atlas.hashicorp.com/ubuntu/trusty32
❶ ==> default: Adding box 'ubuntu/trusty32' (v14.04) for provider: virtualbox
❶     default: Downloading: https://atlas.hashicorp.com/ubuntu/boxes/trusty32/
              versions/14.04/providers/virtualbox.box
❶ ==> default: Successfully added box 'ubuntu/trusty32' (v14.04) for 'virtualbox'!
==> default: Importing base box 'ubuntu/trusty32'...
==> default: Matching MAC address for NAT networking...
==> default: Checking if box 'ubuntu/trusty32' is up to date...
==> default: Setting the name of the VM: new-project-chapter-04_default_1425979386605_81311
==> default: Clearing any previously set forwarded ports...
==> default: Clearing any previously set network interfaces...
==> default: Preparing network interfaces based on configuration...
    default: Adapter 1: nat
❷ ==> default: Forwarding ports...
    default: 22 => 2222 (adapter 1)
==> default: Booting VM...
==> default: Waiting for machine to boot. This may take a few minutes...
    default: SSH address: 127.0.0.1:2222
    default: SSH username: vagrant
    default: SSH auth method: private key
    default: Warning: Connection timeout. Retrying...
    default: Warning: Remote connection disconnect. Retrying...
    default:
    default: Vagrant insecure key detected. Vagrant will automatically replace
    default: this with a newly generated keypair for better security.
    default:
    default: Inserting generated public key within guest...
    default: Removing insecure key from the guest if its present...
    default: Key inserted! Disconnecting and reconnecting using new SSH key...
==> default: Machine booted and ready!
==> default: Checking for guest additions in VM...
❸ ==> default: Mounting shared folders...
    default: /vagrant => /examples/new-project-chapter-04
```

Downloading the ubuntu/trusty32 Base Box from Atlas

The parts marked in Listing 4-3 with ❶ concern downloading and installing the base box. As you know, this is the first stage of $ vagrant up. The box name ubuntu/trusty32 is searched for in the Atlas service:

```
❶ default: URL: https://atlas.hashicorp.com/ubuntu/trusty32
```

Atlas expands the name ubuntu/trusty32 into the URL:

❶   default: Downloading: https://atlas.hashicorp.com/ubuntu/boxes/trusty32/
versions/14.04/providers/virtualbox.box

If you try to download the previous URL with the curl command-line tool like this:

```
$ curl https://atlas.hashicorp.com/ubuntu/boxes/trusty32/versions/14.04/providers/
virtualbox.box
```

you will receive this response:

```
<html>
  <body>
    You are being <a href="http://cloud-images.ubuntu.com/vagrant/trusty/current/trusty-
server-cloudimg-i386-vagrant-disk1.box">redirected</a>.
  </body>
</html>
```

Atlas redirects requests for ubuntu/trusty32 to http://cloud-images.ubuntu.com/vagrant/trusty/
current/trusty-server-cloudimg-i386-vagrant-disk1.box.

The preceding file served by cloud-images.ubuntu.com is downloaded to your computer and installed as a base box.

■ **Note**   You can also download base boxes manually by using curl or wget:

```
$ curl [URL] -o [FILENAME]
$ wget -O [FILENAME] [URL]
```

Here are the commands to download one of my boxes:

```
$ curl http://boxes.gajdaw.pl/apache/apache-v1.0.0.box -o apache-v1.0.0.box
$ wget -O apache-v1.0.0.box http://boxes.gajdaw.pl/apache/apache-v1.0.0.box
```

And here are the commands to download the ubuntu/trusty32 base box:

```
$ curl http://cloud-images.ubuntu.com/vagrant/trusty/current/trusty-server-cloudimg-
i386-vagrant-disk1.box -o trusty-server-cloudimg-i386-vagrant-disk1.box
$ wget -O trusty-server-cloudimg-i386-vagrant-disk1.box http://cloud-images.ubuntu.com/
vagrant/trusty/current/trusty-server-cloudimg-i386-vagrant-disk1.box
```

Default Configuration of a VM

The default configuration of a VM consists of the following:

- *One forwarded port*: Host port 2222 is forwarded to guest port 22.

- *One shared folder*: The folder that contains the Vagrantfile is shared by the host and guest OS.

Forwarding Port 2222 on the Host to Port 22 on the Guest

The exposed port is announced in Listing 4-3 by the output denoted here:

```
➋ ==> default: Forwarding ports...
    default: 22 => 2222 (adapter 1)
```

When you access port number 2222 on the host system, you are redirected to port number 22 inside the guest system. This configuration is necessary; without it, you could not to access the guest OS using SSH. But Vagrant takes the precaution to restrict the access to this port to only requests coming from IP address 127.0.0.1, which prevents access to the guest OS through the network. By default, the SSH session to the guest OS can be opened only from the host machine.

You can verify this by inspecting forwarded ports properties for VM with the VirtualBox application. The procedure to do this is shown in Figures 4-1, 4-2, and 4-3. Open the VirtualBox main window and follow the buttons shown with arrows A, B, C, and D.

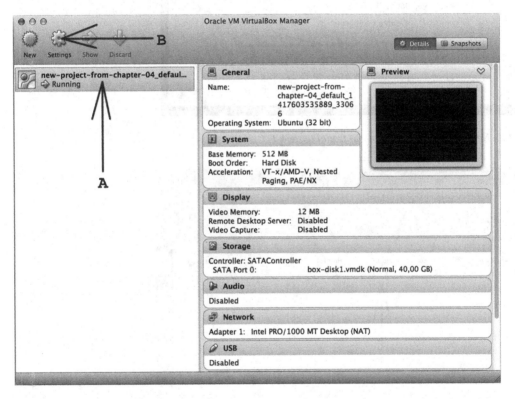

Figure 4-1. *VirtualBox main window with the VM from new-project-chapter-04/ running*

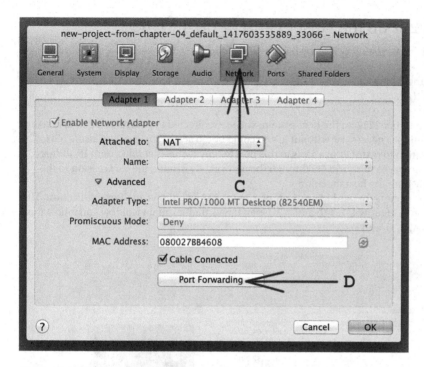

Figure 4-2. *Network properties of the VM from Figure 4-1*

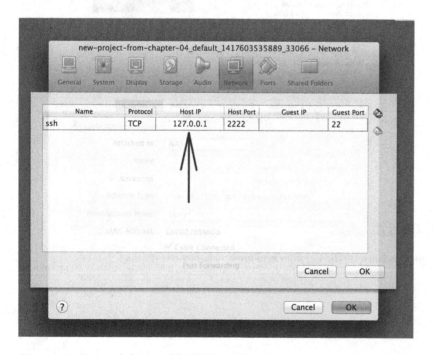

Figure 4-3. *Forwarded ports of the VM from Figure 4-1*

The Host IP value shown in Figure 4-3 is responsible for restricting the machines that can access the forwarded port. This setting can be achieved with the following Vagrantfile entry:

```
config.vm.network :forwarded_port, guest: 22, host: 2222, host_ip: "127.0.0.1"
```

Whenever you use forwarded ports to access services of a guest OS, ensure that you expose the ports only to the host machine unless you know exactly what you are doing.

Security Concern #2

By default, Vagrant exposes only one port of a guest OS. No matter which daemons are running inside a guest OS, the only daemon that can be accessed is sshd. What's more, the sshd running on a guest machine can be accessed only by sessions originating from a host machine.

When dealing with forwarded ports, you should mimic this behavior. Your guest OS should not expose any services to the outside world. One way to do this is to use the host_ip parameter for :forwarded_port rules:

```
config.vm.network :forwarded_port, guest: 80, host: 8888, host_ip: "127.0.0.1"
```

Sharing a Project Directory

When you run $ vagrant up, Vagrant turns on sharing of a project directory by default. This is announced in Listing 4-3 with the following:

```
❸==> default: Mounting shared folders...
    default: /vagrant => /examples/new-project-chapter-04
```

The project directory in the host OS is now available in the guest OS. In my case, I executed $ vagrant up inside the /examples/new-project-chapter-04/ directory, which became available in the guest OS as the /vagrant folder. In other words, the following two directories have exactly the same contents and are synchronized in the background:

```
Host directory                          Guest directory
/examples/new-project-chapter-04/    <===>    /vagrant
```

The changes you make in the host OS are immediately visible in the guest OS. And the changes made in the guest are immediately visible in the host. You can verify this by running the following commands, which will create a file named abc.txt in the host OS:

```
### Here you are in Host OS
$ cd new-project-chapter-04/
$ echo abc > abc.txt
```

The echo command creates a file named abc.txt that contains the text "abc". Open the SSH session to the guest, list the contents of the /vagrant directory, and print the contents of the /vagrant/abc.txt file on the terminal:

```
### Here you are in Host OS
$ vagrant ssh
### Now you are in Guest OS
$ ls /vagrant
$ cat /vagrant/abc.txt
$ logout
### After logout you are in Host OS again
```

The output of $ ls /vagrant will include the abc.txt file, and $ cat /vagrant/abc.txt will print the string "abc".

Thus, the changes you made in the host system inside the /examples/new-project-chapter-04/ directory are visible in the guest OS in the /vagrant directory. It proves the synchronization from host to guest.

Now test the synchronization in the other direction: from guest to host. Run the following commands that change the contents of the abc.txt file inside the guest OS:

```
### Here you are in Host OS
$ vagrant ssh
### Now you are inside Guest OS
$ echo xyz > /vagrant/abc.txt
$ logout
### After logging out you are in Host OS again
```

Take a look at the new-project-chapter-04/ directory. If you list the contents of the abc.txt file in the host OS with the following, you will see the output "xyz":

```
### You are in Host OS
$ cd new-project-chapter-04
$ cat abc.txt
```

Thus, the changes made inside the guest OS are available in the host OS.

You can inspect the properties of a shared folder by using VirtualBox (see Figure 4-4). Run VirtualBox and then click the buttons in Figure 4-4 denoted by the A, B, C, and D arrows.

■ **Note**   Some commands, like for example $ ls, can be executed in both the host and the guest systems.

To avoid confusion, I add comments such as these:

```
### Here you are in Host OS
$ ls
$ vagrant ssh
### Now you are in Guest OS
$ ls
$ logout
### After logout you are in Host OS again
```

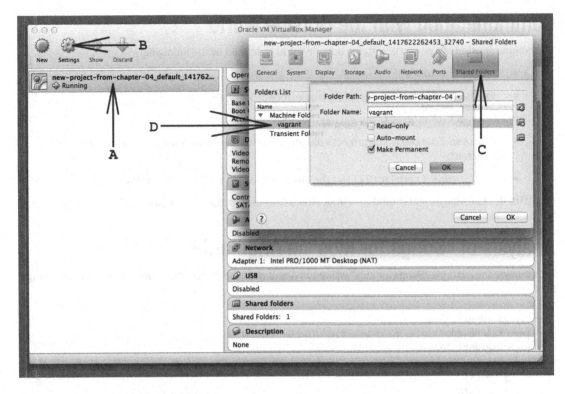

Figure 4-4. *Inspecting a shared folder's properties*

Sharing a project directory is defined in Vagrant with the following configuration settings:

```
config.vm.synced_folder [HOST-PATH], [GUEST-PATH]
```

Here's the example for Windows:

```
config.vm.synced_folder "c:\\dir\\on\\host\\windows", "/dir/on/guest/ubuntu"
```

And here's one for Mac or Linux:

```
config.vm.synced_folder "/dir/on/host/Mac/or/Linux", "/dir/on/guest/ubuntu"
```

■ **Note** There are some very interesting options for the `config.vm.synced_folder` setting (turning on NFS, for example). But because this requires using private networks, I will postpone the discussion until Chapter 8.

Communication with the Outside World

The communication of a guest OS with the outside world is defined by the following:

- Shared directories

- Exposed network resources (for example, forwarded ports)

The new-project-chapter-04/ project has the following:

- *One shared directory*: The project's directory is available in the guest under the name /vagrant.

- *One forwarded port*: Port 2222 on the host is forwarded to port 22 on the guest.

With this knowledge, you should now understand how the examples discussed in Chapter 2 work.

Analysis of "Songs for kids" in AngularJS

Let's analyze the example "Songs for kids" written in AngularJS. The project directory contains the following files:

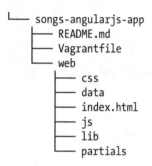

Because a project directory is shared between the host and guest, the files inside the directory (for example, web/index.html) can be edited on the host workstation. You can use an arbitrary editor to change the contents of the file.

The contents of a project's directory are mounted in the guest OS under the name /vagrant. Thus the files available in the host under the web/ directory are present in the guest inside the /vagrant/web/ folder.

Next, port number 8800 on the host is mapped to port number 80 in the guest, thanks to the following line in Vagrantfile:

```
config.vm.network :forwarded_port, guest: 80, host: 8800, host_ip: "127.0.0.1"
```

So when you access http://127.0.0.1:8800 on the host, the request is sent to port number 80 in the guest VM.

The box used in this example, apache-v0.3.3, contains an Apache daemon running in the guest OS. The Apache starts at boot time and serves the contents of /vagrant/web directory over HTTP port 80.

When you run $ vagrant up in this example, you can use your browser to access http://127.0.0.1:8800, which presents the contents of the project's web/ directory.

When you change the contents of a file (for example, web/index.html on the host machine), these changes are at once reflected inside the guest (thanks to host-guest synchronization). When you refresh the page that is displayed, you will see the new contents.

Working with SSH

Secure Shell (SSH) is a mechanism that opens a remote terminal session to a computer running a u*ix-like system. By default, the guest VM is configured so that its ssh daemon is available on the host on port number 2222. This information is included in the output of the $ vagrant up command:

```
❷ ==> default: Forwarding ports...
    default: 22 => 2222 (adapter 1)
```

The usual way to use SSH is to run the ssh command from a command prompt. Use something like the following, where johnny is your username on the example.net server:

```
$ ssh johnny@example.net
```

When you boot the guest OS, you can start the SSH session with the much-simplified $ vagrant ssh command. This process is the simplest way to do it because it takes into account various settings. The configuration of SSH sessions opened by Vagrant can be checked with this command:

```
$ vagrant ssh-config
```

One advantage of using $ vagrant ssh is that Vagrant will take care of port conflicts. If you start more than one guest OS (for example, if you run all the examples from Chapter 2 at the same time), only one guest can use default port mapping: 2222 => 22 for the ssh daemon. Every other guest will have to use a different setting (for example, 2200 => 22) to avoid conflicts with ports that have already been allocated on the guest. Vagrant takes care of such conflicts when you use $ vagrant ssh to open an SSH session.

■ **Note** In case of conflicts, you can verify the port mapping for every VM using the output of $ vagrant up:

```
==> default: Forwarding ports...
    default: 22 => 2222 (adapter 1)
```

You can also use the VirtualBox dialog box shown in Figure 4-3.

You can also use a traditional approach, which is also worth trying because it exposes another important aspect of guest security. The following command opens the SSH session to the guest OS:

```
$ ssh -p2222 vagrant@127.0.0.1
```

To log in, you have to use the following credentials:

```
username: vagrant
password: vagrant
```

After typing the password, you will be granted SSH access to the guest. All the standard base boxes contain the "vagrant" account that is protected by the "vagrant" password.

Working with Multiple Guests

When you work with multiple guests, it is very useful to embed a script that prints the precise information about the box in the guest. I will tell you how to do it in Chapter 6, but for now remember that when you open an SSH session to one of the boxes prepared for the example projects (such as the apache-v1.0.0 box used in the "Songs for kids" project in Chapter 2), you can run this command:

```
### You should open SSH session to guest
### the command should be executed in guest vm
$ guestvm
```

You will see output similar to this:

```
============================================================
gajdaw
/some/path/on/your/host/os/songs-app-angularjs
apache
1.0.0
============================================================
```

The output contains the following:

- *Vendor*: gajdaw
- *Box name*: apache
- *Box version*: 0.3.3
- *Path on the host OS*: /some/path/on/your/host/os/songs-app-angularjs

Security Concern #3

As you may guess a well known built-in account is yet another thing that can be considered a security concern. The guest OS contains the following account:

```
username: vagrant
password: vagrant
```

The account is allowed to use the sudo command, so the Vagrant user has full administrative access to the guest OS. The only restriction that protects the guest OS from remote access is the host_ip requirement set to "127.0.0.1".

So you must remember that you can't make your guest's sshd daemon publicly available until you disable the Vagrant account. The following configuration setting would allow everyone who knows your IP to access the guest OS:

```
config.vm.network :forwarded_port, guest: 22, host: 9999
```

The command to open SSH session to VM configured with the above config entry is the following, where 1.2.3.4 is the IP address:

```
$ ssh -p9999 vagrant@1.2.3.4
```

You can resolve these problems by changing the password for the Vagrant account. To do so, open the SSH session:

```
$ vagrant ssh
```

Then use this command:

```
$ passwd
```

■ **Note** When you destroy the VM with $ vagrant destroy and boot it again with $ vagrant up, the guest OS will use the settings from the original base box. For ubuntu/trusty32, it is username=vagrant, password=vagrant. To make the change permanent, you need to repackage the base box (this will be discussed in Chapter 5).

Using the authorized_keys File for SSH Authorization

The SSH protocol allows two different methods of authorization: username/password and public/private cryptographic keys. This command from the previous section uses the first method:

```
$ ssh -p222 vagrant@127.0.0.1
```

Access is granted if you provide a valid password to the Vagrant account.

The second method relies on two RSA keys: a private key and a public key, stored in separate files. By default, the keys are stored here:

```
~/.ssh/id_rsa     - private key
~/.ssh/id_rsa.pub - public key
```

When you try to open the SSH session to the account johnny@example.net, the access can be granted without having to type the password under one condition: the public key has to be included in the list stored in johnny's authorized_keys file. The file should be saved at the host example.net in johnny's home directory under the name ~/.ssh/authorized_keys. When it is done, the SSH session is opened.

This is the way to avoid having to retype your password for SSH sessions, scp commands, and git push/fetch commands.

And this is the method applied by Vagrant. When you run the following command, the SSH session is authorized with RSA keys:

```
$ vagrant ssh
```

The two keys are stored as follows:

- The private key is stored in the host OS in ~/.vagrant.d/insecure_private_key
- The public key is stored in the guest OS inside /home/vagrant/.ssh/authorized_keys

---

■ **Tip** You can check the path to the host's private key with the $ vagrant ssh-config command.

To change the RSA key pair used by the guest, generate a new pair of keys. The following generates two files: johnny and johnny.pub:

```
# Host
$ ssh-keygen -t rsa -C johnny@example.net -f johhny
```

This is a pair of RSA keys. The first of them contains the private key; the second contains the public key.

Once the keys are generated, append the public key to the authorized_keys file for the Vagrant account in the guest OS by using these commands:

```
# Host
$ cp johnny.pub new-project-chapter-04/
$ vagrant ssh

# Guest
$ cat /vagrant/johnny.pub > ~/.ssh/authorized_keys
$ logout
```

Finally, instruct Vagrant to use the private key from the file named johnny. Inside the Vagrantfile of the project, add the following line:

```
config.ssh.private_key_path = "/path/to/the/key/johnny"
```

When you reload the guest system with the following, Vagrant will use the new RSA keys to authorize access, and the default pair of keys will no longer work:

```
$ vagrant reload
```

Security Concern #4

Publicly available boxes (for example, ubuntu/trusty32) use so-called insecure and publicly known SSH keys. (The insecure private key can be found in the ~/.vagrant.d/insecure_private_key file.) The insecure public key is added to the authorized_keys file for a Vagrant account inside a box (for example, ubuntu/trusty32), which is why you can log in as admin and install software within the guest OS. Be aware that everyone has access to this pair of keys and can use them. For security, use a new pair of RSA keys to authorize access to the guest OS.

The latest versions of Vagrant minimize the risk of using a publicly known key pair. If Vagrant recognizes insecure keys, it replaces them on the fly with a new and randomly generated pair, which is announced during $ vagrant up by the following message shown in Listing 4-3:

```
default: Vagrant insecure key detected. Vagrant will automatically replace
default: this with a newly generated keypair for better security.
default:
default: Inserting generated public key within guest...
default: Removing insecure key from the guest if its present...
default: Key inserted! Disconnecting and reconnecting using new SSH key...
```

■ **Note** When publishing a box, you have to use insecure keys; otherwise, no one can use the box. So you need to turn on SSH key substitution with config.ssh.insert_key = false. You will use this option in Chapters 5 and 7.

Reloading the Guest OS

You might need to change the configuration stored in the Vagrantfile. To apply new changes made in the configuration stored within Vagrantfile, use this:

```
$ vagrant reload
```

This command stops the guest OS and boots it again using the settings read from Vagrantfile. This is the command to use if you want to change port forwarding settings or shared folder configurations.

You can change the configuration in the "Songs for kids" AngularJS example so that the application is available at port 9876. To do this, edit the Vagrantfile by introducing the following change:

```
config.vm.network :forwarded_port, guest: 80, host: 9876, host_ip: "127.0.0.1"
```

Then reload the system with the $ vagrant reload command. When the command finishes rebooting the guest OS, the example application will be available at http://127.0.0.1:9876.

You now know how to resolve the problem of colliding ports. If port 8800 is already used on your host, and you can't start the "Songs for kids" AngularJS example, change the project's configuration in Vagrantfile and reload the guest OS.

Summary

This chapter discussed the potential risks of using Vagrant, with emphasis on the following issues:

- Downloading and running unknown boxes (they can contain malicious software)

- Exposing resources, such as network ports, to the outside world

- Base boxes that contain the Vagrant account with sudo privileges protected by a well-known password

- Base boxes that use a well-known RSA key pair

When you introduce Vagrant in your company, consider doing the following:

- Change the user account used to access the SSH session (or at least change the password to the Vagrant account)

- Change the private/public key pair used for SSH authorization within your box

This chapter also discussed the following:

- Atlas

- Default VM configuration

- SSH

You should know that the name "ubuntu/trusty32" is resolved by the Vagrant service into an arbitrary URL that may point to an arbitrary server (for ubuntu/* boxes, it is http://cloud-images.ubuntu.com). You should also be able to download boxes manually by using wget or curl.

Default VM configuration concerns include these:

- Port forwarding

- Directory sharing

If the Vagrantfile contains no entries other than the box name (as in Listing 4-2), host-guest communication is reduced to the following:

- One shared folder (the host's folder with Vagrantfile is available in the guest as /vagrant)

- One host port (2222 by default) mapped to the guest's 22 port with host_ip restricted to 127.0.0.1

Remember that changes you make to the configuration file Vagrantfile can be applied with the $ vagrant reload command.

If you get lost when working with multiple VMs, use the following command:

```
$ guestvm
```

It is available in my boxes; in Chapter 6, I will explain to you how you can embed similar commands inside your boxes.

In the Next Chapter, You Will Learn . . .

The guest OS created in this chapter was not very interesting because it was a bare Ubuntu without any daemons installed. In Chapter 5, you will learn how to customize the box with the software you might need for your next project. You will learn how to install software inside the guest and how to package the obtained system into an image file to be used by others. Using this knowledge, you will be able to make permanent changes within a guest OS.

Reading List

For more information about SSH, visit Wikipedia: `http://en.wikipedia.org/wiki/Secure_Shell` and check the SSH manual:

```
$ man ssh
```

Test Yourself

1. What are the potential risks of using Vagrant?

2. How do you open a SSH session to the guest OS by using Vagrant commands?

3. How do you check SSH settings for a current project?

4. How do you open an SSH session to the guest OS in a traditional way?

5. How do you initialize a new project using Vagrant?

6. What flags of `$ vagrant init` do you know? What are their roles?

7. What is the sole purpose of the `$ vagrant init` command?

8. How do you define port forwarding from port 1234 on the host to the service running inside the guest using port 9876?

9. How does the `$ vagrant up` command inform the forwarding port host's port 55555 about the service running in the guest VM on port 80?

10. How do you restrict access to the forwarded port to only sessions originating from the host machine?

11. How do you generate a new pair of RSA keys?

12. How do you use a new pair of RSA keys to authorize access to the guest OS?

13. How do you apply any changes done in Vagrantfile?

Exercises

1. Start a new project using the `puppetlabs/debian-7.8-64-puppet` base box.

2. Start a new project using `chef/fedora-21`.

3. Boot two VMs: "Songs for kids" in AngularJS and "Songs for kids" in Django. Open the SSH session to each guest and run the `$ guestvm` command.

■ ■ ■

## CHAPTER 5

Your First Box

The time has come to create your first box. In this chapter, you will adopt a manual procedure: initialize a new base box using the pristine Ubuntu 14.04 and then install the software by hand, running appropriate commands. Once the guest contains the necessary packages and tools, you will export it to a file. This is a basic solution to generate a new base box. Even though it can be a tedious process, the possibilities it offers are just great. With your box at hand, you can introduce Vagrant in your workflow. I will show you how to do this by creating an imaginary project called "Corporate Blog."

The Task at Hand

Suppose that you are responsible for setting up the development environment for the next project your company wants to launch: a blog coauthored by all the staff. The blogging platform will be Jekyll, which is a tool that works offline to process a set of text files written in MarkDown language with some templates and configuration files into a complete set of HTML static files that can be served to clients.

You are responsible for setting up the development environment so that it does the following:

- Contains all the tools necessary to process source files into the HTML to be served

- Enables you to inspect how the blog looks at any given moment with a web browser at http://localhost:8080

The exercise in this chapter will involve two activities carried out in two different folders:

- ~/first-box-factory/

- ~/corporate-blog/

In the introductory step, you will work in the ~/first-box-factory/ directory to produce a boxed VM. This work will be carried out by system engineers.

In the second stage, you will work in ~/corporate-blog/ to create a blog using the box prepared in the first step. This part of the work is assigned to a developer.

■ **Note**   To avoid confusion, turn off all guest VMs that may be already running on your host.

Choosing a Base Box and Initializing a New Project

Suppose that you are a system engineer and your role is to set up the development environment. The result of your work should be a single box file that developers will use to work on a project.

When you need to produce a new box, the easiest solution is to extend one of the existing base boxes. If you want to prepare a development environment running Ubuntu, you can choose one of the boxes supported by Ubuntu:

- ubuntu/trusty64

- ubuntu/trusty32

- ubuntu/precise32

- ubuntu/precise64

If you prefer CentOS, Debian, Fedora, or FreeBSD, you can use boxes supported by Chef Software, Inc.:

- chef/centos-6.5

- chef/debian-7.4

- chef/fedora-20

- chef/freebsd-9.2

More boxes can be found on the atlas.hashicorp.com site. I will stick with 32-bit version of Ubuntu 14.04, but the approach to the task is exactly the same, no matter what your platform is. The only difference is the way you install the software in the guest OS.

When you decide which base box you want to use, go to your home directory and create a new folder named first-box-factory/:

```
# Host
$ cd
$ mkdir first-box-factory
$ cd first-box-factory
```

Initialize a new project using Vagrant:

```
# Host
$ vagrant init -m ubuntu/trusty32
```

Bring up the VM:

```
# Host
$ vagrant up
```

Installing the Necessary Software

When the guest OS is ready, you can start the SSH session and install the necessary software. Because Jekyll relies on the Ruby and JavaScript runtime, you have to install the following:

- NodeJS

- Ruby

- Jekyll

You will also install Lynx, which is a web browser that runs in a terminal. Lynx is a useful tool to test web sites served by a guest OS within an SSH session. And because you are using Ubuntu, the first thing you have to do is update the system.

The complete set of commands you need to run is presented in Listing 5-1.

Listing 5-1. Commands to Install Jekyll and Lynx on Ubuntu 14.04

```
# Host
$ vagrant ssh

# Guest
$ sudo apt-get update -y
$ sudo apt-get install nodejs -y
$ sudo apt-get install lynx-cur -y
$ sudo apt-get install ruby1.9.1-dev -y
$ sudo gem install jekyll
```

Let's run the commands from Listing 5-1, and I will explain the role of each command as we go. Because the VM was already started, you can open the SSH session as follows:

```
# Host
$ vagrant ssh
```

Once in the guest OS, update the system and install the NodeJS and Lynx packages:

```
# Guest
$ sudo apt-get update -y
$ sudo apt-get install nodejs -y
$ sudo apt-get install lynx-cur -y
```

Install the latest version of Ruby header files for compiling extension modules:

```
# Guest
$ sudo apt-get install ruby1.9.1-dev -y
```

The last thing to do is to install Jekyll like this:

```
# Guest
$ sudo gem install jekyll
```

When the installation is finished, you can verify that Jekyll is available on your guest system:

```
# Guest
$ jekyll --version
```

You can close the SSH session. VM is now ready to be boxed.

Generating a Box

Now you have the guest OS running, which includes all the necessary software. It is time to create the box that will result in exactly the same guest machine when booted. To do so, run this command:

```
# Host
$ vagrant package --output first-box-jekyll.box
```

Vagrant offers the $ vagrant package subcommand for boxing. It should be executed in a directory containing the guest OS (i.e., in a directory that contains a Vagrantfile).

The $ vagrant package command can be used for a VM that is running or halted. If the VM is running, it will be gracefully shut down. The command then produces a file that contains the boxed VM.

When run without any parameters, the command creates a file named package.box:

```
# Host
$ vagrant package
```

With the --output parameter, you can change the name and location of the file.

As soon as $ vagrant package has finished working, you can run $ ls to verify that the file named first-box-jekyll.box has been successfully created. The boxed development environment is ready. The box file is ready, and your work as a system engineer is finished.

Listing, Installing, and Removing Boxes

Now you will start to work as a developer. As you already know, boxes have to be installed in your system before they can be used by Vagrant. Box management is achieved with the following subcommands:

```
# Host
$ vagrant box list
$ vagrant box add
$ vagrant box remove
```

Unlike $ vagrant up and $ vagrant package, these subcommands can be executed in an arbitrary directory because they affect a global Vagrant installation, not the particular VM instance.

The first command lists the boxes that have already been installed in your system. Depending on your previous actions, the following command:

```
# Host
$ vagrant box list
```

may produce the following results:

```
gajdaw/rails              (virtualbox, 0.3.3)
gajdaw/sinatra            (virtualbox, 0.1.2)
ubuntu/trusty32           (virtualbox, 14.04)
```

The listing contains the following:

- Box name (e.g., gajdaw/rails)

- Provider name (e.g., virtualbox)

- Box version (e.g., 14.04)

The boxes listed in the output of $ vagrant box list come from the directory discussed in Chapter 3: either ~/.vagrant.d/boxes/ or $VAGRANT_HOME/.vagrant.d/boxes/, depending on the configuration. The listing of one of these directories should resemble (to some extent) the output of $ vagrant box list:

```
# Host
$ ls -la ~/.vagrant.d/boxes/
$ ls -la $VAGRANT_HOME/.vagrant.d/boxes/
```

To add a new box to your .vagrant.d/boxes/ directory, you need to use the $ vagrant box add command. It takes two parameters: box name and box URL, as follows:

```
# Host
$ vagrant box add [NAME] [ADDRESS]
```

The NAME is the label that you want to assign to the newly installed box; ADDRESS points to the file that contains the box (usually with the *.box extension). The ADDRESS can take one of these forms:

- Vendor/Name

- http:// . . .

- file:/// . . .

- A local filename

■ **Tip** When the NAME has the form Vendor/Name, the box comes from the cloud service atlas.hashicorp.com.

To add your box stored in the first-box-jekyll.box file under the name first-box-jekyll, use this command:

```
# Host
$ vagrant box add first-box-jekyll first-box-jekyll.box
```

When `$ vagrant box add` finishes, you can run the following again:

```
# Host
$ vagrant box list
```

The output should contain this:

```
first-box-jekyll          (virtualbox, 0)
```

And, of course, the `.vagrant.d/boxes/` directory should now contain another item: the subdirectory `first-box-jekyll/`.

To remove a box, you can use this command:

```
# Host
$ vagrant box remove NAME
```

The `NAME` parameter passed to this command is the name of the box as printed by `$ vagrant box list`. Because Vagrant supports multiple providers and box versioning, this command can also take two more optional parameters:

```
# Host
$ vagrant box remove NAME --provider PROVIDER --box-version VERSION
```

These parameters set the provider and version of the box to be removed. For example, the following command removes version 1.2.3 of the box labelled as abc:

```
# Host
$ vagrant box remove abc --box-version 1.2.3
```

But versioning works only for boxes that are hosted remotely, either in an Atlas or HTTP server with specially created versioning information.

To remove the box that you created in the previous section, use this:

```
# Host
$ vagrant box remove first-box-jekyll
```

If you use it, remember to add it again because you need the box to proceed with the task:

```
# Host
$ vagrant box add first-box-jekyll first-box-jekyll.box
```

■ **Note** The mysterious lack of symmetry between the `$ vagrant up` and `$ vagrant destroy` commands that was discussed in Chapter 3 is thus solved. When executed, `$ vagrant up` invokes `$ vagrant box add` if the box is not installed already. The `$ vagrant destroy` command does not run `$ vagrant box remove`. Thus, when you run the two commands `$ vagrant up` and `$ vagrant destroy`, your system will remain in the state as it would be after using `$ vagrant box add`. The box that was installed during `$ vagrant up` was not removed by `$ vagrant destroy`; it is still present in the system. You can verify it with `$ vagrant box list`.

Using the Box

If you proceeded with the example up to this point, you should have the box installed in the system and ready to be used. The following command:

```
# Host
$ vagrant box list | grep jekyll
```

should produce the single line:

```
first-box-jekyll             (virtualbox, 0)
```

Go to your home directory and create another folder in which the corporate blog project will be stored:

```
# Host
$ cd
$ mkdir corporate-blog
$ cd corporate-blog
```

This project should use the box named first-box-jekyll. To achieve this result, run this command:

```
# Host
$ vagrant init -m first-box-jekyll
```

You can now boot the VM and open the SSH session:

```
# Host
$ vagrant up
$ vagrant ssh
```

Once in the guest OS, go to the shared directory:

```
# Guest
$ cd /vagrant
```

Generate the first version of the corporate blog:

```
# Guest
$ jekyll new -f .
```

■ **Note**   The command to generate a new blog contains a dot after the -f parameter. This dot stands for current directory.

The previous command generates the source code of the blog in Jekyll internal format. To build the HTML version, run this:

```
# Guest
$ jekyll build
```

The command to build the site with Jekyll should be run in the directory that contains the Jekyll source files. In this case, it is the /vagrant folder (in the guest OS, of course). The HTML files built on the basis of configuration, MarkDown, and templates are stored under the _site/ directory. You can serve the HTML files from the _site/ directory using Jekyll's built-in HTTP server by running the following:

```
# Guest
$ jekyll serve -H 0.0.0.0 --detach
```

Among other things, the output of the command informs you how to access the site and how to stop the server:

```
Server address: http://0.0.0.0:4000/
Server detached with pid '2159'. Run 'kill -9 2159' to stop the server.
```

By default, Jekyll's HTTP server listens on port 4000. To visit the generated site inside your guest OS, run this:

```
# Guest
$ lynx 127.0.0.1:4000
```

You will see a page like the one shown in Figure 5-1.

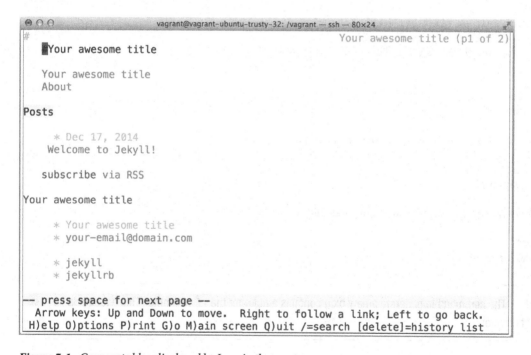

Figure 5-1. *Corporate blog displayed by Lynx in the guest*

Now you can proceed with the last step that will allow to access the blog from the host OS. Not surprisingly, you need to forward ports.

■ **Note** The -H parameter of the $ `jekyll serve -H 0.0.0.0` command defines the IP addresses that are allowed to connect to the HTTP server. The `0.0.0.0` value allows connections that originate at any host. But the HTTP server runs in guest and, by default, no connections are allowed from the outside world to the guest's daemons. So you should not be afraid to use -H `0.0.0.0`. We will filter the incoming request using the `host_ip` restriction for the forwarded port.

Forwarding Ports

To reconfigure port forwarding, you need to edit the Vagrantfile like this:

```
# Host
$ vi ~/corporate-blog/Vagrantfile
```

■ **Tip** If you are comfortable with vi, you can also edit the Vagrantfile within a guest system with the $ `vi /vagrant/Vagrantfile` command.

Change its contents by adding port forwarding. Host port 8080 should be forwarded to guest port 4000. This is the purpose of the `config.vm.network` entry shown in Listing 5-2.

Listing 5-2. Vagrantfile for Corporate Blog Project with Forwarded Ports

```
Vagrant.configure(2) do |config|
  config.vm.box = "first-box-jekyll"
  config.vm.network :forwarded_port, guest: 4000, host: 8080, host_ip: "127.0.0.1"
end
```

To apply the new changes, you have to reload the guest OS with this:

```
# Host
$ vagrant reload
```

After rebooting the system, you have to start the built-in Jekyll server again:

```
# Host
$ vagrant ssh
# Guest
$ cd /vagrant
$ jekyll serve -H 0.0.0.0 --detach
```

Now, if you run the web browser on your host and access `http://localhost:8080`, you will be forwarded to the guest's port number 4000. The page displayed by your browser will look like Figure 5-2.

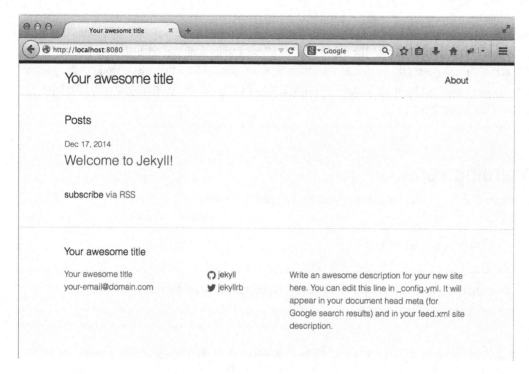

Figure 5-2. Corporate blog displayed by Firefox running in the host

Advantages of Boxing

You are already aware of the most important aspect of boxing, which was the purpose of the examples presented in Chapter 2. The development environment can be reproduced with a single command:
`$ vagrant up`. No special knowledge is required to do this, no matter how difficult and time-consuming the process of preparing the boxed VM might have been.

But that's not the end of boxing advantages. It speeds up your work tremendously, especially when you want to start afresh using a given development environment. Two possible scenarios I have in mind are these:

- You made some changes to your guest OS and don't know how to revert them

- You want to create another Jekyll-driven web site in the `~/my-personal-blog/` directory

In the first scenario, all you have to do is to run this:

```
# Host
$ cd ~/corporate-blog
$ vagrant destroy
$ vagrant up
```

In the second case, you can use these commands:

```
# Host
$ cd
$ mkdir my-personal-blog
$ cd my-personal-blog
$ vagrant init -m create-your-first-box
$ vagrant up
```

Because the box is already installed in the system, in both cases the $ vagrant up command will skip the longest stage: the downloading of the box.

From a practical point of view, I consider boxing much more important than automatic provisioning, which will be discussed in Chapter 6. Do not misunderstand me: I do not advise you to abandon or underestimate provisioning. Definitely not. What I mean is that boxing and manual software installation provide a workflow that can be satisfactorily used in practice, even when used without automated provisioning.

It was not until I introduced boxed solutions that using Vagrant for my classes and courses became possible. Two key tricks are using boxed solutions and sharing installed boxes by setting VAGRANT_HOME, as explained in Chapter 1.

Serving Boxes over the Network

The box you created is just one large first-box-jekyll.box file. You can distribute it any way you like, for example using shared directories, FTP servers, CD-ROMs, DVDs, and so on. Your collaborators can copy the file using the $ cp command and arbitrary media.

But with these solutions, you have to instruct your colleagues what to do with the file (i.e., how to add the box to Vagrant). And regardless of how easy the process is, it will always cause some trouble, questions, and inconvenience. (And, of course, we would not say that the development environment is built with a single $ vagrant up command anymore.)

The best approach to distribute the box is to use the network and internal Vagrant feature to automatically download and install the box if it is missing. All you need is an HTTP server or shared network drive. Assuming that you have read/write access to http://example.net server, upload the box so that it is available under http://example.net/first-box-jekyll.box.

Change the name of the box inside ~/corporate-blog/Vagrantfile to this:

```
config.vm.box = "http://example.net/first-box-jekyll.box"
```

Now, if anyone runs $ vagrant up in this project, the command automatically downloads and installs the box without any interaction from the user. It relieves the burden of instructing your colleagues about boxes.

You can also use shared and mapped drives to achieve the same purpose, as with the following:

```
config.vm.box = "/net/drive/mounted/first-box-jekyll.box"
```

■ **Tip** Boxes hosted over HTTP can be downloaded with the help of curl or wget. The command to download the file with curl looks like this:

```
$ curl http://example.net/first-box-jekyll.box > first-box-jekyll.box
```

Securing Your Boxes

Yes, you should apply the security considerations discussed in Chapter 4 into practice. You should do the following:

- Change the Vagrant user's password
- Change the SSH key used to authenticate in guest

All these changes should be done in guest before you run the `$ vagrant package` command, of course. To change the Vagrant user's password, run this command:

```
# Guest
$ passwd
```

■ **Tip**   Refer to Chapter 4 to see the procedure to replace SSH keys.

Repackaging Boxes

Your system now contains the `first-box-jekyll.box` box twice, which is stored in the `first-box-jekyll.box` file and installed in the `.vagrant.d/boxes/` directory.

The boxes that you installed in your system can be deleted from your hard drive:

```
$ rm first-box-jekyll.box
```

In case you need the boxes again, you can always create a `*.box` file from the box installed in `.vagrant.d/boxes/` with this:

```
$ vagrant box repackage NAME PROVIDER VERSION
```

To re-create the `first-box-jekyll` box, run this command:

```
$ vagrant box repackage first-box-jekyll
```

The command will save the box in file named `package.box`.

Summary

In Chapter 2, you learned how to use the box that has already been prepared. This is the approach applied by developers in your company. They want to work on a given project (i.e., to write some code) and they need a working development environment.

In this chapter, you learned about Vagrant from the perspective of a system engineer. Vagrant involves the cooperation of both developers and system engineers. It all begins with the work done by system engineers, who are responsible for preparing the box. When the box is ready, developers start to work on a project using the box at hand.

You learned the most basic method to prepare the box, which consists of four steps:

1. Choose the appropriate base box (Ubuntu, Fedora, Debian, FreeBSD, and so on).

2. Boot the base box.

3. Install the software within the guest OS (e.g., $ `sudo apt-get install` and $ `sudo yum install`).

4. Package the box with the $ `vagrant package` command.

This is a natural and simple solution that you can apply immediately.

To distribute the box, the best approach is to upload it to the HTTP server and update the `config.vm.box` configuration entry in your project's Vagrantfile. Vagrant will take care of downloading and installing the box on your workstation. (In fact, this is the method used in Chapter 2.)

The following Vagrant commands that you learned to use in this chapter will help you manage the boxes:

```
$ vagrant box list
$ vagrant box add
$ vagrant box remove
$ vagrant box repackage
$ vagrant package
```

In the Next Chapter, You Will Learn . . .

Chapter 6 will get rid of the tedious and error-prone manual installation phase and replaces the necessity of issuing commands to install the software within a guest OS with automatic scripts. The procedure of creating a box will become semiautomatic; the only steps done by humans will be booting and boxing.

Reading List

Jekyll is a tool that belongs to Static Site Generators (SSGs). The comprehensive list of SSGs can be found at `https://staticsitegenerators.net/`.

The Jekyll documentation is available at `http://jekyllrb.com/`

You can always access the syntax of $ `vagrant box` and $ `vagrant package` with the following:

```
$ vagrant box help
$ vagrant package help
```

Test Yourself

1. What are two advantages of using boxes?

2. How do you package a guest OS into a `my-new-box.box` file?

3. How do you list the boxes installed on your workstation?

4. Where are the boxes internally stored by Vagrant?

5. How do you manually install a new box stored in the `abc.box` file?

6. How do you remove a box named xyz that is installed on your system?

7. Are the commands $ vagrant up and $ vagrant destroy symmetrical? Do they perform exactly the same actions in reverse order?

8. How do you create a *.box file for one of the boxes already installed on your system?

9. Where can you find base boxes for various OSs?

10. How can you distribute the boxed development environment among those who work on the project?

Exercises

1. Create a new Ubuntu 14.04 box containing the apache daemon. Follow the manual approach described in Chapter 5.

2. Create a new CentOS 7 box containing the nginx daemon. Follow the manual approach described in Chapter 5.

3. Create a new Fedora 21 box containing Python and Django. Follow the manual approach described in Chapter 5.

4. Create a new Debian box containing Ruby and Ruby on Rails. Follow the manual approach described in Chapter 5.

CHAPTER 6

■ ■ ■

Provisioning

Whenever you want to prepare a new development environment, the first approach is probably a manual one. By running the commands in the pristine guest OS, you should find all the steps you need to install required packages. (That's the approach used in Chapter 5.) To find out the exact procedure of setting up the desired development environment we booted the clean Ubuntu and ran various commands to install Jekyll.

After you know all the necessary commands and steps that tune the new system for the next project, you don't have to run them by hand. You can automate this process by using configuration management software (CMS), which is what you will learn about in this chapter.

It can be helpful, at least for beginners, to think about creating boxes in terms of two separate stages:

- Manual

- Automatic

First, you will start a new project in a new directory and proceed with a manual procedure, which will resemble what you did in previous chapters. When the manual phase is finished, which means that you know all the commands necessary to set up a guest VM, you will create another project in a new directory. It is a completely new project and does not depend on the first one. This time you will save the commands in special scripts that will be automatically executed during $ vagrant up. This automatic process is called *provisioning*.

Vagrant has built-in support for many popular configuration management tools. In this chapter, you will learn how to automate the task of setting up the VM with the following:

- Shell scripts

- Puppet

- Ansible

- Chef

To give each of them a try, you will create four projects:

- vagrant-jekyll-shell

- vagrant-jekyll-puppet

- vagrant-jekyll-ansible

- vagrant-jekyll-chef

Every one of these projects will be responsible for creating an identical development environment that was used for the corporate Jekyll-powered blog in Chapter 5.

Working with provisioners opens new possibilities. Not only it does lead to a procedure that is repeatable and free of manually introduced errors but it also facilitates versioning. This chapter shows you how to version your environment with git.

Provisioners

In Vagrant's terminology, the process of automatic installation and configuration of software within the guest OS during $ vagrant up is called *provisioning* and the tools to perform this operation are called *provisioners*. A provisioner can execute arbitrary commands; it can, for example,[1] install Apache like so:

```
$ sudo apt-get install apache2
```

It can also start the service:

```
$ sudo service apache2 restart
```

It can also download the Ruby source code:

```
$ curl ftp://ftp.ruby-lang.org/pub/ruby/2.2/ruby-2.2.0.tar.gz > ruby.tar.gz
```

And it can also recompile and install Ruby:

```
$ make
$ make install
```

There are no restrictions; all the commands that you usually run within an SSH session to reconfigure your system can be performed by provisioners.

There are many different approaches to provision VMs. You can provision the guest OS by writing shell scripts or using more sophisticated tools such as Puppet, Ansible, and Chef. Out-of-the-box Vagrant supports the following provisioners:

- File
- Shell scripts
- Ansible
- CFEngine
- Chef
- Docker
- Puppet
- Salt

As of now, Puppet, Chef, and Ansible are generally considered the most popular open – source configuration management solutions available on the market. Although I decided to include them all in this book, you can confine yourself to just the one you need, or you might want to try them all and then choose the one that most appeals to you. Vagrant offers the perfect environment for getting acquainted with configuration-management software.

---

[1]The following examples are for the Ubuntu system.

■ **Note** Provisioning is the process of automatic software installation and configuration during $ `vagrant up`.

Configuring Provisioning

Provisioning configuration is stored in a Vagrantfile. Here is the general syntax to configure provisioning:

```
Vagrant.configure(2) do |config|
  ...
  config.vm.provision "THE-NAME-OF-THE-PROVISIONER" ...
end
```

The first parameter of `config.vm.provision` is the name of the provisioner you want to use. Replace "THE-NAME-OF-THE-PROVISIONER" with one of the built-in provisioners, such as the following:

- shell

- puppet

- ansible

- chef-solo

Other parameters of `config.vm.provision` depend on the provisioner you have chosen. Each takes different parameters, and some provisioners (Puppet, for example) don't have any obligatory parameters because all the options have reasonable default values. To use Puppet, you can simply write the following:

```
Vagrant.configure(2) do |config|
  ...
  config.vm.provision "puppet"
end
```

Other provisioners, such as shell, need at least one additional parameter. For the shell provisioner, you have to define the shell script to be executed:

```
Vagrant.configure(2) do |config|
  ...
  config.vm.provision "shell", path: "script.sh"
end
```

Because provisioners do not share any common options except the first parameter, they will be discussed separately.

Multiple Provisioners

Remember that a single project can use more than one provisioner. You can use shell and Puppet and Ansible in one project like this:

```
Vagrant.configure(2) do |config|
  ...
  config.vm.provision "shell", path: "script.sh"
  config.vm.provision "puppet"
  config.vm.provision "ansible", playbook: "playbook.yml"
end
```

Provisioners are executed in the order in which they are defined in the Vagrantfile. Mixing different provisioners proves to be very useful. You will learn why in Chapter 9, which will dissect real-life examples.

When Does Provisioning Happen?

By default, provisioning is executed only during the first run of $ vagrant up. When you run $ vagrant up for the very first time after $ vagrant init or $ vagrant destroy, the system is in a pristine state — it does not contain the packages installed by provisioners. Thus, Vagrant boots the system and runs the provisioners defined in the Vagrantfile.

If you halt the system using $ vagrant halt or $ vagrant suspend, the next run of $ vagrant up will skip the provisioners. Vagrant assumes that provisioners were already executed and all the necessary packages are already installed.

You can change the default behavior in a number of ways. First, you can enable and disable provisioning during $ vagrant up by using the --provision and --no-provision flags:

```
$ vagrant up --provision
$ vagrant up --no-provision
```

The first command, $ vagrant up --provision, boots the system and runs provisioners, even if they were already applied. The second command, $ vagrant up --no-provision, turns off provisioners even if it is the first time $ vagrant up is being executed.

You can also enable provisioners by type. The following command enables only provisioners x, y, and z, disabling all the others:

```
$ vagrant up --provision-with x, y, z
```

To boot the system with shell provisioners only, you can use $ vagrant up like this:

```
$ vagrant up --provision-with shell
```

Another way to run provisioners is to run the $ vagrant provision command, which is especially useful when you work on provisioning scripts and want to try many different settings. The command is supposed to be run for the guest OS that has already been booted. Instead of booting and provisioning the system with $ vagrant up, you can, for example, boot the system without running provisioners:

```
$ vagrant up --no-provision
```

and then run the provisioners:

```
$ vagrant provision
```

The `$ vagrant provision` command can be invoked with the `--provision-with x,y,z` option to enable only some provisioners. To run modified provisioning scripts, you don't have to reboot the system; you can run provisioners again and again with `$ vagrant provision`.

The last command that can be executed with or without running provisioners is `$ vagrant reload`, which can be run with the `--provision`, `--no-provision` and `--provision-with x, y, z` parameters:

```
$ vagrant reload --provision
$ vagrant reload --no-provision
$ vagrant reload --provision-with shell
```

Versioning Boxes with git

Working with provisioners to automate the system configuration process boils down to writing various scripts. No matter which provisioners you eventually choose, you will end up creating text files. Over a period of time, your scripts will surely evolve: you will add new components, change settings, and probably remove obsolete items. At some point, you will get a satisfactory solution that needs to be assigned a unique tag. Looking forward to this scenario, the best approach is to put the VM configuration under version control, which will lead you to workflows in which you can version the infrastructure build with Vagrant the same way you version the code.

For this purpose, git will be used. To proceed with the examples in this chapter, you will have to issue some basic git commands. But don't worry; I will give you all the necessary explanations about how to do it and the exact role of every command used. Working with git, you will be able to do the following:

- Version the development environments

- Tag various versions

To start using git for versioning your VMs, you have to do the following:

- Install the git distribution appropriate for your system

- Set up the basic configuration options

The installation was already explained in Chapter 1. To commit your changes using git, you have to set up your name and e-mail address with the following commands:

```
$ git config --global user.name "Włodzimierz Gajda"
$ git config --global user.email gajdaw@gajdaw.pl
```

Of course, you have to substitute your name and your e-mail for `"Włodzimierz Gajda"` and `gajdaw@gajdaw.pl`. And please remember to use quotation marks around your first name and surname. After you have done this, the following commands should print your data:

```
$ git config --global user.name
$ git config --global user.email
```

■ **Tip** Git stores users' global configuration in the `~/gitconfig` file. You can edit this file using any text editor you like.

Jekyll Box with the Shell Provisioner

Let's start the first project: a Vagrant box for Jekyll–driven web sites configured with a shell provisioner. (All the commands necessary to build this box were already discussed in Chapter 5 and shown in Listing 5-1.) The task at hand is to automate the process of running these commands with a shell provisioner. The goal is to define the VM configuration so that after a single $ vagrant up command, you will have a guest OS with Ruby and Jekyll already installed. Then you will create the box file.

■ **Note** The work in this section is to be done by system engineers. Developers are not involved.

Box Source Code

Create the empty directory for this project:

```
# Host OS
$ cd folder/with/examples
$ mkdir vagrant-jekyll-shell
```

Inside this directory, create two files: the Vagrantfile and `script.sh`. They are shown in Listings 6-1 and 6-2.

Listing 6-1. Vagrantfile for a Jekyll Box with Shell Provisioning

```
Vagrant.configure(2) do |config|
  config.vm.box = "ubuntu/trusty32"
  config.vm.provision "shell", path: "script.sh"
end
```

Listing 6-2. Bash Script script.sh for a VM with Shell Provisioning

```
#!/usr/bin/env bash

echo "Installing: nodejs, lynx, ruby and jekyll..."
apt-get update -y >>/tmp/provision-script.log 2>&1
apt-get install nodejs -y >>/tmp/provision-script.log 2>&1
apt-get install lynx-cur -y >>/tmp/provision-script.log 2>&1
apt-get install ruby1.9.1-dev -y >>/tmp/provision-script.log 2>&1
gem install jekyll >>/tmp/provision-script.log 2>&1
```

The Vagrantfile sets the name of the base box to be ubuntu/trusty32 and enables automatic provisioning with a shell script named script.sh. The following line instructs Vagrant to provision the box running the shell script named script.sh:

```
config.vm.provision "shell", path: "script.sh"
```

In other words, when you boot the system with $ vagrant up, Vagrant will run the script.

The filename can be arbitrary, and the path to the file is a path in your host system. It is relative with regard to the directory that contains the Vagrantfile.

Let's dissect the bash script named script.sh. It starts with a portable shebang for bash:

```
#!/usr/bin/env bash
```

Next, it uses the echo command to print a message that will be visible in the Vagrant output:

```
"Installing: nodejs, lynx, ruby and jekyll..."
```

The commands that follow install NodeJS, Lynx, Runy and Jekyll. This time, you don't need to prepend sudo before each command because provisioning scripts are executed with root's privileges. The second modification is to redirect all the output produced by the commands to a file named /tmp/privision-script.log with the following appended to every command:

```
>>/tmp/provision-script.log 2>&1
```

The two >> characters redirect the output of the command to a file. The 2>&1 part is responsible for redirecting errors (file descriptor 2) to the same file as the standard output (&1). If the file /tmp/provision-script.log doesn't exist, it will be created by the first of the commands.

The two files shown in Listings 6-1 and 6-2 can be seen as the source code for the box you are to create.

First Run of the Shell Provisioner

When you have created the two files shown in Listings 6-1 and 6-2, you can test the box. Enter the directory that contains these files:

```
# Host OS
$ cd vagrant-jekyll-shell
```

and run the command:

```
# Host OS
$ vagrant up
```

The provisioning script shown in Listing 6-2 downloads Jekyll and various gems and recompiles them (among other processes). It might take more than 10 minutes, so you have to be patient.

■ **Warning** Using provisioner scripts such as the one shown in Listing 6-2 within your projects will only make your collaborators furious. Would you like to wait 30 minutes to run each of the example projects that I showed you in Chapter 2? Probably not. Provisioning scripts should be run by system engineers when they build the box. Developers should work with a box that contains all the necessary software baked inside. (Best practices will be discussed in Chapter 9.)

You will see the old Vagrant output with two new elements at the very end. One of them will be the message ❶ about running the shell provisioner; the other is the message ❷ about installing NodeJS, Lynx, Ruby, and Jekyll:

```
Bringing machine 'default' up with 'virtualbox' provider...
==> default: Importing base box 'ubuntu/trusty32'...
...
❶==> default: Running provisioner: shell...
==> default: stdin: is not a tty
❷==> default: Installing: nodejs, lynx, ruby and jekyll...
```

■ **Note** The output contains one red warning: "`stdin: is not a tty`". This is a completely minor issue and you can safely ignore it. It will be discussed after you complete the `vagrant-jekyll-shell` project.

Now your guest OS is running, which you can verify with the following command:

```
# Host OS
$ vagrant status
```

Open the SSH session to the guest OS with this:

```
# Host OS
$ vagrant ssh
```

You can verify that Jekyll is installed and ready with the following:

```
# Guest OS
$ jekyll --version
```

You don't have to run any commands to install Ruby or Jekyll; it was already done by the `script.sh` shell script. You can destroy the system with this:

```
# Host OS
$ vagrant destroy
```

And bring it back to life with this:

```
# Host OS
$ vagrant up
```

The operation of booting the system and installing the software is automatic, but the installation takes place every time you destroy and boot the system again. You can reboot a guest OS, but the time necessary to get it running again is annoyingly long—usually about 30 minutes.

There are two important aspects of provisioning to be aware of. The first is that the installation of the software within the guest OS was done automatically. The second is that the whole process of booting the guest OS lasts much longer than anything in Chapters 2 or 3. Depending on the software that you want to provision, it can last for hours.

The first feature of this approach, automatization, is an obvious advantage. The second, the slowness of the process, is a severe disadvantage. Although there is nothing you can do when you boot the project for the very first time—the software has to be downloaded and installed anyway—you can speed up each following $ vagrant up by generating a box that contains all the software baked inside. That's where you are heading, but you first have to enable version control for your first project.

> ■ **Note** Keep in mind the two most important aspects of provisioning: it runs automatically, but it usually takes a lot of time to provision the pristine system.

Versioning the Box Source Code

When your environment is ready, which means that the system boots and is provisioned without any errors, you can put the configuration under the control of git, which will help you track changes.

Enter the directory in which you created the project:

```
# Host OS
$ cd vagrant-jekyll-shell
```

Initialize a new git repository:

```
# Host OS
$ git init
```

As discussed in earlier chapters, when you boot the guest OS, Vagrant creates a special directory named .vagrant, which should be excluded from version control. Create a file named .gitignore that contains a single line:

```
.vagrant
```

It will force git to ignore the .vagrant directory. Use the following command:

```
# Host OS
$ echo .vagrant > .gitignore
```

To avoid inadvertent box commits, ignore all the files with the *.box extension. Run the following command, which will append the line "*.box" to the .gitignore file:

```
# Host OS
$ echo "*.box" >> .gitignore
```

Now you can commit your changes with these two commands:

```
# Host OS
$ git add -A
$ git commit -m "Initial version"
```

The first of the preceding commands selects all the files in the project and prepares them for the next commit. In git terminology, this process is called *staging changes*. The $ git add -A command stages three new files: the Vagrantfile, script.sh, and .gitignore. The .vagrant directory is excluded, so it will not be staged.

The second command creates the revision titled "Initial version", which will include the three new files that were just staged: the Vagrantfile, script.sh, and .gitignore.

Finally, you can assign a name to this version of the environment. Semantic versioning strategy suggests that the initial version of a new project should have the number 0.1.0. To assign this version to the first commit, use the following git command:

```
# Host OS
$ git tag -a v0.1.0 -m "Release 0.1.0"
```

It creates a v0.1.0 tag with the caption "Release 0.1.0". Once it is done, you can check available versions with this:

```
$ git tag
```

To print the complete history of the project with the tag list, use this command:

```
# Host OS
$ git log --oneline --decorate
```

Now the git repository is in a clean state, which means that all the files were checked in and saved in the git database. To verify it, use one of these commands:

```
# Host OS
$ git status
$ git status -sb
```

Generating a Box

The manual procedure to generate a box consists of two basic steps (refer to Chapter 5):

- Booting the guest OS

- Running the $ vagrant package command

Here are the commands to produce a box for the vagrant-jekyll-shell project (remember that $ vagrant up can take more than 30 minutes):

```
# Host OS
$ cd vagrant-jekyll-shell
$ vagrant up
$ vagrant package --output vagrant-jekyll-shell-v0.1.0.box
```

When the `vagrant-jekyll-shell-v0.1.0.box` file is ready, you can use it as you used the box generated in Chapter 5. It can be seen as the *compiled* version of the source code. And, of course, this procedure is done only by system engineers; developers just use `vagrant-jekyll-shell-v0.1.0.box`.

It is very convenient to append the tag, for example `v0.1.0`, to the filename used for the box. It helps to avoid confusion and allows you to host various versions of the same box.

■ **Note** The box source code consists of the Vagrantfile and `script.sh`. The `vagrant-jekyll-shell-v0.1.0.box` file can be seen as the binary version of the box.

Using the Shell-Provisioned Box

The box is ready, so you can change the role; now you will perform the developer's work. First, you have to install the box in the system with the following command:

```
# Host OS
$ vagrant box add vagrant-jekyll-shell-v0.1.0 vagrant-jekyll-shell-v0.1.0.box
```

You have to execute this command in the folder that contains the `vagrant-jekyll-shell-v0.1.0.box` file generated in the previous section. Alternatively, you can prepend the path to the file:

```
# Host OS
$ vagrant box add vagrant-jekyll-shell-v0.1.0 /some/path/vagrant-jekyll-shell-v0.1.0.box
```

The output of this command should now contain the `vagrant-jekyll-shell` entry:

```
# Host OS
$ vagrant box list
```

So far, so good. Let's create a new project named `flowers-vagrant-jekyll-shell`, which will be a Jekyll–driven web site titled Flowers:

```
# Host OS
$ cd folder/with/examples
$ mkdir flowers-vagrant-jekyll-shell
$ vagrant init -m vagrant-jekyll-shell-v0.1.0
```

Notice that the name of the box that was installed with the `$ vagrant box add` command is passed to the `$ vagrant init` command. Now edit the Vagrantfile and add a directive to configure port forwarding. The complete Vagrantfile for the `flowers-vagrant-jekyll-shell` project is shown in Listing 6-3.

Listing 6-3. Vagrantfile for the flowers-vagrant-jekyll-shell Project

```
Vagrant.configure(2) do |config|
  config.vm.box = "vagrant-jekyll-shell-v0.1.0"
  config.vm.network :forwarded_port, guest: 4000, host: 8100, host_ip: "127.0.0.1"
end
```

When the Vagrantfile is ready, you can boot the VM with this:

```
# Host OS
$ vagrant up
```

This time, the procedure to boot the system will be reasonably short: about one minute. You don't have to run the provisioners; it was done by a system engineer when the box file was created. Ruby and Jekyll are baked inside the box, and the developer doesn't have to download, recompile, or install them.

The development environment is ready. You can create a new project and serve it over the forwarded port:

```
# Guest
$ cd /vagrant
$ jekyll new -f .
$ jekyll build
$ jekyll serve -H 0.0.0.0 --detach
$ logout
```

Thanks to directory sharing, the flowers-vagrant-jekyll-shell/ host directory now contains the source code of the flowers site. And because of the forwarded_port entry in Listing 6-3, you can use your browser to access http://127.0.0.1:8100/. You will see the same page as the one shown in Figure 5-2.

Now the flowers-vagrant-jekyll-shell project is configured so that you have to run $ jekyll serve -H 0.0.0.0 --detach every time you boot the VM. You can avoid it with the shell provisioner. Modify the Vagrantfile by introducing the changes shown in Listing 6-4.

Listing 6-4. Shell Provisioner to Start the HTTP Server at Boot

```
Vagrant.configure(2) do |config|
  config.vm.box = "vagrant-jekyll-shell-v0.1.0"
  config.vm.network :forwarded_port, guest: 4000, host: 8100, host_ip: "127.0.0.1"

$script = <<SCRIPT

cd /vagrant
jekyll serve -H 0.0.0.0 --detach

SCRIPT

  config.vm.provision "shell", inline: $script, run: "always"

end
```

The Vagrantfile shown in Listing 6-4 contains a variable named $script. The part between <<SCRIPT and SCRIPT is a text assigned to the $script variable, which is, of course, the code of the shell script that consists of two commands: cd /vagrant and jekyll serve. Thanks to config.vm.provision, this script will be automatically executed when you boot the guest VM.

Now destroy the guest VM and boot it again:

```
# Host OS
$ vagrant destroy
$ vagrant up
```

This time, the URL http://127.0.0.1:8100 is available right after $ vagrant up. You don't have to open the SSH session and start the HTTP server by hand.

SYSTEM ENGINEER'S ROLE VS. DEVELOPER'S ROLE

The following comparison can help you get started with Vagrant in the most efficient manner:

- Different roles

  - System engineer creates a box file

  - Developer uses a box file

- Different timings

  - Booting the guest OS can last for hours when you run provisioners that install software

  - Booting the guest OS without installing anything takes about one minute

- Differences in configuration

  - System engineer's Vagrantfile (refer to Listing 6-1) doesn't contain port forwarding, but contains provisioners that install software

  - Developer's Vagrantfile (refer to Listing 6-3) contains port forwarding, but doesn't contain provisioners that install software; it may contain provisioners that perform some fast actions, such as starting and stopping the HTTP server (refer to Listing 6-4)

- Re-creating (i.e., $ vagrant destroy -f && vagrant up)

  - To re-create the guest VM, system engineer needs a lot of time (half an hour, an hour, or even more)

  - Developer can re-create the guest VM in a minute or so

- Reconfiguring

  - To change the Vagrantfile (for example, forwarded ports) and reload the guest VM, system engineer might need an hour

  - Developer can modify the Vagrantfile and apply the changes in a minute

Of course, there are many different scenarios for using Vagrant, and I don't know them all. There are probably cases in which the preceding rules won't apply directly, so don't take them literally. But if you start your adventure with Vagrant, they can help you avoid disappointment.

Annoying "not a tty" Problem

Shell provisioners that run on some boxes, for example ubuntu/trusty32, print this red message:

```
==> default: stdin: is not a tty
```

This message is displayed by the following command, which is included in the /root/.profile script in the ubuntu/trusty32 box:

```
mesg n
```

The role of the mesg n command is to disable messages sent by other users with the $ write and $ wall commands. Because the guest system won't be used by others (there are no user accounts), you can safely remove mesg n from the /root/.profile script, and the red message will vanish. (That's what you will do in Chapter 9.)

To verify what I told you above create a new project called verify-tty-problem:

```
# Host OS
$ mkdir verify-tty-problem
$ cd verify-tty-problem
$ vagrant init -m ubuntu/trusty32
```

Edit the Vagrantfile by adding three inline shell provisioners:

```
Vagrant.configure(2) do |config|
  config.vm.box = "ubuntu/trusty32"
  config.vm.provision "shell", inline: "echo abc"
  config.vm.provision "shell", inline: "echo def"
  config.vm.provision "shell", inline: "echo ghi"
end
```

Boot the guest with this:

```
# Host OS
$ vagrant up
```

You will see the red message displayed three times, once for every run of the shell provisioner:

```
==> default: Running provisioner: shell...
    default: Running: inline script
==> default: stdin: is not a tty
==> default: abc
==> default: Running provisioner: shell...
    default: Running: inline script
==> default: stdin: is not a tty
==> default: def
==> default: Running provisioner: shell...
    default: Running: inline script
==> default: stdin: is not a tty
==> default: ghi
```

To run the provisioners again, use this command:

```
# Guest OS
$ vagrant provision
```

The red messages will be printed each time you run the $ vagrant provision command. Now log in to the guest:

```
# Host OS
$ vagrant ssh
```

Display the /root/.profile file:

```
# Guest OS
$ sudo cat /root/.profile
```

You should see mesg n at the very end of the output. Remove the mesg n command from the /root/.profile file with this:

```
# Guest OS
$ sudo sed -i "/mesg n/d" /root/.profile
```

You can verify that the /root/.profile file no longer contains the mesg n with the command:

```
# Guest OS
$ sudo cat /root/.profile
```

To find out the final effect of removal, close the SSH session:

```
# Guest OS
$ logout
```

Run the provisioners:

```
# Host OS
$ vagrant provision
```

The output is free of the annoying "not tty" warnings. When you create your own boxes, just remove the mesg n command from /root/.profile and you will be just fine.

Diving into this issue will give you a pretext to do the following:

- Use multiple shell provisioners
- Learn about inline shell provisioners
- See the $ vagrant provision command in action

I always prefer a practical approach; there's nothing better than to get your hands dirty. That's why you should proceed with this experiment.

Jekyll Box with the Puppet Provisioner

This second example presents the Puppet provisioner in action. Again, you now enter the realm of the system engineer.

Box Source Code

Start with an empty directory:

```
# Host OS
$ cd folder/with/examples
$ mkdir vagrant-jekyll-puppet
```

Create two files (the Vagrantfile and `manifests/default.pp`) with the contents shown in Listings 6-5 and 6-6. Note that `default.pp` is to be stored inside a directory named `manifests/`. The Vagrantfile doesn't contain a directive to define port forwarding.

Listing 6-5. Vagrantfile for Jekyll Box with Puppet Provisioning

```
Vagrant.configure(2) do |config|
  config.vm.box = "ubuntu/trusty32"
config.vm.provision "puppet"
end
```

Listing 6-6. Puppet Script default.pp to Provision a VM

```
exec { 'apt-get update':
    command => '/usr/bin/apt-get update -y'
}

package { 'nodejs':
    require => Exec['apt-get update']
}

package { 'lynx-cur':
    require => Exec['apt-get update']
}

package { 'ruby1.9.1-dev':
    require => Exec['apt-get update']
}

exec { 'Install Jekyll':
    command => '/usr/bin/gem install jekyll',
    require => Package['ruby1.9.1-dev']
}
```

Apart from the following line to set up provisioning, there is nothing new in the Vagrantfile:

```
config.vm.provision "puppet"
```

With the default configuration, Puppet looks for a file named `manifests/default.pp` and executes it. Puppet manifests consist of resources such as exec or package:

```
exec {
}
package {
}
```

Manifests can contain an arbitrary number of resources, and resources can be processed by Puppet in an arbitrary order—not necessarily in the order in which they are declared. The first string that appears inside the braces is a unique label that identifies the resource.

The following resource has the label `'apt-get update'`:

```
exec { 'apt-get update':
    command => '/usr/bin/apt-get update -y'
}
```

When applied, this resource executes a command to update the system. The next resource installs the nodejs package:

```
package { 'nodejs':
    require => Exec['apt-get update']
}
```

For package resources, the label identifies the package to be installed. This resource should be applied after the first resource that updated the system. Resource ordering is achieved with the `required` entry.

The following key forces Puppet to apply the `package{'nodejs': }` resource after the `exec{ 'apt-get update': }` resource:

```
require => Exec['apt-get update']
```

The following two resources will be applied after the system has been updated:

```
package { 'nodejs':
    require => Exec['apt-get update']
}

package { 'lynx-cur':
    require => Exec['apt-get update']
}
```

The order in which `nodejs` and `lynx-cur` are installed is not defined, so you can't assume that `nodejs` will be installed before `lynx-cur`.

The last two resources are responsible for installing Ruby dev package and Jekyll. The `require` keys set the following ordering of the resources:

- First to be applied: exec { 'apt-update': }

- Second to be applied: package { 'ruby1.9.1-dev': }

- Last to be applied: exec { 'Install Jekyll': }

First Run of the Puppet Provisioner

The commands to run the environment are exactly the same as they were for the shell provisioner. The following commands might require half an hour or more to finish:

```
# Host OS
$ cd folder/with/examples
$ cd vagrant-jekyll-puppet
$ vagrant up
```

This time, the output will contain the Puppet's messages, denoted with ❶. They will be printed once in a while:

```
Bringing machine 'default' up with 'virtualbox' provider...
==> default: Importing base box 'ubuntu/trusty32'...
...
❶==> default: Running provisioner: puppet...
❶==> default: Running Puppet with default.pp...
❶==> default: stdin: is not a tty
❶==> default: Notice: Compiled catalog for vagrant-ubuntu-trusty-32 in environment
production in 0.10 seconds
❶==> default: Notice: /Stage[main]/Main/Exec[apt-get update]/returns: executed successfully
❶==> default: Notice: /Stage[main]/Main/Package[lynx-cur]/ensure: ensure changed 'purged'
to 'present'
❶==> default: Notice: /Stage[main]/Main/Package[nodejs]/ensure: ensure changed 'purged' to
'present'
❶==> default: Notice: /Stage[main]/Main/Package[ruby1.9.1-dev]/ensure: ensure changed
'purged' to 'present'
❶==> default: Notice: /Stage[main]/Main/Exec[Install Jekyll]/returns: executed successfully
❶==> default: Notice: Finished catalog run in 174.26 seconds
```

As you can see, Puppet prints a notice about every resource, and every message contains the label of the resource. The provisioning lasted for 174.26 seconds, which is quite long when compared with the time necessary to boot a guest VM.

The 174-second timing was achieved on a Mac Book Pro i7/8GB RAM/SSD. Windows running i5/4 GB RAM/SATA reported 260.77 seconds. But network transfer has some impact on these results, so your benchmarks can differ.

■ **Note** When you use the Puppet provisioner, you might encounter the following red warning:

```
warning: could not retrieve fact fqdn
```

It means that there is a problem with getting a fully qualified domain name (FQDN) for your machine. You will encounter this message, for example, when you boot the guest machine that uses the Puppet provisioner on a computer that isn't connected to the Internet. By default, Puppet tries to set the hostname of a guest VM using an FQDN. You can resolve this issue with the following entry in the Vagrantfile:

```
config.vm.hostname = "abc.example.net"
```

It sets the guest's hostname; Puppet will not try to resolve the FQDN anymore.

Versioning the Box Source Code

The procedure to version the box is the same, no matter which provisioner you use:

1. Change the current directory.

2. Initialize the new repository with `git init`.

3. Create the `.gitignore` file.

4. Commit all the files.

5. Tag the initial version with the `v0.1.0` annotated tag.

Here are the commands:

```
# Host OS
$ cd vagrant-jekyll-puppet
$ git init
$ echo .vagrant > .gitignore
$ echo "*.box" >> .gitignore
$ git add -A
$ git commit -m "Initial version"
$ git tag -a v0.1.0 -m "Release 0.1.0"
```

The initial version of the source code of the box is ready.

Generating a Box

Generate the box named `vagrant-jekyll-puppet-v0.1.0.box` with the following commands:

```
# Host OS
$ cd vagrant-jekyll-puppet
$ vagrant up
$ vagrant package --output vagrant-jekyll-puppet-v0.1.0.box
```

Using a Puppet-Provisioned Box

■ **Note**   Again, you switch the role. Here you work as a developer.

The procedure to use the `vagrant-jekyll-puppet-v0.1.0.box` is exactly the same as the procedure described for the shell-provisioned box. The only difference is when you install the box:

```
# Host OS
$ vagrant box add vagrant-jekyll-puppet-v0.1.0 vagrant-jekyll-puppet-v0.1.0.box
```

And when you initialize a project:

```
# Host OS
$ vagrant init -m vagrant-jekyll-puppet-v0.1.0
```

Apart from these two diversions, both procedures are exactly the same. You should be able to proceed with the `flowers-vagrant-jekyll-puppet` exercise on your own.

Jekyll Box with the Chef Provisioner

■ **Note**   Here you work as a system engineer.

The third example presents the Chef provisioner in action. To proceed with this example, you need to install Chef on your host. You will find the necessary packages for your host at `https://downloads.chef.io`.

Box Source Code

Create the new directory:

```
# Host OS
$ cd folder/with/examples
$ mkdir vagrant-jekyll-chef
```

Populate it with two files: the Vagrantfile and `cookbooks/jekyll/recipes/default.rb` (see Listings 6-7 and 6-8). Ensure that you store the `default.rb` file in the appropriate directory: `cookbooks/jekyll/recipes`. (You have to create the `cookbooks/jekyll/recipes` directory).

Listing 6-7. Vagrantfile for a Jekyll Box with Chef Solo Provisioning

```
Vagrant.configure(2) do |config|
  config.vm.box = "ubuntu/trusty32"
  config.vm.provision "chef_solo" do |chef|
    chef.add_recipe "jekyll"
  end
end
```

Listing 6-8. Chef Script default.pp to Provision a VM

```
execute 'apt-get update'
package 'nodejs'
package 'lynx-cur'
package 'ruby1.9.1-dev'
execute 'gem install jekyll'
```

This project uses the `chef_solo` provisioner with one recipe named "jekyll":

```
config.vm.provision "chef_solo" do |chef|
  chef.add_recipe "jekyll"
end
```

The name of the recipe sets the name of the directory in which the Ruby default.rb. script is stored. By default, all recipes should reside in the cookbooks/ directory. Then goes the name of the recipe: jekyll/ in this case. Inside the recipe directory, another folder named recipes is needed. Thus the complete path to default.rb is this:

cookbooks/jekyll/recipes/default.rb

The default.rb script consists of a list of instructions that are executed in the same order in which they appear in the file. The instructions from Listing 6-8 either execute a command or install a package.

First Run of the Chef Provisioner

As you already know, it takes some time to install Ruby and Jekyll. Chef requires as much time as the shell and Puppet provisioners. But don't expect miracles; Chef requires as much time as the shell and Puppet provisioners.

To start the VM, run these commands:

```
# Host OS
$ cd vagrant-jekyll-chef
$ vagrant up
```

This time, the output will contain Chef messages, which are denoted with ❶:

```
Bringing machine 'default' up with 'virtualbox' provider...
==> default: Importing base box 'ubuntu/trusty32'...
...
❶==> default: Running provisioner: chef_solo...
❶Generating chef JSON and uploading...
❶==> default: Running chef-solo...
❶==> default: stdin: is not a tty
❶==> default: [2015-04-18T07:52:35+00:00] INFO: Forking chef instance to converge...
❶==> default: [2015-04-18T07:52:35+00:00] INFO: *** Chef 12.2.1 ***
❶==> default: [2015-04-18T07:52:35+00:00] INFO: Chef-client pid: 2421
❶==> default: [2015-04-18T07:52:42+00:00] INFO: Setting the run_list to ["recipe[jekyll]"]
from CLI options
❶==> default: [2015-04-18T07:52:42+00:00] INFO: Run List is [recipe[jekyll]]
❶==> default: [2015-04-18T07:52:42+00:00] INFO: Run List expands to [jekyll]
❶==> default:  [2015-04-18T07:52:42+00:00]  INFO:  Starting Chef Run for vagrant-ubuntu-trusty-32
❶==> default: [2015-04-18T07:52:42+00:00] INFO: Running start handlers
❶==> default: [2015-04-18T07:52:42+00:00] INFO: Start handlers complete.
❶==> default: [2015-04-18T07:52:52+00:00] INFO: execute[apt-get update] ran successfully
❶==> default: [2015-04-18T07:53:01+00:00] INFO: apt_package[nodejs] installed nodejs at
0.10.25~dfsg2-2ubuntu1
❶==> default: [2015-04-18T07:53:07+00:00] INFO: apt_package[lynx-cur] installed lynx-cur
at 2.8.8pre4-1
❶==> default: [2015-04-18T07:53:14+00:00] INFO: apt_package[ruby1.9.1-dev] installed
ruby1.9.1-dev at 1.9.3.484-2ubuntu1.2
❶==> default: [2015-04-18T07:55:34+00:00] INFO: execute[gem install jekyll] ran successfully
❶==> default: [2015-04-18T07:55:34+00:00] INFO: Chef Run complete in 171.99255357 seconds
❶==> default:  [2015-04-18T07:55:34+00:00]  INFO:  Skipping removal of unused files from the cache
❶==> default: [2015-04-18T07:55:34+00:00] INFO: Running report handlers
❶==> default: [2015-04-18T07:55:34+00:00] INFO: Report handlers complete
```

For every entry in the default.rb file, Chef prints a notice with the information about whether the command succeeded. The whole process of provisioning with Chef took 171.99 seconds for me.

Versioning the Box Source Code

As before, version the source code using git:

```
# Host OS
$ cd vagrant-jekyll-chef
$ git init
$ echo .vagrant > .gitignore
$ echo "*.box" >> .gitignore
$ git add -A
$ git commit -m "Initial version"
$ git tag -a v0.1.0 -m "Release 0.1.0"
```

The repository is ready.

Generating a Box

To generate the box named vagrant-jekyll-chef-v0.1.0.box, run these commands:

```
$ cd vagrant-jekyll-chef
$ vagrant up
$ vagrant package --output vagrant-jekyll-chef-v0.1.0.box
```

Jekyll Box with the Ansible Provisioner

The last example presents the basic use of the Ansible provisioner. Before you can use Ansible, you have to install it.

On OS X, run this:

```
$ brew update
$ brew install ansible
```

If you work on Ubuntu, use these commands:

```
$ sudo apt-get install software-properties-common
$ sudo apt-add-repository ppa:ansible/ansible
$ sudo apt-get update
$ sudo apt-get install ansible
```

For other platforms, refer to the Ansible documentation at http://docs.ansible.com/intro_installation.html.

■ **Note**   As of now, there is no Ansible installer for Windows platform.

Box Source Code

Start with the empty directory:

```
# Host OS
$ cd folder/with/examples
$ mkdir vagrant-jekyll-ansible
```

Create the two files shown in Listings 6-9 and 6-10: the Vagrantfile and playbook.yml.

Listing 6-9. Vagrantfile for a Jekyll Box with Ansible Provisioning

```
Vagrant.configure(2) do |config|
  config.vm.box = "ubuntu/trusty32"
  config.vm.provision "ansible", playbook: "playbook.yml"
end
```

Listing 6-10. Ansible playbook.yml to Provision a VM

```
- hosts: all
  sudo: true
  tasks:

    - name: Update apt
      apt: update_cache=yes

    - name: Install nodejs
      apt: name=nodejs state=present

    - name: Install lynx
      apt: name=lynx-cur state=present

    - name: Install ruby1.9.1-dev
      apt: name=ruby1.9.1-dev state=present

    - name: Install Jekyll
      shell: 'gem install jekyll'
```

To activate the Ansible provisioner, the Vagrantfile contains the following:

```
config.vm.provision "ansible", playbook: "playbook.yml"
```

This entry sets the name of the file with the configuration to playbook.yml. The file, which is written in YAML format, contains a list of tasks to be run that are stored under a tasks key. Each task consists of a name and one more key that defines the action. In the playbook shown in Listing 6-10, three different actions are used:

- apt is responsible for running the apt-get commands
- command is responsible for running arbitrary commands
- shell is responsible for running arbitrary commands in a shell environment

First Run of the Ansible Provisioner

To start the VM, run these commands (they will need some time, maybe even half an hour, to finish):

```
# Host OS
$ cd vagrant-jekyll-ansible
$ vagrant up
```

The output produced by Ansible is denoted with ❶:

```
Bringing machine 'default' up with 'virtualbox' provider...
==> default: Importing base box 'ubuntu/trusty32'...
...
❶==> default: Running provisioner: ansible...
...
❶PLAY [all] *********************************************************

❶GATHERING FACTS ***************************************************
ok: [default]

❶TASK: [Update apt] ***********************************************
ok: [default]

❶TASK: [Install nodejs] *******************************************
changed: [default]

❶TASK: [Install lynx] *********************************************
changed: [default]

❶TASK: [Install ruby1.9.1-dev] ************************************
changed: [default]

❶TASK: [Install Jekyll] *******************************************
changed: [default]

❶PLAY RECAP ********************************************************
default    : ok=6    changed=4    unreachable=0    failed=0
```

The notices produced by Ansible contain the name of each task.

Versioning the Box Source Code

To store the project with Ansible provisioner in git, use the following:

```
# Host OS
$ cd vagrant-jekyll-ansible
$ git init
$ echo .vagrant > .gitignore
$ echo "*.box" >> .gitignore
$ git add -A
$ git commit -m "Initial version"
$ git tag -a v0.1.0 -m "Release 0.1.0"
```

Generating a Box

Finally, `vagrant-jekyll-ansible-v0.1.0.box` can be generated with this:

```
$ cd vagrant-jekyll-ansible
$ vagrant up
$ vagrant package --output vagrant-jekyll-ansible-v0.1.0.box
```

Workflow

Remember from now on that the workflow for creating and using Vagrant boxes splits into two diverse procedures:

- The procedure to create the box is carried out by system engineers.

- The procedure to use the box is carried out by developers.

This chapter updated the workflow used by system engineers to create the box. Now the code of the box is versioned, and booting of the box is automatic. The procedure to build the box is repeatable, and new versions of the box can be released in the same way as software.

There is only one final step that still requires manual interaction. Right now, to produce a box, you have to run two commands manually: `$ vagrant up` and `$ vagrant package`. (This topic will be discussed in Chapter 9.)

From the system administrator's perspective, the cost of using this workflow is the following:

1. The admin has to boot the VM with provisioning (it has to be done only once).

2. The admin has to package the VM into the box file.

3. The box file has to be uploaded to globally accessible storage.

All three of these steps have to be executed for every new release of the box.

From the developers' perspective, each new release will force them to do the following:

- Download the box file from globally accessible storage to their laptops.

- Destroy and boot the VM again (using the updated box).

And no matter how many projects use the new release of the box, the procedure to update the box needs to be run just once. Because the procedure to update the box can be done semiautomatically, this workflow is extremely convenient and efficient.

Summary

Automatic installation and configuration of software within a guest OS is called provisioning in Vagrant terminology. It is a huge step forward because VMs can be developed as if they were the code.

You were introduced to four different provisioners: shell scripts, Puppet, Chef, and Ansible. As of now, these are the most popular and frequently used software configuration solutions on the market. Ansible currently has a lot of attention because it has been described as the easiest-to-learn SCM tool yet invented.

To be sure, this chapter was only an introduction, and you will have to refer to documentation for a more in-depth discussion. But you should understand the overall view of provisioners: what purposes they serve, how to include them in Vagrantfiles, and how to use them for some simple tasks. As you can see, Vagrant-controlled VMs act as a perfect sandbox to play with Puppet, Chef, or Ansible.

When you have a basic grasp of one of the provisioners, take care to use a version control system (VCS) for your boxes. I personally prefer to use git, but there are others (for example, Bazaar and Mercurial) that you can choose from.

Using a VCS system for boxes help you keep track of box releases. The approach that I use is to tag a version that can be automatically booted without any human interaction and to store the box in a file using a filename that contains the version number. It is a very simple trick, yet it helps to avoid confusion when you update your boxes.

Keep in mind that if developers use a box that contains all the software inside (as in `vagrant-jekyll-shell-v0.1.0.box`), they can reboot and destroy the box without any penalty. The process of destroying and booting a completely new VM-based box that contains all the software inside and does not need to run provisioners in order to download, compile, and install packages is not time-consuming. Although there is an upfront cost to produce the box, you can then re-create the environment in a fraction of the time required to perform a complete provisioning.

In the Next Chapter, You Will Learn . . .

In this chapter, you modified the `ubuntu/trusty32` box. But how can you start from scratch? How was the `ubuntu/trusty32` box created? Is it an updated and reconfigured version of some other box? How can you create a new box without falling back on any box? These are the main topics of Chapter 7.

Reading List

Vagrant documentation contains an extended chapter that explains the whole purpose of provisioning and gives various examples of how to use it: `https://docs.vagrantup.com/v2/provisioning/index.html`. The documentation contains a complete reference of options for each provisioner.

To learn more about each provisioner, Ansible, Chef and Puppet, refer to their documentation on Wikipedia:

- Ansible

    - `http://en.wikipedia.org/wiki/Ansible_%28software%29`

    - `www.ansible.com/home`

    - `www.ansible.com/get-started`

- Chef

    - `http://en.wikipedia.org/wiki/Chef_%28software%29`

    - `www.chef.io/`

    - `https://learn.chef.io/`

- Puppet

    - `http://en.wikipedia.org/wiki/Puppet_%28software%29`

    - `http://puppetlabs.com/`

    - `http://puppetlabs.com/download-learning-vm`

Wikipedia shows a comprehensive comparison of open source SCM tools at `http://en.wikipedia.org/wiki/Comparison_of_open-source:configuration_management_software`.

Shebang and portable shebang are described at `http://en.wikipedia.org/wiki/Shebang_%28Unix%29`.

For the `mesg` command, see `http://en.wikipedia.org/wiki/Mesg`. The `"not a tty"` "thing" is explained in issue 1673 of the Vagrant GitHub repository: `https://github.com/mitchellh/vagrant/issues/1673`.

For resources on git, refer to `http://git-scm.com/`. You will see, among many other resources, the most famous Pro Git book: `http://git-scm.com/book/en/v2`.

Semantic versioning is specified in the document at `http://semver.org`. The note about starting your project at 0.1.0 can be found in the FAQs (this is the first entry).

Finally, for the specification of the YAML format, visit `http://www.yaml.org`.

Test Yourself

1. What is the purpose of provisioning?

2. Can you name at least four provisioners supported by Vagrant?

3. What is the Vagrantfile configuration entry to configure provisioning with a shell script saved in a separate file?

4. What is the Vagrantfile configuration entry to configure provisioning with an inline shell script?

5. What is the Vagrantfile configuration entry to configure provisioning with Puppet?

6. What is the Vagrantfile configuration entry to configure provisioning with Chef?

7. What is the Vagrantfile configuration entry to configure provisioning with Ansible?

8. What is shebang?

9. Can you write a shell script that updates the system and installs an arbitrary package (e.g., git, lynx, mc)?

10. Can you write a Puppet manifest that updates the system and installs an arbitrary package (e.g., git, lynx, mc)?

11. Can you write a Chef recipe that updates the system and installs an arbitrary package (e.g. git, lynx, mc)?

12. Can you write an Ansible playbook that updates the system and installs an arbitrary package (e.g., git, lynx, mc)?

13. Can you define the terms "source code of the box" and "binary version of a box"?

14. How can you use git to version control the source code of the box?

15. How do you build a binary version of a box?

16. What is the advantage of using binary boxes with all the software baked in instead of running provisioners to install the software each time you boot the guest VM?

Exercises

1. Create the `flowers-vagrant-jekyll-puppet` project, which should use the
    `vagrant-jekyll-puppet` box. For instructions on how to do it, refer to the "Using
    the Shell-Provisioned Box" section. When you finish this exercise, your web
    browser should display a page like the one shown in Figure 5-2. The box used by
    the project should be generated with the Puppet provisioner.

2. Create the `flowers-vagrant-jekyll-chef` project, which should use the
    `vagrant-jekyll-chef` box. For instructions on how to do it, refer to the "Using
    Shell-Provisioned Box" section. When you finish this exercise, your web browser
    should display a page like the one shown in Figure 5-2. The box used by the
    project should be generated with the Chef provisioner.

3. Create the `flowers-vagrant-jekyll-ansible` project, which should use the
    `vagrant-jekyll-ansible` box. For instructions on how to do it, refer to the
    "Using Shell-Provisioned Box" section. When you finish this exercise, your web
    browser should display a page like the one shown in Figure 5-2. The box used by
    the project should be generated with the Ansible provisioner.

CHAPTER 7

■ ■ ■

Creating Boxes from Scratch

By now, it should be completely clear to you that Vagrant boxes are preinstalled OSs stored in files with a `*.box` extension, and you can easily download and start them using Vagrant. To perform automated downloads and booting of VMs, you need to create a Vagrantfile containing a `config.vm.box` entry like the following and then run the `$ vagrant up` command:

```
config.vm.box = "ubuntu/trusty32"
config.vm.box = "puppetlabs/centos-6.6-64-puppet"
```

To download the box manually, you can use `curl` or `wget` like this:

```
$ curl http://cloud-images.ubuntu.com/vagrant/trusty/current/trusty-server-cloudimg-i386-
vagrant-disk1.box -o trusty-server-cloudimg-i386-vagrant-disk1.box
```

```
$ wget -O trusty-server-cloudimg-i386-vagrant-disk1.box http://cloud-images.ubuntu.com/
vagrant/trusty/current/trusty-server-cloudimg-i386-vagrant-disk1.box
```

In Chapters 5 and 6, you learned how to build your own customized solution based on one of the existing boxes, for example ubuntu/trusty32. The procedure is quite simple: boot the predefined box, change its configuration, and export it to a new file with a `*.box` extension using the `$ vagrant package` command.

But how were these public boxes, such as ubuntu/trusty32, created? What can you do if you need to run an atypical guest OS and can't find any base box for it?

This chapter will get to the very bottom of this problem. You'll create boxes by installing OSs using ISO CD-ROM and DVD images distributed by producers. And the whole process will be completely automatic.

Packer

Packer is a command-line tool produced by HashiCorp, which is the company behind Vagrant. The main purpose of Packer is to automate the creation of preinstalled VMs for various operating systems and providers. You will use it to generate Vagrant boxes.

How does Packer work? It starts by downloading the ISO CD or DVD image of the OS you want to install. Then it runs the installation program and applies the default configuration. When that finishes, Packer uses provisioners (shell, Chef, Puppet, or Ansible) to customize the system. Finally, it exports the system and converts it into a single box file. The whole process can be described in five steps:

1. Download the ISO image for the OS.

2. Install the system using preconfigured options read from configuration files.

3. Run provisioners to customize the system.

4. Export the system.

5. Pack the exported OS into a single *.box file.

This procedure can be used for the following purposes:

- To produce arbitrary systems—for example, Ubuntu, CentOS, FreeBSD, Windows 7

- To create a box for arbitrary providers—for example, VirtualBox, VMware, Parallel

Before you dive deeper into the details of how Packer works, you can start by building your first box.

Installing Packer

Packer distributions are available for download at https://www.packer.io/downloads.html. Just download a package appropriate for your platform and unzip it. The files you unzip can reside anywhere on your drive, but the directory that contains the Packer binary should be available in the path.

If you work on OS X, you can also use brew to install Packer. Here are the commands to use:

```
$ brew tap homebrew/binary
$ brew install packer
```

In case of a problem, refer to Packer's documentation here: https://www.packer.io/docs/installation.html.

When the installation is finished, you can verify that Packer is ready by running this command:

```
$ packer version
```

Before you start using Packer, it is worthwhile to change some settings. By default, Packer caches downloaded files on a per-project basis, and cached files are stored in a subdirectory named packer_cache. It is very convenient to reconfigure Packer to work with the global packer_cache directory, which will allow you to share downloaded ISO files between different projects instead of downloading them again.

You can change Packer's behaviour concering the cache with the following environment variable:

```
PACKER_CACHE_DIR
```

To change the location of cached files run the command:

```
$ PACKER_CACHE_DIR=/some/dir/packer_cache
$ export PACKER_CACHE_DIR
```

If you want to run them during every shell session, you can put them in your shell configuration file—for example, in ~/.profile.

Building Boxes Using the chef/bento Project

The most popular project with Packer definitions is chef/bento, which is available on GitHub here: https://github.com/chef/bento. It contains boxes published by Chef Software, Inc. here: https://atlas.hashicorp.com/chef. And you can also find them here: http://chef.github.io/bento/.

To use those definitions, simply clone the chef/bento project:

```
# Host OS
$ cd folder/with/examples
$ git clone https://github.com/chef/bento.git
```

Enter the packer/ subdirectory inside the cloned project:

```
$ cd bento
$ cd packer
```

You are done. The current directory contains a lot of JavaScript Object Notation (JSON) files. To verify it, run this command:

```
$ ls
```

Each JSON file contains definitions of how to build a given OS for many different providers. By using Packer and the JSON files, you can build many different base boxes: Ubuntu, Debian, Fedora, and FreeBSD, among others.

■ **Note** Building a box with Packer consists of many stages, one of which is an unintended installation of an OS. As you might expect, it takes a lot of time—longer than any operations you have performed so far. You need a lot of patience; the command to build Ubuntu 14.04 runs for almost an hour.

To build the Ubuntu 14.04 box for the VirtualBox provider, run this:

```
$ packer build -only=virtualbox-iso ubuntu-14.04-i386.json
```

■ **Note** When you run the preceding command, observe the windows that appear on your screen: you will see an unintended installation of Ubuntu. One of the windows will, at some point, contain the boot command shown in Listing 7-5. The window will act as if someone were typing the command for you.

When it finally finishes, you should be able to find the following file on your system:

```
bento/builds/virtualbox/opscode_ubuntu-14.04-i386_chef-provisionerless.box
```

This is an Ubuntu 14.04 box that was built without any preexisting box; it was installed using an ISO image downloaded from the Ubuntu distribution site.

Using a different JSON file as the last parameter for the Packer command, you can build boxes for other OSs and other providers:

```
$ packer build -only=vmware-iso fedora-21-i386.json
```

The boxes produced by chef/bento definitions are bare; they do not contain anything that is not necessary for the system to run. They are stripped of various programs and tools, and they don't even contain provisioning tools such as Puppet or Chef. This makes them a perfect starting point for personalized customizations.

Using the Box Generated with chef/bento

Once you have created a box you can use it. The box for Ubuntu 14.04 is stored in:

`bento/builds/virtualbox/opscode_ubuntu-14.04-i386_chef-provisionerless.box`

The procedure to generate this box is very time-consuming and nerve-straining experience. But when the box is ready, you need only a minute or two to give it a try.

First, you have to install the box in your system. It can be done with the $ `vagrant box add` command, preceded by the appropriate $ `cd` commands:

```
# Host OS
$ cd folder/with/examples
$ cd bento
$ cd builds/virtualbox
$ vagrant box add bento-ubuntu opscode_ubuntu-14.04-i386_chef-provisionerless.box
```

Note that the first parameter of the $ `vagrant box add` command can be just an arbitrary string. I used bento-ubuntu. Now the list printed by the following command should include, among other things, the bento-ubuntu box:

```
$ vagrant box list
```

Go to the directory with your examples and create a new project:

```
# Host OS
$ cd folder/with/examples
$ mkdir using-bento-ubuntu-box
$ cd using-bento-ubuntu-box
$ vagrant init -m bento-ubuntu
```

Finally, you can boot the VM with this:

```
# Host OS
$ vagrant up
```

The procedure to build the box lasted for half an hour, but booting consumes only about a minute. Now open the SSH session:

```
# Host OS
$ vagrant ssh
```

Print the contents of one file:

```
# Guest OS
$ cat /home/vagrant/.vbox_version
```

You will see the version of VirtualBox that you used to generate the box, which is very handy.

When you finish, close the SSH session and destroy the box to avoid complications:

```
# Guest OS
$ logout
# Host OS
$ vagrant destroy
```

Building Boxes Using the boxcutter Project

Another interesting initiative for building base boxes with Packer is the boxcutter project available at https://github.com/boxcutter. You will find many subprojects there, each one for a different OS. Boxcutter builds boxes that are equipped with the Puppet, Chef, and Salt provisioners. The build is governed by the GNU make program.

INSTALLATION OF MAKE ON WINDOWS

If you work on Windows, you have to install the make program. Go to http://cygwin.com/install.html and run setup-x86.exe. Follow the instructions; when you are asked about packages to install, select Development Tools and Make. When the installation finishes, you will find the C:\cygwin directory that contains the make program. To run the program in git bash, use this command:

```
$ /c/cygwin/bin/make.exe
```

If you add the /c/cygwin/bin directory to your path, you can use the make command like this:

```
$ make
```

The prefix /c/cygwin/bin is necessary only if your path doesn't contain the /c/cygwing/bin folder.

To build an Ubuntu 14.04 box equipped with the latest version of Puppet, clone this project:

```
# Host OS
$ cd folder/with/examples
$ git clone https://github.com/pro-vagrant/ubuntu.git
```

The previous command creates a directory named folder/with/examples/ubuntu. Enter this directory:

```
$ cd ubuntu
```

Create a new file named Makefile.local with the following contents:

```
CM := puppet
UPDATE := true
```

You can do this by running these two commands:

```
$ echo "CM := puppet" > Makefile.local
$ echo "UPDATE := true" >> Makefile.local
```

You can also use your favorite text editor. When the `Makefile.local` file is ready, run this command (be patient; the command will run for an hour):

```
$ make virtualbox/ubuntu1404-i386
```

■ **Note**   If you work on Windows, you might need to use this command:

```
$ /c/cygwin/bin/make.exe virtualbox/ubuntu1404-i386
```

It will run for about half an hour and should create the file named box/virtualbox/ubuntu1410-i386-puppetlatest-1.0.16.box. The version of the file, which in my case is 1.0.16, may be different.

The boxes built with boxcutter configuration files contain one provisioner that you can choose using the `Makefile.local` file. The CM configuration variable stands for Configuration Manager and can take the following values: puppet, chef, salt, and nocm. The following line:

```
CM := puppet
```

can be replaced with this:

```
CM := chef
```

or this:

```
CM := salt
```

As of now, there is no support for Ansible, though.

■ **Note**   To list the boxes that can be built with Boxcutter/Ubuntu, run the following:

```
$ make list
```

Or run this:

```
$ /c/ygwin/bin/make.exe list
```

By using other repositories available in https://github.com/boxcutter, such as the following, you can build boxes for other systems:

- https://github.com/boxcutter/centos
- https://github.com/boxcutter/fedora

Using the Box Generated with the boxcutter Project

The procedure to use the box should be straightforward. The box is stored in:

```
box/virtualbox/ubuntu1410-i386-puppetlatest-1.0.16.box
```

Install the box in your system:

```
# Host OS
$ cd folder/with/examples
$ cd ubuntu
$ cd box/virtualbox
$ vagrant box add boxcutter-ubuntu ubuntu1410-i386-puppetlatest-1.0.16.box
```

Verify that the box named boxcutter-ubuntu is available:

```
$ vagrant box list
```

Go to the directory with your examples and create a new project:

```
# Host OS
$ cd folder/with/examples
$ mkdir using-boxcutter-ubuntu-box
$ cd using-boxcutter-ubuntu-box
$ vagrant init -m boxcutter-ubuntu
```

Boot the VM:

```
# Host OS
$ vagrant up
```

Booting should last for a minute or so. Finally, close the SSH session and destroy the box:

```
# Guest OS
$ logout
# Host OS
$ vagrant destroy
```

How Does Packer Work?

Just like Vagrant, Packer knows a couple of subcommands that perform certain actions. The subcommand you used to build a box was build, which takes the mandatory argument TEMPLATE:

```
$ packer build TEMPLATE
```

TEMPLATE is the name of a JSON file that defines precisely how to build a box. The basic structure of a template file is shown in Listing 7-1.

```
A ONE-MINUTE INTRODUCTION TO JSON
```

JSON files are text files that contain hashes, tables, and scalar values. To define a hash with two keys, the following syntax is used:

```
{
    "name": "John",
    "surname": "Doe"
}
```

JSON for an array with two strings looks like this:

```
[
    "First string",
    "Second string"
]
```

You can nest both structures in an arbitrary number of levels:

```
{
    "persons": [
        { "name": "John", "surname": "Doe" },
        { "name": "Ann", "surname": "Moo" }
    ],
    "cities": [
        "London", "New York", "Berlin"
    ]
}
```

Listing 7-1. Basic Structure of a Packer Template File

```
{
  "variables": {
    "mirror": "http://releases.ubuntu.com",
    ...
  },
  "builders": [
    {
      "type": "virtualbox-iso",
      ...
    },
    {
      "type": "vmware-iso",
      ...
    },
    {
      "type": "parallels-iso",
    }
  ],
```

```
"provisioners": [
  {
    "scripts": [
      "scripts/ubuntu/update.sh",
      "scripts/common/sshd.sh",
      "scripts/ubuntu/networking.sh",
      ...
    ],
    "type": "shell"
  }
],
"post-processors": [
  {
    "type": "vagrant",
    ...
  }
]
}
```

■ **Note** The template file is in JSON format, which means that the entries can be reordered. The following order was used here: variables, builders, provisioners, post-processors. It reflects the order of processing.

The template contains a list of the following:

- Variables
- Builders
- Provisioners
- Post-processors

Variables define some global settings—for example, URLs for OS distribution. Builders are the most complicated part of the configuration: they define the procedure to boot VMs and perform unattended installation. Provisioners allow you to install additional packages and customize running VMs. And post-processors shut the VM down and transform it into a box file.

Every builder has a mandatory key type. In Listing 7-1, you can see three types: virtualbox-iso, vmware-iso, and parallels-iso. Each section with type defines one box. When you run $ packer build command, feeding it with just the name of the template, as follows, you ask Packer to build all the builders:

```
$ packer build ubuntu-14.04-i386.json
```

For the template shown in Listing 7-1, Packer would run three builders:

- virtualbox-iso
- vmware-iso
- parallel-iso

The algorithm to process the template file is just an iteration that for every builder X runs four steps: variables, a particular builder X, all the provisioners, and post-processors. And because the VM for every build is completely independent, all the boxes can be produced in parallel.

The -only=virtualbox-iso parameter that you used to produce the Ubuntu box filters the builders:

```
$ packer build -only=virtualbox-iso ubuntu-14.04-i386.json
```

The previous command will run only the virtualbox-iso builder.

The most interesting part of processing happens in the builder. Crucial parts of the VirtualBox builder for Ubuntu 14.04 are shown in Listing 7-2. The excerpts shown in Listing 7-2 come from the chef/bento file packer/ubuntu-14-04-i386.json, but they are reordered for clarity.

Listing 7-2. VirtualBox Builder for Ubuntu 14.04

```
{
  "type": "virtualbox-iso",

  "iso_checksum": "976044842804eafc18390505508958b559c131211160ecae5e60694bdf171f78",
  "iso_checksum_type": "sha256",
  "iso_url": "{{user `mirror`}}/14.04.1/ubuntu-14.04.1-server-i386.iso",

  "disk_size": 40960,
  "vboxmanage": [
    [
      "modifyvm",
      "{{.Name}}",
      "--memory",
      "384"
    ],
    [
      "modifyvm",
      "{{.Name}}",
      "--cpus",
      "1"
    ]
  ],

  "boot_wait": "10s",

  "http_directory": "http",

  "boot_command": [
    "<esc><wait>",
    "<esc><wait>",
    "<enter><wait>",
    "/install/vmlinuz<wait>",
    " auto<wait>",
    " console-setup/ask_detect=false<wait>",
    " console-setup/layoutcode=us<wait>",
    " console-setup/modelcode=pc105<wait>",
    " debconf/frontend=noninteractive<wait>",
    " debian-installer=en_US<wait>",
    " fb=false<wait>",
    " initrd=/install/initrd.gz<wait>",
```

```
    " kbd-chooser/method=us<wait>",
    " keyboard-configuration/layout=USA<wait>",
    " keyboard-configuration/variant=USA<wait>",
    " locale=en_US<wait>",
    " netcfg/get_domain=vm<wait>",
    " netcfg/get_hostname=vagrant<wait>",
    " noapic<wait>",
    " preseed/url=http://{{ .HTTPIP }}:{{ .HTTPPort }}/ubuntu-14.04/preseed.cfg<wait>",
    " -- <wait>",
    "<enter><wait>"
  ],

  "virtualbox_version_file": ".vbox_version",
  "guest_additions_path": "VBoxGuestAdditions_{{.Version}}.iso",

  "ssh_password": "vagrant",
  "ssh_port": 22,
  "ssh_username": "vagrant",
  "ssh_wait_timeout": "10000s",

  "shutdown_command": "echo 'vagrant'|sudo -S shutdown -P now",

  "output_directory": "packer-ubuntu-14.04-i386-virtualbox",

}
```

The processing starts with downloading two files: VirtualBox Guest Additions and the Ubuntu installation ISO file. The following entry is expanded with the mirror variable defined in the variables section of Listing 7-1:

```
"iso_url": "{{user `mirror`}}/14.04.1/ubuntu-14.04.1-server-i386.iso",
```

It produces this URL: http://releases.ubuntu.com/14.04.1/ubuntu-14.04.1-server-i386.iso.

If the file cannot be found in PACKER_CACHE_DIR, it is downloaded from the network. Two additional keys are relevant to this operation: iso_checksum and iso_checksum_type. They define the checksum of the file, which is used to verify the file's integrity.

When the ISO installation file is ready, Packer starts the VM using this file as an image. Two modifyvm entries under the vboxmanage key modify the memory and CPU of the VM that is started. Disk size for this VM is defined with the disk_size key. Then Packer waits the amount of time defined with the boot_wait parameter.

In the meantime, Packer starts the HTTP server that allows access to the directory defined with the http_directory entry. The subdirectory http/ contains a preseed.cfg file that is necessary to automate the install. This HTTP server is a one-way communication channel from host machine to guest VM that is used to transfer this file.

When the amount of time defined with boot_wait has expired, Packer types the command defined with boot_command into the VM. The command contains special sequences such as <esc>, <enter>, and <wait>. The sequences <esc> and <enter> send the ESC and ENTER key codes to the VM. The <wait> sequence waits for a couple of seconds. Thus, the boot command acts as if it did the following:

1. Pressed ESC and waited

2. Pressed ESC and waited

3.   Typed the long command waiting from time to time

4.   Finally pressed Enter

The command contains some basic parameters for Ubuntu installation, such as keyboard layout and hostname. But no matter which parameters are defined here, the installation procedure asks a couple of questions. To skip all the questions, use the preseed.cfg file stored in the http/ directory. This file contains answers to questions that are asked by the installation program. The following fragment of the boot command forces the installation program to fetch the preseed.cfg file via HTTP:

```
" preseed/url=http://{{ .HTTPIP }}:{{ .HTTPPort }}/ubuntu-14.04/preseed.cfg<wait>",
```

■ **Note**   Packer replaces the variables .HTTPIP and .HTTPPort with the actual values for the HTTP server instance that was started.

You will wait a long time while the system is being installed. When it finishes, Packer logs in to the guest OS using the following credentials:

```
"ssh_password": "vagrant",
"ssh_port": 22,
"ssh_username": "vagrant",
"ssh_wait_timeout": "10000s",
```

The user account vagrant with the password vagrant was created by the keystrokes stored in the preseed.cfg file. After a successful login, Packer uploads VirtualBoxGuestAdditions to the guest machine and creates a special text file that contains the version of VirtualBox. These two operations are governed by the following:

```
"virtualbox_version_file": ".vbox_version",
"guest_additions_path": "VBoxGuestAdditions_{{.Version}}.iso",
```

The system is ready to be provisioned, so Packer runs all the provisioners defined by entries under the key "provisioners": [ ] shown in Listing 7-1.

Finally, Packer does the following:

1.   Halts the system using the command defined with shutdown_command

2.   Exports the VM to a directory defined with output_directory

3.   Runs the post-processor defined in Listing 7-1 with "post-processors": [ ]

The output produced by Packer when generating the VirtualBox Ubuntu 14.04 box is presented in Listing 7-3. You should be able to correlate most of the messages with the appropriate fragments of either Listing 7-1 or Listing 7-2.

Listing 7-3. Output Produced by Packer During Ubuntu Box Production

```
==> virtualbox-iso: Downloading or copying Guest additions
    virtualbox-iso: Downloading or copying: file:///.../VBoxGuestAdditions.iso
==> virtualbox-iso: Downloading or copying ISO
    virtualbox-iso: Downloading or copying:
        http://releases.ubuntu.com/14.04.1/ubuntu-14.04.1-server-i386.iso
```

```
==> virtualbox-iso: Starting HTTP server on port 8134
==> virtualbox-iso: Creating virtual machine...
==> virtualbox-iso: Creating hard drive...
==> virtualbox-iso: Creating forwarded port mapping for SSH (host port 4229)
==> virtualbox-iso: Executing custom VBoxManage commands...
    virtualbox-iso: Executing: modifyvm packer-ubuntu-14.04-i386 --memory 384
    virtualbox-iso: Executing: modifyvm packer-ubuntu-14.04-i386 --cpus 1
==> virtualbox-iso: Starting the virtual machine...
==> virtualbox-iso: Waiting 10s for boot...
==> virtualbox-iso: Typing the boot command...
==> virtualbox-iso: Waiting for SSH to become available...
==> virtualbox-iso: Connected to SSH!
==> virtualbox-iso: Uploading VirtualBox version info (4.3.18)
==> virtualbox-iso: Uploading VirtualBox guest additions ISO...
==> virtualbox-iso: Provisioning with shell script: scripts/ubuntu/update.sh
...
==> virtualbox-iso: Provisioning with shell script: scripts/common/minimize.sh
==> virtualbox-iso: Gracefully halting virtual machine...
==> virtualbox-iso: Preparing to export machine...
    virtualbox-iso: Deleting forwarded port mapping for SSH (host port 4229)
==> virtualbox-iso: Exporting virtual machine...
    virtualbox-iso: Executing: export packer-ubuntu-14.04-i386 ...
==> virtualbox-iso: Unregistering and deleting virtual machine...
==> virtualbox-iso: Running post-processor: vagrant
==> virtualbox-iso (vagrant): Creating Vagrant box for 'virtualbox' provider
Build 'virtualbox-iso' finished.
```

Customizing Boxes Generated with chef/bento

If you want to produce a modified version of any of the boxes included in the chef/bento project, the simplest procedure is to add one more provisioning script.

In this section, you again work in the chef/bento project. To avoid confusion, change the current directory to your clone of the chef/bento project:

```
# Host OS
$ cd folder/with/examples
$ cd bento
```

To customize Ubuntu builds, create a packer/scripts/ubuntu/customize.sh file with the following contents:

```
#!/bin/bash -eux

apt-get install git
apt-get install mc
```

As you may guess, the preceding instructions install git and mc tools. Then add to the provisioners' section shown in Listing 7-1 the name of the newly created script ❶:

```
"provisioners": [
  {
    ...
    "scripts": [
      "scripts/ubuntu/update.sh",
      "scripts/common/sshd.sh",
      "scripts/ubuntu/networking.sh",
      "scripts/ubuntu/sudoers.sh",
      "scripts/common/vagrant.sh",
      "scripts/common/vmtools.sh",
      "scripts/common/chef.sh",
❶    "scripts/ubuntu/customize.sh",
      "scripts/ubuntu/cleanup.sh",
      "scripts/common/minimize.sh"
    ],
    "type": "shell"
  }
],
```

The next time you build an Ubuntu 14.04 box, it will include git and mc.

By modifying existing configuration files and scripts, you can also change all other settings for the generated box. For example, you can modify the SSH key used for authorization and username/password credentials. The user account is created in the pressed.cfg file. Here are the code lines responsible for this operation:

```
d-i passwd/user-fullname string vagrant
d-i passwd/user-uid string 900
d-i passwd/user-password password vagrant
d-i passwd/user-password-again password vagrant
d-i passwd/username string vagrant
```

By changing these lines in the preseed.cfg file into the following, you create a default user account called johnny with the password THISISSECRET:

```
d-i passwd/user-fullname string johnny
d-i passwd/user-uid string 900
d-i passwd/user-password password THISISSECRET
d-i passwd/user-password-again password THISISSECRET
d-i passwd/username string johnny
```

VirtualBox Guest Additions

If you work a with VirtualBox provider, you might have encountered the message about a mismatched version of VirtualBox Guest Additions. Vagrant displays this message when you boot the guest OS that was built with a version of VirtualBox different from the one you are using. Listing 7-4 presents the warning printed by Vagrant.

Listing 7-4. Warning About Mismatched VirtualBox Guest Additions

```
default: The guest additions on this VM do not match the installed version of
default: VirtualBox! In most cases this is fine, but in rare cases it can
default: prevent things such as shared folders from working properly. If you see
default: shared folder errors, please make sure the guest additions within the
default: virtual machine match the version of VirtualBox you have installed on
default: your host and reload your VM.
default:
default: Guest Additions Version: 4.1.12
default: VirtualBox Version: 4.3
```

Mismatched VirtualBox Guest Additions can sometimes result in severe problems (for example, the inability to mount shared folders). How can you avoid this kind of issue? The first step is to make certain that your host and guest use the same version of Guest Additions.

One of the benefits of building boxes with Packer is that the resulting box contains the Guest Additions copied from the VirtualBox installation directory. Thus, the Guest Additions version in a generated box always matches the version of VirtualBox that you have installed on your computer. The boxes generated with chef/bento definitions also include a file named /home/vagrant/.vbox_version, which contains the VirtualBox version used to generate the box. So when you open the SSH session to the guest using one of the boxes generated with chef/bento, you can check the version of VirtualBox with this:

```
# Guest OS generated with chef/bento project
# This is the instruction that we run in
# "Using the box generated with bento project"
# section.
$ cat /home/vagrant/.vbox_version
```

The name of the .vbox_version file is defined with the following configuration entry shown in Listing 7-2:

```
"virtualbox_version_file": ".vbox_version",
```

Creating a Box Manually

If you really want to take a closer look at the commands and actions executed by Packer, you can follow the procedure by hand. Even though this is not a method that you will use in practice, I still advise you to try it at least once up to the point shown in Figure 7-9 because it is helpful for understanding the box-generation procedure.

Downloading ISO Images

Where do the CD/DVD ISO images come from? They are published and distributed by OS producers. Here are websites to download Ubuntu, CentOS, Debian and Fedora ISO images:

Ubuntu:

```
http://releases.ubuntu.com/
http://releases.ubuntu.com/14.04/ubuntu-14.04.1-server-i386.iso
```

CentOS:

```
http://mirrors.kernel.org/centos/
http://mirrors.kernel.org/centos/7.0.1406/isos/x86_64/CentOS-7.0-1406-x86_64-Minimal.iso
```

Debian:

```
http://cdimage.debian.org/cdimage/archive/
http://cdimage.debian.org/cdimage/archive/6.0.10/i386/iso-cd/debian-6.0.10-i386-CD-1.iso
```

Fedora:

```
http://download.fedoraproject.org/pub/fedora/linux
http://download.fedoraproject.org/pub/fedora/linux/releases/21/Server/i386/iso/Fedora-
Server-DVD-i386-21.iso
```

■ **Note**   You will find more URLs in the chef/bento project.

To copy a file available at http://releases.ubuntu.com/14.04/ubuntu-14.04.1-server-i386.iso onto your drive, use the curl command:

```
# Host OS
$ cd folder/with/examples
$ mkdir manually-downloaded-boxes
$ cd manually-downloaded-bxes
$ curl http://releases.ubuntu.com/14.04/ubuntu-14.04.1-server-i386.iso -o ubuntu-14.04.1-
server-i386.iso
```

After some minutes, you should see a file named ubuntu-14.04.1-server-i386.iso in your manually downloaded files. This is the file that you will use in the dialog box shown in Figure 7-8.

If you proceeded with the previous Packer examples, you should find a file with a name that begins with the following characters in the packer_cache directory:

```
90a2489db0fb9bf8...
```

This is the ubuntu-14.04.1-server-i386.iso cached file. The filename used by Packer is a SHA256 hash of the URL used to download the file. You can verify it by running the following command:

```
# Host OS
$ echo -n "http://releases.ubuntu.com/14.04/ubuntu-14.04.1-server-i386.iso" | openssl dgst
-sha256
```

This command should print the hash that starts with this:

```
90a2489db0fb9bf8e4062a05cd...
```

The first step performed by Packer is to download the ISO DVD image and store it under this funny name in the cache directory.

Booting ISO Images

The second step performed by Packer is to start the VM using the downloaded ISO DVD image file. The process for doing it manually is described in the Figures 7-1 through 7-8.

Start VirtualBox and press the New button available in the main toolbar. You can also choose Machine/New from the main menu. You should see the dialog box shown in Figure 7-1. Type the name **manual-ubuntu** and choose Linux/Ubuntu 32 OS.

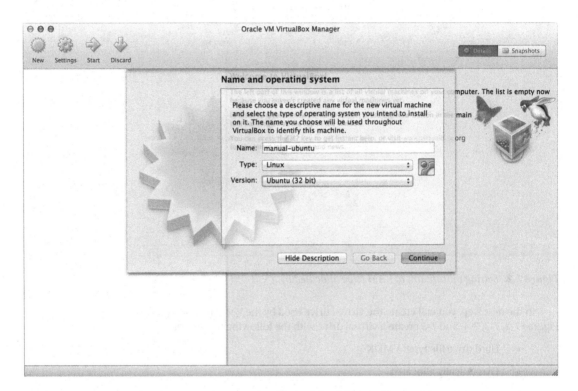

Figure 7-1. *Setting the name of the VM in the VirtualBox dialog box*

When you finish with the first dialog box, press the Continue button. You will be forwarded to a second dialog box, which is responsible for setting the RAM of the VM. It is equivalent to the entries in Listing 7-2:

```
[
    "modifyvm",
    "{{.Name}}",
    "--memory",
    "384"
]
```

Thus, you can set the amount of RAM to 384 MB (see Figure 7-2).

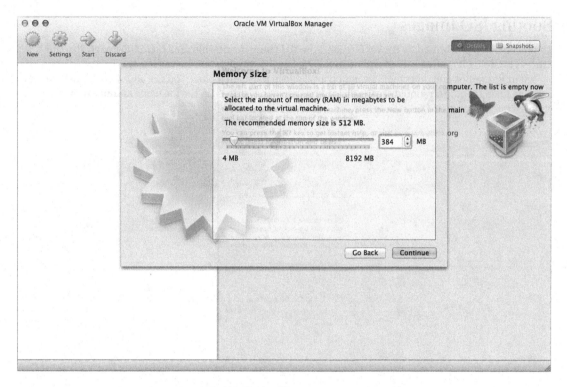

Figure 7-2. *Setting the amount of RAM to be allocated by a VM*

In the next step, you will create the virtual drive used by the VM. The dialog boxes shown in Figures 7-2, 7-3, 7-4, and 7-5 create a virtual drive with the following properties:

- Hard drive file type: VMDK

- Dynamically allocated

- File location and size: manual-ubuntu, 40 GB

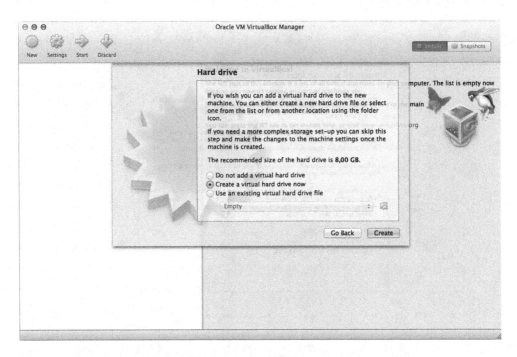

Figure 7-3. *Creating a virtual hard drive*

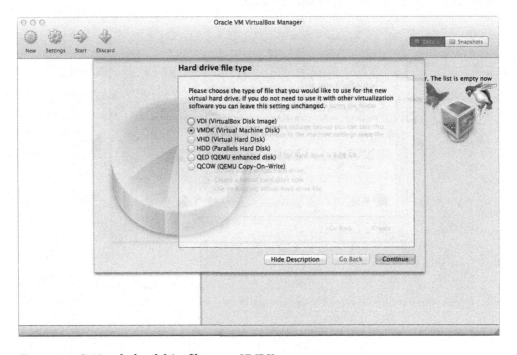

Figure 7-4. *Setting the hard drive file type to VMDK*

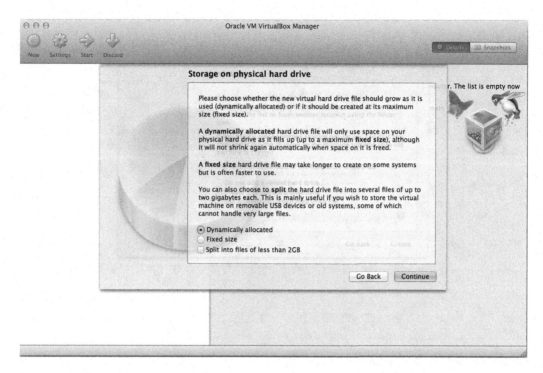

Figure 7-5. *Chosing a dynamically allocated virtual hard drive*

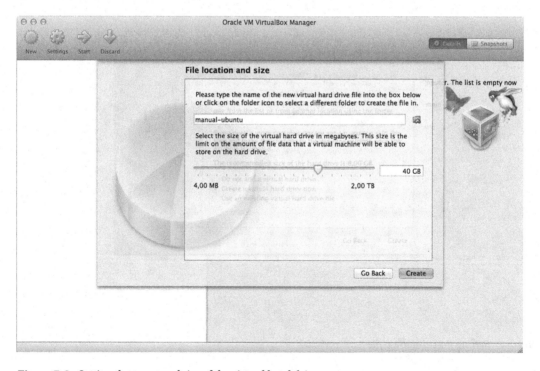

Figure 7-6. *Setting the name and size of the virtual hard drive*

In the template file shown in Listing 7-2, the file size is defined with this:

```
"disk_size": 40960,
```

Press the Create button to close the last dialog box; you will be redirected to the VirtualBox main window shown in Figure 7-7. As you can see, the VM configuration was successfully created.

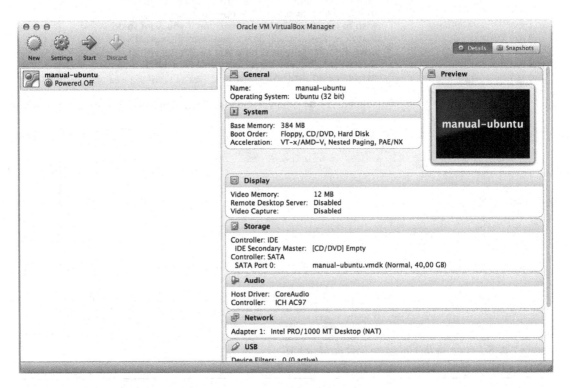

Figure 7-7. *Newly created VM appears in the VirtualBox main window*

At this point, you can customize VM properties. For example, you might want to disable audio drivers because they probably won't be necessary.

■ **Note** The VirtualBox main window can contain many other VMs, depending on your previous actions. Before creating Figure 7-7, I destroyed all VMs with the $ `vagrant destroy` command, which is why the window is so empty.

To boot the VM, double-click its name or select it with single click and run Machine/Start. When you do this for the first time, you will be asked to select the ISO file (see Figure 7-8). Choose the file that you manually downloaded with the `curl` command in the "Downloading ISO Images" section. The filename, which is `ubuntu-14.04.1-server-i386.iso`, should be available in the `manually-downloaded-boxes` directory.

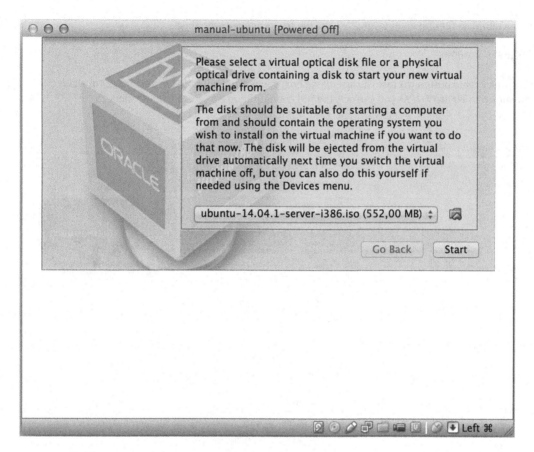

Figure 7-8. *Selecting an ISO image to boot inside a VM*

■ **Note** You can also use files cached by Packer. The ubuntu-14.04.1-server-i386.iso file is available in the Packer cache directory under the name that starts with 90a2489db0fb9bf8....

Press the Start button to begin the procedure of booting the system. If you chose the Ubuntu 14.04 ISO file, you should see a window like the one shown in Figure 7-9.

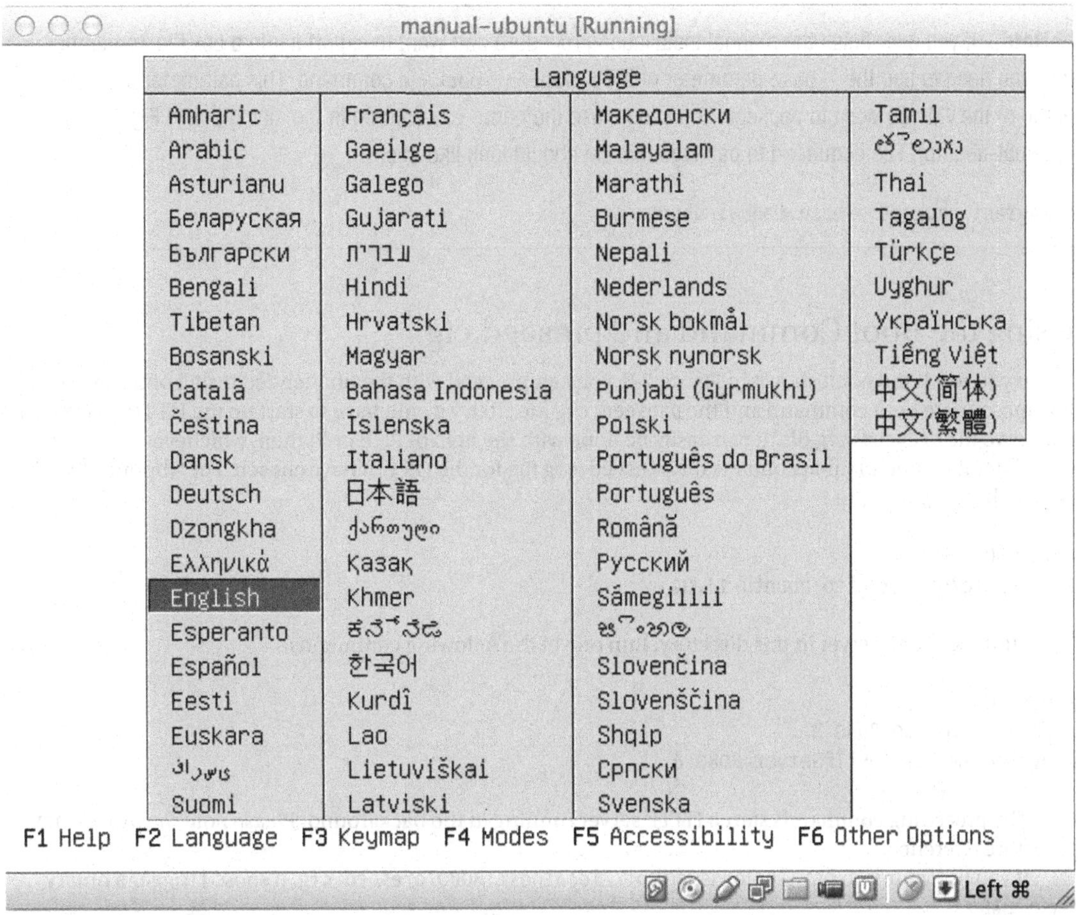

○ ○ ○   manual-ubuntu [Running]

Language

Amharic	Français	Македонски	Tamil
Arabic	Gaeilge	Malayalam	తెలుగు
Asturianu	Galego	Marathi	Thai
Беларуская	Gujarati	Burmese	Tagalog
Български	עברית	Nepali	Türkçe
Bengali	Hindi	Nederlands	Uyghur
Tibetan	Hrvatski	Norsk bokmål	Українська
Bosanski	Magyar	Norsk nynorsk	Tiếng Việt
Català	Bahasa Indonesia	Punjabi (Gurmukhi)	中文(简体)
Čeština	Íslenska	Polski	中文(繁體)
Dansk	Italiano	Português do Brasil	
Deutsch	日本語	Português	
Dzongkha	ქართული	Română	
Ελληνικά	Қазақ	Русский	
English	Khmer	Sámegillii	
Esperanto	ಕನ್ನಡ	සිංහල	
Español	한국어	Slovenčina	
Eesti	Kurdî	Slovenščina	
Euskara	Lao	Shqip	
اردو	Lietuviškai	Српски	
Suomi	Latviski	Svenska	

F1 Help F2 Language F3 Keymap F4 Modes F5 Accessibility F6 Other Options

⬇ Left ⌘

Figure 7-9. *First step of installating Ubuntu 14.04*

You can now manually install Ubuntu 14.04. Although the installation is not necessary to complete, I wanted to show you how it can be done. You can stop this exercise at this point by going to the VirtualBox main window and using the Machine/Close/Power Off menu option.

Remember that if you want to create a box to be used by Vagrant, you have to do the following:

- Enable NAT Networking for the first adapter (these are default settings; you can check them using Machine/Settings/Network for the VM displayed in Figure 7-7)

- Manually install VirtualBox Guest Additions inside the guest VM

- Create vagrant user with the vagrant password

- Use the Vagrant insecure private key for the authorization SSH

All these operations are fully automated with Packer and chef/bento definitions.

■ **Note** If you ever finish the manual installation procedure and want to export it into a box file, remember that you need to use the `--base` parameter of the `$ vagrant package` command. This parameter sets the name of the VM you want to package. You should use the name you entered in the dialog box in Figure 7-1 (manual-ubuntu). The command to package this VM should look like this:

```
$ vagrant package --base manual-ubuntu
```

Using the Boot Command and preseed.cfg

When you reach the point shown in Figure 7-9, you can proceed with the unattended install of Ubuntu using the appropriate boot command and the `preseed.cfg` file. To try it, you have to start up the HTTP server that will serve the `preseed.cfg` file. It can easily be done with the help of PHP or Python, whichever you prefer.

Enter the directory that contains the `preseed.cfg` file for the OS you have chosen. For Ubuntu 14.04, it is the following:

```
# Host OS
$ cd bento/packer/http/ubuntu-14.04
```

Start the HTTP server in this directory. Run one of the following commands:

```
# Host OS
$ php -S 0.0.0.0:8080 &
$ python -m SimpleHTTPServer 8080 &
```

The preceding commands start a HTTP server running in the background. Please note the process ID for future reference.

If you use your web browser to visit `http://localhost:8080/preseed.cfg`, it should trigger a binary file transfer.

■ **Note** When you finish, you can stop the HTTP server started with PHP or Python by running the `$ kill NNN` command, where *NNN* is the ID of the process started with one of these commands:

```
$ php -S 0.0.0.0:8080 &
$ python -m SimpleHTTPServer 8080 &
```

Next, use the `ifconfig` command to find out your IP address:

```
$ ifconfig
```

Assuming that your IP is `10.20.30.40`, and the HTTP server is running, go to VirtualBox and restart the system shown in Figure 7-9. When you are in the window shown in Figure 7-9, press the ESC key on your keyboard twice. You will see the message shown in Figure 7-10.

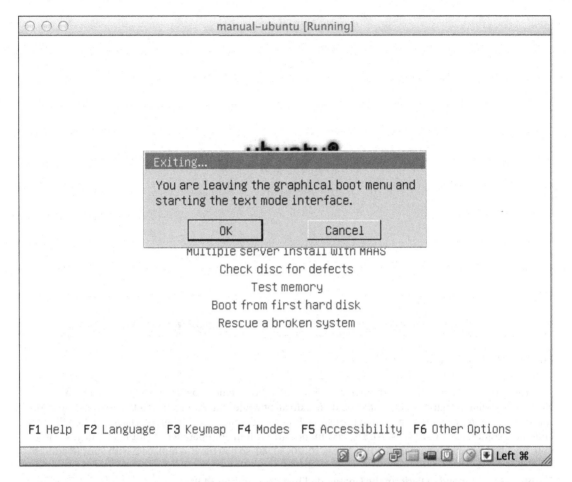

Figure 7-10. *Warning about entering the text mode interface during Ubuntu 14.04 installation*

When you close the dialog box shown in Figure 7-10 by pressing the OK button, you will see the text mode interface presented in Figure 7-11.

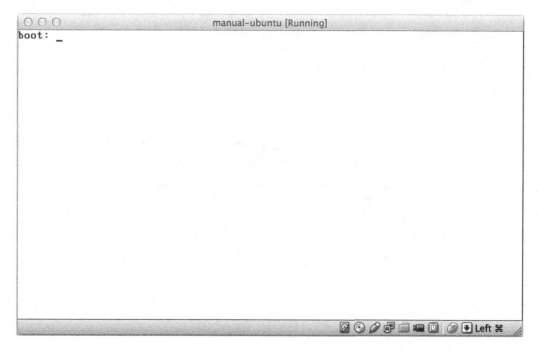

Figure 7-11. *Text mode interface of Ubuntu 14.04*

You can proceed with the unattended install. Type the command shown in Listing 7-5 inside the window depicted in Figure 7-11. (While you do it, skip all newline characters.) Instead of pressing Enter, use spaces to separate the lines displayed in the listing. Press Enter only once—when you have reached the very end of the command (two dashes --). The commands are written on separate lines for readability. Please note that the commands contain the IP address 10.20.30.40, so you have to replace it with your IP address.

Listing 7-5. Command to Perform the Unattended Install of Ubuntu 14.04

```
/install/vmlinuz
auto
console-setup/ask_detect=false
console-setup/layoutcode=us
console-setup/modelcode=pc105
debconf/frontend=noninteractive
debian-installer=en_US
fb=false
initrd=/install/initrd.gz
kbd-chooser/method=us
keyboard-configuration/layout=USA
keyboard-configuration/variant=USA
locale=en_US
netcfg/get_domain=vm
netcfg/get_hostname=vagrant
noapic
preseed/url=http://10.20.30.40/preseed.cfg
--
```

After you have typed the command shown in Listing 7-5, the window should look like Figure 7-12. Press Enter and enjoy the unattended install of Ubuntu 14.04.

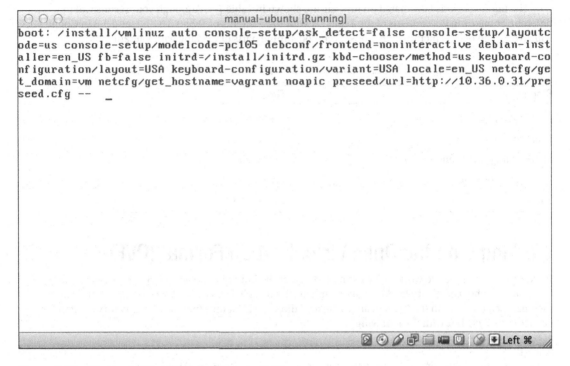

```
boot: /install/vmlinuz auto console-setup/ask_detect=false console-setup/layoutc
ode=us console-setup/modelcode=pc105 debconf/frontend=noninteractive debian-inst
aller=en_US fb=false initrd=/install/initrd.gz kbd-chooser/method=us keyboard-co
nfiguration/layout=USA keyboard-configuration/variant=USA locale=en_US netcfg/ge
t_domain=vm netcfg/get_hostname=vagrant noapic preseed/url=http://10.36.0.31/pre
seed.cfg --  _
```

Figure 7-12. *Unattended installation of Ubuntu 14.04*

You can interrupt or stop this activity at any point. I just wanted to provide you with a complete description of how an OS can be installed from scratch in a completely unattended manner.

■ **Note** You can now repeat the automatic generation of the Ubuntu box procedure with bento definitions. Run the following command and take a closer look at the VM window:

```
$ packer build -only=virtualbox-iso ubuntu-14.04-i386.json
```

You will see that to perform an unattended install, Packer types the command shown in Listing 7-5 within the VM window.

Timing

Generating freshly built boxes with Packer takes a lot of time; it is the longest operation you have encountered so far. First, you need to download the ISO CD/DVD image, which might last a couple of minutes, depending on your Internet connection. Then you have to perform an unattended install, which usually lasts for half an hour.

The freshly built system will then be configured and provisioned, which consumes another 10 (or even more) minutes. Finally, the provisioned system will be exported and post-processed into a box file. This operation, as you may remember from the previous chapter, takes another couple of minutes.

The timing periods I estimated on my Mac are shown in Table 7-1. Although your results will be different, comparing the contents of the Table 7-1 with the contents of Tables 3-1, 3-2, and 3-3 in Chapter 3 will give you an overall picture of the most time-consuming parts of working with Vagrant.

Table 7-1. *Timing of the $ packer build -only=virtualbox-iso ubuntu-14.04-i386.json Command*

Stage	Time
Downloading ISO CD	6 minutes
Unattended install	10 minutes
Provisioning and configuration	6 minutes
Exporting a box file	1 minute
Total	23 minutes

Working with the Open Virtualization Format (OVF)

Packer can also be used to work with existing VMs. After the initial $ vagrant up run for a given box (for example, ubuntu/trusty32), Vagrant downloads the box file from the network, unzips it, and stores the unzipped contents in the ~/.vagrant.d/boxes/ directory. List the contents of a directory created for ubuntu/trusty32 box with the following:

```
# Host OS
$ ls .vagrant.d/boxes/ubuntu-VAGRANTSLASH-trusty32/14.04/virtualbox
```

You will see the following output:

```
Vagrantfile
box-disk1.vmdk
box.ovf
metadata.json
```

The box.ovf file can be used as the entry point of Packer instead of ISO CD/DVD images. The complete example template file is shown in Listing 7-6.

Listing 7-6. Template File to Work with Existing Boxes in OVF Format

```
{
    "builders": [{
        "name": "vagrant-jekyll-packer-ovf-shell",
        "type": "virtualbox-ovf",
        "source:path": "/Users/gajdaw/.vagrant.d/boxes/ubuntu-VAGRANTSLASH-trusty32/14.04/
        virtualbox/box.ovf",
        "ssh_username": "vagrant",
        "ssh_password": "vagrant",
        "ssh_wait_timeout": "30s",
        "shutdown_command": "echo 'packer' | sudo -S shutdown -P now"
    }],
```

```
    "provisioners": [{
        "type": "shell",
        "script": "script.sh"
    }],
    "post-processors": [{
        "type": "vagrant"
    }]
}
```

Working with the OVF format is similar to the procedure that you applied in Chapter 6. It is the way to modify one of the existing boxes.

Summary

This chapter gave you basic knowledge about practical methods you can use to create Vagrant boxes from scratch. The quickest path to achieve satisfactory results is to use Packer and the chef/bento or boxcutter templates. Because I wanted to explain actions performed by Packer, I showed you how to create boxes manually in VirtualBox without the need to refer to either Packer or any templates. This is not a practical approach, however; you should stick with Packer and the chef/bento and boxcutter templates, customizing them when necessary.

In this chapter, VirtualBox Guest Additions were discussed for the first time. This software contains drivers that have to be installed in a guest OS. The important thing to know is that Guest Additions are published for every version of VirtualBox. If you work with VirtualBox 4.3.18 on your host, you will get the best VirtualBox experience if your Vagrant boxes contain Guest Additions v4.3.18. The simplest way to achieve it is to generate Vagrant boxes from scratch using Packer. Other solution is to use vbguest plugin mentioned in Chapter 10.

Finally, you learned how to apply Packer to use existing base boxes (stored on your system in OVF format) as a starting point for Packer. You can use Packer to extend boxes the way you did manually in Chapter 6.

In the Next Chapter, You Will Learn . . .

Your knowledge of Vagrant is now very broad. Chapter 7 will discuss various configuration options that you can include in the Vagrantfile.

Reading List

Documentation available at http://www.packer.io is the best source of knowledge concerning Packer. For a quick remainder about commands and their syntax, use the built-in manual:

```
$ packer
$ packer build --help
```

Packer is quite a new product: its first commit was dated March 22, 2013. Another project named Veewee performs similar operations, and because it was started on November 9, 2010, it can be seen as a predecessor of Packer.

The source code of both Packer and Veewee are available on GitHub:

```
https://github.com/mitchellh/packer
https://github.com/jedi4ever/veewee
```

Packer is written in Go; Veewee is written in Ruby.

The JSON file format is specified at http://json.org/. If you are new to JSON, you might be interested in the Wikipedia entry about this format: http://en.wikipedia.org/wiki/JSON.

For more information about Virtual Box Guest Additions, see the VirtualBox documentation at https://www.virtualbox.org/manual/ch04.html.

Test Yourself

1. What is the purpose of using Packer?

2. In which situations is this tool indispensable?

3. What is the name of the most popular GitHub project that contains a large collection of Packer templates of many different OSs for various providers?

4. What is the command to produce an Ubuntu 14.04 box using Packer and bento definitions?

5. Where does Packer store downloaded ISO images by default?

6. How do you change the location of the Packer cache?

7. Why does the Packer cache folder contain files with strange names that consist of hexadecimal numbers?

8. How to calculate SHA 256 hash of an arbitrary string?

9. Create an example JSON file that contains a list of five persons, with each person having two attributes: name and surname?

10. What are the four top-level keys used in the Packer template JSON file?

11. How does Packer perform an unattended install of Ubuntu 14.04 using the ISO CD/DVD distribution downloaded from the Ubuntu web site?

12. How can you manually download an ISO image from the Ubuntu web site?

13. What are the necessary steps to create, from scratch, a complete box that can be used by Vagrant?

Exercises

1. Build a box for a FreeBSD 10.1 (32-bit) system using the chef/bento project. Use the freebsd-10.1-i386.json file.

2. Build a box for a Fedora 21 (32-bit) system using the chef/bento project. Use the fedora-21-i386.json file.

3. List all the boxes that can be generated with boxcutter/ubuntu templates.

4. Build a box for an Ubuntu 12.04 (32-bit) system using the boxcutter/ubuntu project. The box should contain Puppet SCM tool.

5. List all the boxes that can be generated with boxcutter/centos templates.

6. Build a box for CentOS 6.5 (32-bit) system using the boxcutter/centos project. The box should contain the Chef SCM tool.

CHAPTER 8

■ ■ ■

Configuring Virtual Machines

This chapter will analyze and classify the most important configuration settings that can be used within the Vagrantfile. In particular, you will learn about the following:

- VirtualBox-related configuration

    - VM name

    - GUI mode

    - Physical properties, such as RAM and number of CPUs

- General VM settings

    - Hostname

    - Post-up message

    - Booting and halting timeouts

    - SSH settings

    - X11 forwarding

    - Box-related configuration

- Networking

    - Port forwarding

    - Private networks

    - Public networks

- Sync folders

    - Performance

    - Types: VirtualBox, NFS, rsync, SMB

- Defining platform-specific configuration

VirtualBox-Related Configuration

VirtualBox allows you to redefine the following configuration settings:

- VM name
- Graphical user interface (GUI) mode
- Physical properties of a VM

VM Name

To set the VM name to `my-fantastic-project`, use the code shown in Listing 8-1. In other words, the `v.name` variable allows you to interact with the name defined in Figure 7-1 in Chapter 7.

Listing 8-1. Setting the VM Name to my-fantastic-project

```
Vagrant.configure(2) do |config|
  config.vm.box = "ubuntu/trusty32"
  config.vm.provider "virtualbox" do |v|
    v.name = "my-fantastic-project"
  end
end
```

When you boot the machine using the Vagrantfile from Listing 8-1 with `$ vagrant up`, the output will include the following message:

```
==> default: Setting the name of the VM: my-fantastic-project
```

What happens if you use the same name in two different projects? Nothing interesting. You will see this error message:

```
A VirtualBox machine with the name 'my-fantastic-project' already exists.
Please use another name or delete the machine with the existing name, and try again.
```

The name of the machine is displayed inside VirtualBox, as shown in Figure 8-1.

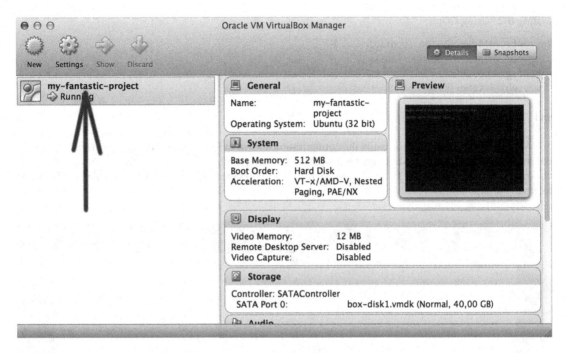

Figure 8-1. *VM name within VirtualBox*

The name of the machine is very important in one situation: when you want to package a box, as described in Chapter 7 in the section "Booting ISO Images." Boot the VM using this command:

```
$ vagrant up
```

You can package the box with this:

```
$ vagrant package
```

Vagrant is clever enough to find the VM that was started in the current directory.

But if the VM is started without the `$ vagrant up` command (for example, using ISO images distributed by Ubuntu.com), you have to pass the name of the box to the `$ vagrant package` command:

```
$ vagrant package --base my-fantastic-project
```

GUI Mode

By default, VirtualBox starts the machines in headless mode, which means that there is no interface to access the guest OS. The only way to do it is to use SSH. You can change this behavior using the `gui` configuration variable, as shown in Listing 8-2.

Listing 8-2. Using GUI

```
Vagrant.configure(2) do |config|
  config.vm.box = "ubuntu/trusty32"
  config.vm.provider "virtualbox" do |v|
    v.gui = true
  end
end
```

When you boot the machine using the configuration shown in Listing 8-2, VirtualBox will start the console shown in Figure 8-2. Although it is a typical terminal that doesn't offer any advantages over the SSH console, it can be useful when something goes wrong. The messages shown in the GUI console may help you to pin the problem down.

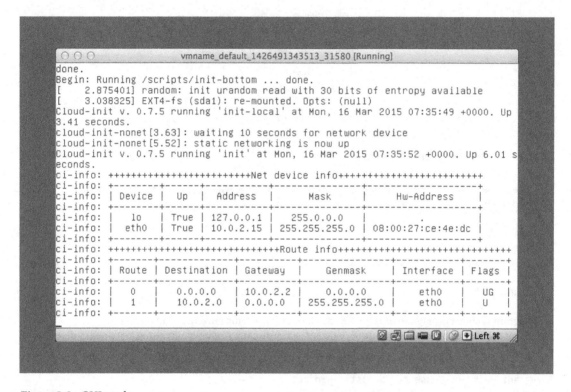

Figure 8-2. *GUI mode*

■ **Note**   In case of problems with booting the VM you can also use the debug flag:

```
$ vagrant up --debug
```

RAM

The amount of RAM assigned to a VM can be defined with the memory variable. The guest using the configuration from Listing 8-3 has 4 GB of RAM.

Listing 8-3. Setting the Amount of RAM to 4 GB

```
Vagrant.configure(2) do |config|
  config.vm.box = "ubuntu/trusty32"
  config.vm.provider "virtualbox" do |v|
    v.memory = 4096
  end
end
```

When you boot the machine configured with Listing 8-3, you can verify the amount of RAM within the guest with the following commands:

```
# Guest OS
$ free m
$ cat /proc/meminfo
$ sudo lshw
```

VirtualBox displays the amount of RAM assigned for the VM inside the Settings/System/Motherboard dialog box, as shown in Figure 8-3 (the screenshot was generated for a machine configured with the v.memory = 4096 value).

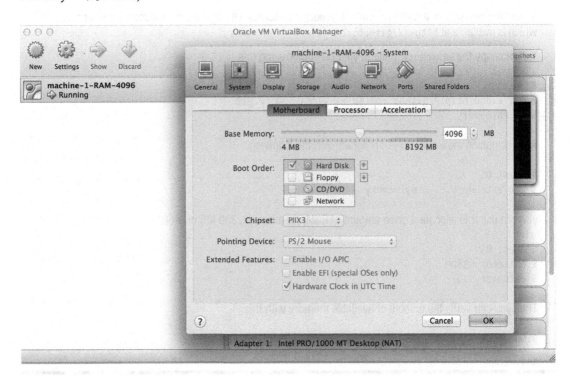

Figure 8-3. *Amount of RAM assigned to the VM*

By default, Vagrant allocates 512 MB for each VM. So if you skip the memory variable, it is equivalent to this:

```
v.memory = 512
```

How much RAM should you assign to your VM? You need to take a few factors into consideration:

- How much physical RAM your machine has
- How much RAM the tools you use consume

Of course, you have to leave enough memory for your host to run smoothly. You will get the best performance when your system doesn't have to use the swap file, and can fit all the applications and processes within the physical memory limit. When I boot my Mac OS system, the activity window displays the information that the processes consume about 3.7 GB of physical memory. Starting the web browser, integrated development environment (IDE), and some tools increases this amount to more than 4 GB. So I prefer to reserve 5 GB for my host. Having 8 GB of RAM, it leaves 3 GB for guests, so I don't exceed the limit of 3 GB assigned to guests. It helps keep my swap file size at 0.

Another problem is the amount of RAM needed by the guest OS, which depends on the software you want to use within a VM. For running just a basic HTTP server, as you did in Chapter 2, the default amount of 512 MB of RAM is more than enough. But some applications might need more RAM. For example, if you want to use composer (a dependency manager for PHP projects), you will have to increase the amount of RAM to 1 GB. In practice, I usually use 1 GB for VMs.

EATMEMORY PROGRAM

To test the behavior of a guest OS under memory constraints, you can use the eatmemory program, which is available at `https://github.com/julman99/eatmemory`.

You can copy the `eatmemory.c` file to your computer using this:

```
# Host OS
$ git clone http://github.com/julman99/eatmemory.git
$ cd eatmemory
```

After compiling the `eatmemory.c` program with the following:

```
# Guest OS
$ gcc eatmemory.c -o eatmemory
```

you can use it to allocate a given amount of RAM; for example, 380 MB or 1 GB:

```
# Guest OS
$ eatmemory 380M
$ eatmemory 1G
```

Then you can verify the amount of available memory with this:

```
# Guest OS

$ free m
```

GUEST'S VIRTUAL MEMORY

By default, the `ubuntu/trusty32` guest OS does not use swap files for virtual memory. Thus, the various processes that you run within the guest can allocate the amount of memory only up to the limit defined with the `v.memory` setting. You can enable virtual memory within a guest running Linux using the following commands:

```
# Guest OS
$ /bin/dd if=/dev/zero of=/var/swap.1 bs=1M count=1024
$ /sbin/mkswap /var/swap.1
$ /sbin/swapon /var/swap.1
```

These instructions come from the Composer documentation: `https://getcomposer.org/doc/articles/troubleshooting.md`.

Number of CPUs

If you work on a multiprocessor machine, you can restrict the number of CPUs to be used by the guest system with the configuration shown in Listing 8-4.

Listing 8-4. Setting RAM and Number of CPUs

```
Vagrant.configure(2) do |config|
  config.vm.box = "ubuntu/trusty32"
  config.vm.provider "virtualbox" do |v|
    v.cpus = 2
  end
end
```

With the configuration shown in Listing 8-4, VirtualBox will use only two processors to run this particular VM, even if your machine has four of them. In most cases, you should use all the CPUs. And, of course, using the value that is greater than the number of CPUs installed on your computer won't do any good because VirtualBox will decrease it.

■ **Note** Try to use VirtualBox/Settings/System dialog box shown in Figure 8-3. Go to the Processor tab and use the slider titled Processors. As you can see, VirtualBox doesn't allow you to set the value greater than the actual number of processors installed on your computer.

Other Physical Properties

There are some other low-level properties of a guest OS that you may find useful. (For a full list, see the VirtualBox documentation at `www.virtualbox.org/manual/ch08.html#vboxmanage-modifyvm`.)
Vagrant allows you to set those low-level properties with the following syntax:

```
v.customize ["modifyvm", :id, "NAME", "VALUE"]
```

For example, to set the value of parameter named --cpuexecutioncap to 50, use the code shown in Listing 8-5.

Listing 8-5. Setting --cpuexecutioncap parameter to 50

```
Vagrant.configure(2) do |config|
  config.vm.box = "ubuntu/trusty32"
  config.vm.provider "virtualbox" do |v|
    v.customize ["modifyvm", :id, "--cpuexecutioncap", "50"]
  end
end
```

For the VM created with the Vagrantfile shown in Listing 8-5, VirtualBox will constrain the processors' execution time to 50 percent.

■ **Note** The following configuration:

```
v.memory = 758
v.cpus = 4
```

is a shorthand for the following:

```
v.customize ["modifyvm", :id, "--memory", "758"]
v.customize ["modifyvm", :id, "--cpus", "4"]
```

General Settings

This is the general configuration of a VM:

- Hostname
- Post-up message
- Booting and halting timeouts
- SSH configuration
- Base box settings

Hostname

To set the name of your host to abc.example.lh, use the code shown in Listing 8-6.

Listing 8-6. Setting the Hostname

```
Vagrant.configure(2) do |config|
  config.vm.box = "ubuntu/trusty32"
  config.vm.hostname = "abc.example.lh"
end
```

If the Vagrantfile contains the `config.vm.hostname` variable, `$ vagrant up` will output the following message:

```
==> default: Setting hostname...
```

As you may remember from the Puppet section in Chapter 6, an undefined hostname might result in warning about an unresolved fully qualified domain name:

```
warning: could not retrieve fact fqdn
```

Suppose that you define a name for your host as `abc.example.lh`:

```
config.vm.hostname = "abc.example.lh"
```

Within the guest OS, the following command:

```
# Guest OS
$ hostname -f
```

will produce this output:

```
abc.example.lh
```

The name `abc.example.lh` is available in the guest, but not in the host. To enable it in the host, you have to modify the `/etc/hosts` file. By appending the following line to your `/etc/hosts` file, you can make the name `abc.example.lh` available in your host:

```
127.0.0.1 abc.example.lh
```

The application available in the guest will be available under `http://abc.example.lh`.

■ **Note** If you work on Windows, your `hosts` file is located under `C:\windows\system32\drivers\etc\hosts`. To edit the file, you have to run the editor with administrator privileges.

Post-up Messages

The `config.vm.post_up_message` variable can be used to display a message when booting is finished. This is a perfect place to show your users how to access the application. The example usage is shown in Listing 8-7.

Listing 8-7. Setting the Hostname

```
Vagrant.configure(2) do |config|
  config.vm.box = "ubuntu/trusty32"
  config.vm.post_up_message = "The application is available at http://abc.example.lh:8765"
end
```

When you boot the VM using Listing 8-7, Vagrant will display this message:

```
==> default: Machine 'default' has a post `vagrant up` message. This is a message
==> default: from the creator of the Vagrantfile, and not from Vagrant itself:
==> default:
==> default: The application is available at http://abc.example.lh:8765
```

Booting and Halting Timeouts

Two variables shown in Listing 8-8 set the timeout for booting and halting the guest VM. Both values are in seconds, and the defaults are 300 and 60:

```
config.vm.boot_timeout = 300
config.vm. graceful_halt_timeout = 60
```

Listing 8-8. Booting and Halting Timeouts

```
Vagrant.configure(2) do |config|
  config.vm.box = "ubuntu/trusty32"
  config.vm.boot_timeout = 1
  config.vm. graceful_halt_timeout = 5
end
```

If the system can't boot within the period defined by boot_timeout, you will see the following message (this is just an excerpt, not a complete message):

```
Timed out while waiting for the machine to boot. This means that
Vagrant was unable to communicate with the guest machine within
the configured ("config.vm.boot_timeout" value) time period.
```

The graceful_halt_timeout value is the number of seconds Vagrant waits after issuing a halt signal before shutting the guest down.

SSH

Basic properties of SSH sessions opened by the $ vagrant ssh command are governed by the following settings:

```
config.ssh.username
config.ssh.password
config.ssh.host
config.ssh.port
config.ssh.private_key_path
```

They define username, password, host, port, and private key. With those options, you can avoid using predefined and publicly known credentials.

One more important option is this:

```
config.ssh.insert_key
```

It is a Boolean value that, when set to true, will instruct Vagrant to replace publicly known SSH keys with a new, randomly generated pair. The operation of inserting a new randomly generated pair is shown with the following comment displayed during $ vagrant up:

```
default: Vagrant insecure key detected. Vagrant will automatically replace
default: this with a newly generated keypair for better security.
default:
default: Inserting generated public key within guest...
default: Removing insecure key from the guest if its present...
default: Key inserted! Disconnecting and reconnecting using new SSH key...
```

It makes using publicly known keys much more secure. But remember that you have to turn it off when you package a new box. Otherwise, you will generate a box that can't be accessed with well-known SSH keys. To turn off the operation that inserts new random SSH keys, use the configuration shown in Listing 8-9.

Listing 8-9. Turning Off Random SSH Keys Insertion

```
Vagrant.configure(2) do |config|
  config.vm.box = "ubuntu/trusty32"
  config.ssh.insert_key = false
end
```

X11 Forwarding

Turning on the feature of X11 forwarding allows you to run X11 applications within a guest system with windows displayed by the host system. To try this, you need to install the X11 server:

- On OS X, use XQuartz: https://support.apple.com/en-us/HT201341

- On Windows, use Xming: http://sourceforge.net/projects/xming/

On OS X, the X11 server will start automatically. Windows users have to start Xming/XLaunch manually. Once you start XLaunch, its icon will be displayed in the system tray (systray) in the right-bottom corner of your Windows main screen (see Figure 8-4).

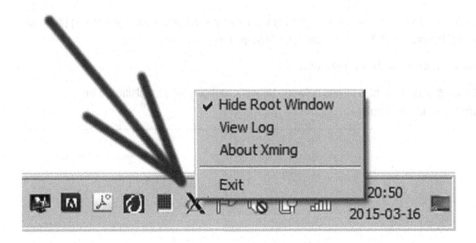

Figure 8-4. *On Windows, the XMing icon is displayed in the systray*

Create the Vagrantfile shown in Listing 8-10. When it is ready, boot the guest VM with $ vagrant up.

Listing 8-10. Forwarding X11

```
Vagrant.configure(2) do |config|
  config.vm.box = "ubuntu/trusty32"
  config.vm.network "private_network", ip: "192.168.50.4"
  config.ssh.forward_x11 = true
end
```

When the guest VM is ready, open the SSH session:

```
# Host OS
vagrant ssh
```

Install X11 applications and run the xeyes program:

```
# Guest OS
$ sudo apt-get update -y
$ sudo apt-get install x11-apps -y
$ xeyes
```

The xeyes application will be displayed by your host OS. In the same way, you can run the Firefox browser within the guest OS:

```
# Guest OS
$ sudo apt-get install firefox -y
$ firefox
```

■ **Note**   If you work on Windows, you need to set the DISPLAY environment variable:

```
# Guest OS
$ export DISPLAY="192.168.0.100:0.0"
$ xeyes
```

You have to replace the IP address 192.168.0.100 with the value that you will find in Xming/View Log (the View Log option is displayed in Figure 8-4). The IP is contained within the line that looks like this:

```
XdmcpRegisterConnection: newAddress 192.168.0.100
```

The Vagrant file in Listing 8-10 contains a private network. Network configuration is explained in the "Networking" section, later in this chapter.

Base Box

There are two important variables that configure the base box:

```
config.vm.box
config.vm.box_url
```

The first one defines the name of the box. The value assigned to `config.vm.box` can take one of three forms:

- The `vendor/name` (for example, `ubuntu/trusty32`); this name is resolved into an URL by `atlas.hashicorp.com`

- The valid URL; for example, `http://boxes.gajdaw.pl/apache/apache-v1.0.0.box`

- The name, such as `rails-my-shop`; the name of the box already installed in the system

These three cases are illustrated in Listings 8-11, 8-12, and 8-13.

Listing 8-11. The Name ubuntu/trusty32 Resolved by atlas.hashicorp.com

```
Vagrant.configure(2) do |config|
  config.vm.box = "ubuntu/trusty32"
end
```

Listing 8-12. Using a URL as a Box Name

```
Vagrant.configure(2) do |config|
  config.vm.box = "http://boxes.gajdaw.pl/apache/apache-v1.0.0.box"
end
```

Listing 8-13. Using the Box That Is Already Installed

```
Vagrant.configure(2) do |config|
  config.vm.box = "apache-v1.0.0"
end
```

If you boot the VM defined in Listing 8-11 or Listing 8-12 for the first time, Vagrant will install the given box in the system. In case of `ubuntu/trusty32`, the URL to download the box file will be resolved by the Atlas service. You will be notified by the message displayed during `$ vagrant up`:

```
==> default: Loading metadata for box 'ubuntu/trusty32'
    default: URL: https://atlas.hashicorp.com/ubuntu/trusty32
==> default: Adding box 'ubuntu/trusty32' (v14.04) for provider: virtualbox
    default: Downloading: https://atlas.hashicorp.com/ubuntu/boxes/trusty32/versions/14.04/
providers/virtualbox.box
```

For Listing 8-12, the box will be installed in the system under the name identical to the URL, which is usually very long and not easy to type. You can change this behavior with the `box_url` parameter. Using both box and `box_url`, instruct Vagrant to install the box under the given name. During the booting of the machine shown in Listing 8-14, Vagrant would at some point issue this command:

```
$ vagrant box add apache-v1.0.0 http://boxes.gajdaw.pl/apache/apache-v1.0.0.box
```

The box would be installed under the name apache-v1.0.0.

Listing 8-14. Using the box and box_url Variables

```
Vagrant.configure(2) do |config|
  config.vm.box = "apache-v1.0.0"
  config.vm.box_url = "http://boxes.gajdaw.pl/apache/apache-v1.0.0.box"
end
```

Remember that to boot the machine from Listing 8-13, the box named apache-v1.0.0 has to be already installed on your host system; otherwise, $ vagrant up will fail.

Using Checksums for Boxes

Two additional variables can be used to validate boxes using checksums:

```
config.vm.box_download_checksum
config.vm.box_download_checksum_type
```

The example configuration is shown in Listing 8-15. (Of course, the 01234567890 value shown in Listing 8-15 is not a real SHA-256 checksum of the apache-v1.0.0.box file.)

Listing 8-15. Validating the Box with Checksums

```
Vagrant.configure(2) do |config|
  config.vm.box_download_checksum_type = "sha256"
  config.vm.box_download_checksum = "01234567890"
  config.vm.box = "http://boxes.gajdaw.pl/apache/apache-v1.0.0.box"
end
```

During the booting of the VM shown in Listing 8-15, Vagrant downloads the apache-v1.0.0.box file, calculates the SHA-256 checksum of the downloaded file, and compares the calculated value with the value given as downloaded_checksum. If the values differ (as is the case for the data in Listing 8-15), Vagrant fails and prints this message:

```
The checksum of the downloaded box did not match the expected
value. Please verify that you have the proper URL setup and that
you're downloading the proper file.

Expected: 019238457
Received: 091eb90af1bce5dd1dc936ed9db9ef65631e7428c29e60b395025a2d21cdc463
```

___

■ **Note** To calculate SHA-256 checksums, you can use the following commands:

```
# OS X
$ shasum -a 256 filename.box
# On Windows
$ openssl dgst -sha256 filename.box
```

Some distributions of Vagrant contain a bug, and a comparison of checksums is skipped. I could produce the message "The checksum of the downloaded box did not match" only when I used this command:

```
# Host OS
$ vagrant box add \
    apache-v1.0.0 \
    --checksum-type sha256 \
    --checksum 019238457 \
    http://boxes.gajdaw.pl/apache/apache-v1.0.0.box
```

Vagrant also supports box versioning. You learn more about versioning boxes in Chapter 10.

Networking

There are three ways to communicate with your guest VM using the network:

- Port forwarding

- Private networks

- Public networks

Port Forwarding

This is the simplest approach to set up host-guest communication. It has two advantages over other methods: Vagrant doesn't ask any questions during booting, and you don't need administrator privileges to boot the machine. (That's why I prefer to use this solution for the examples that accompany this book.) But it also has some drawbacks:

- You have to define each forwarded port manually.

- It is a communication channel that originates on the host side; you cannot use it for NFS or X11 because port forwarding doesn't allow the guest to communicate with services running on the host.

The example shown in Listing 8-16 shows how to forward the requests sent to the host's port 8800 to the guest's port 80. The configuration shown in Listing 8-16 changes the behavior of VirtualBox, and all traffic coming to the port 8800 on the host is routed to the service running on port 80 in the guest.

Listing 8-16. Requests Sent to the Host's Port 8800 Are Handled by Guest's Daemon Running on Port 80

```
Vagrant.configure(2) do |config|
  config.vm.box = "ubuntu/trusty32 "
  config.vm.network :forwarded_port, guest: 80, host: 8800
end
```

When you boot the VM, Vagrant informs you about the forwarded ports:

```
==> default: Forwarding ports...
    default: 80 => 8800 (adapter 1)
    default: 22 => 2222 (adapter 1)
```

As discussed in Chapter 4, to allow SSH connections to the guest, Vagrant configures the forwarding host's port 2222 to the guest's port 22 by default.

The following syntax means that the requests sent to the host's port 456 will be serviced by the daemon running in the guest on port 123:

```
default: 123 => 456 (adapter 1)
```

Forwarding can be further customized with the following five parameters:

```
guest
guest_ip
host
host_ip
protocol
```

The guest and host parameters define the port numbers. For host, you should use a number greater than 1024, unless Vagrant runs with administrator privileges. guest_ip and host_ip can be used to restrict IP addresses. Use the following to forbid remote access to the forwarded port:

```
host_ip: "127.0.0.1"
```

■ **Note** Remember that the configuration shown in Listing 8-16 allows everyone who knows your IP address to access the web server. Suppose that your IP is 10.20.30.40; the web server would then be available at http://10.20.30.40:8800.

The last parameter, protocol, can be used to restrict forwarded protocols to either TCP or UDP.

How many ports can you forward? Well, as many as you like. The following configuration:

```
config.vm.network :forwarded_port, guest: 80, host: 8800
config.vm.network :forwarded_port, guest: 81, host: 8801
config.vm.network :forwarded_port, guest: 82, host: 8802
config.vm.network :forwarded_port, guest: 83, host: 8803
config.vm.network :forwarded_port, guest: 84, host: 8804
config.vm.network :forwarded_port, guest: 85, host: 8805
...
```

results in the following messages:

```
default: 80 => 8800 (adapter 1)
default: 81 => 8801 (adapter 1)
default: 82 => 8802 (adapter 1)
default: 83 => 8803 (adapter 1)
default: 84 => 8804 (adapter 1)
default: 85 => 8805 (adapter 1)
...
```

Port Collision

One port on your host can be assigned to only one service. If the port number 8000 is already in use, you can't use it again. If you try to boot the machine defined in Listing 8-16 twice (you have to copy the same Vagrantfile to two different folders and use $ vagrant up in both folders), the second attempt will fail with this message:

```
Vagrant cannot forward the specified ports on this VM, since they
would collide with some other application that is already listening
on these ports. The forwarded port to 8800 is already in use
on the host machine.

To fix this, modify your current projects Vagrantfile to use another
port. Example, where '1234' would be replaced by a unique host port:

  config.vm.network :forwarded_port, guest: 80, host: 1234

Sometimes, Vagrant will attempt to auto-correct this for you. In this
case, Vagrant was unable to. This is usually because the guest machine
is in a state which doesn't allow modifying port forwarding.
```

To boot the second machine, you have to use a different port on your host.

Vagrant can automatically avoid the conflict, which is done with the auto_correct option set to true (see Listing 8-17).

Listing 8-17. Autocorrecting Port Collisions

```
Vagrant.configure(2) do |config|
  config.vm.box = "ubuntu/trusty32 "
  config.vm.network :forwarded_port, guest: 80, host: 8800, auto_correct: true
end
```

Booting two VMs, the one shown in Listing 8-16 and the second shown in Listing 8-17, results in the following messages:

```
==> default: Fixed port collision for 80 => 8800. Now on port 2200.
==> default: Fixed port collision for 22 => 2222. Now on port 2201.
...
==> default: Forwarding ports...
    default: 80 => 2200 (adapter 1)
    default: 22 => 2201 (adapter 1)
```

During bootup, Vagrant tries to allocate the host's port number 8800. But the port is already occupied. Thanks to auto_correct: true, Vagrant avoids the collision; instead of 8800, it allocates the host's port number 2200. So the service running in guest on port 80 can be accessed from the host using port 2200. Vagrant can successfully boot the system, and you won't see any error message.

As you may guess, Vagrant performs autocorrection for the SSH service. By default, the SSH session uses the host's port 2200. But if this port is already allocated (i.e., another VM is running), Vagrant resolves the conflict automatically. If you use the $ vagrant ssh command to start the SSH session, it won't bother you. But if you use some other SSH client (e.g., putty), you will have to adjust the client configuration.

The range of ports used for autocorrection is defined with config.vm.usable_port_range. It defaults to 2200..2250.

Private Networks

By using private networks, you can do the following:

- Avoid typing the configuration of each forwarded port separately

- Avoid using port numbers such as 8800 for well-known services

- Use the same port numbers in different projects

- Communicate between multiple guests

- Use NFS for shared directories

These are the main advantages. The most important disadvantage is that depending on your host OS and its configuration, you might have to answer some questions during booting, which may be an issue for you.

Private networks can be configured manually or with the VirtualBox built-in DHCP server. The example shown in Listing 8-18 shows how to configure private network manually; Listing 8-19 shows the way to configure private networking with DHCP. Remember that when you provide the IP address manually, you have to use the address from the private space: http://en.wikipedia.org/wiki/Private_network#Private_IPv4_address_spaces.

Listing 8-18. Manual Configuration of Private Networking

```
Vagrant.configure(2) do |config|
  config.vm.box = "ubuntu/trusty32"
  config.vm.network "private_network", ip: "10.20.30.40"
end
```

Listing 8-19. Private Networking Configured with DHCP

```
Vagrant.configure(2) do |config|
  config.vm.box = "ubuntu/trusty32 "
  config.vm.network "private_network", type: "dhcp"
end
```

Before dissecting the internals, let's take a more detailed look at the advantages of private networks. First, although Listings 8-18 and 8-19 do not contain any forwarded_port options, all the ports in the guest are available in the host — no matter how many you want to use. For forwarding, you have to add one forwarding rule per each service (one for HTTP, one for MySQL, one for FTP, and so on).

The second advantage is that with private networks, every project can use default port numbers. For HTTP, every project can use port 80. If the guest runs an HTTP server at default port 80, you can access this port with your browser using this URL: http://10.20.30.40.

If you have multiple projects, you can run them all at the same time. The projects will be accessible under different IPs:

```
http://10.20.30.40
http://192.168.0.123
```

For private networks configured with DHCP, you may need to find out the IPs assigned to guests.

With private networking, all the guest machines running on your host can communicate with each other because they share the IP address space. And because the IPs are private, you don't have to worry about security: the traffic from the remote machines is not routed to or from the guests.

Now that you know the advantages of private networks, you can dive into the internals. When you boot the machine configured with private networks, Vagrant creates a new network interface in the host's configuration. With each new VM and IP address, the list of network interfaces on the host system will be expanded. After booting the machine shown in Listing 8-18, the output of the ifconfig command on the host:

```
# Host OS
$ ifconfig
```

will include the interface named vboxnet0:

```
vboxnet0: flags=8843<UP,BROADCAST,RUNNING,SIMPLEX,MULTICAST> mtu 1500
          ether 0a:00:27:00:00:00
          inet 10.20.30.1 netmask 0xffffff00 broadcast 10.20.30.255
```

The IP address 10.20.30.1 indicates that this is the interface for the private network 10.20.30/255 defined in Listing 8-18.

Now open the SSH session to the guest system and list the guest's interfaces:

```
# Guest OS
$ ifconfig
```

You will see, among other things, the following interface within the guest system:

```
eth1      Link encap:Ethernet  HWaddr 08:00:27:a6:7e:b9
          inet addr:10.20.30.40  Bcast:10.20.30.255  Mask:255.255.255.0
          inet6 addr: fe80::a00:27ff:fea6:7eb9/64 Scope:Link
          UP BROADCAST RUNNING MULTICAST  MTU:1500  Metric:1
          RX packets:0 errors:0 dropped:0 overruns:0 frame:0
          TX packets:8 errors:0 dropped:0 overruns:0 carrier:0
          collisions:0 txqueuelen:1000
          RX bytes:0 (0.0 B)  TX bytes:648 (648.0 B)
```

The IP address 10.20.30.40 indicates that this interface is created by the configuration from Listing 8-18.

If you booted the following two new VMs configured with two different IPs:

```
172.29.253.190
192.168.77.88
```

the list of interfaces on your host would include three interfaces: vboxnet0, vboxnet1 and vboxnet2. The output of the following:

```
# Host OS
$ ifconfig
```

would include vboxnet0, vboxnet1 and vboxnet2:

```
vboxnet0: flags=8843<UP,BROADCAST,RUNNING,SIMPLEX,MULTICAST> mtu 1500
          ether 0a:00:27:00:00:00
          inet 10.20.30.1 netmask 0xffffff00 broadcast 10.20.30.255
vboxnet1: flags=8843<UP,BROADCAST,RUNNING,SIMPLEX,MULTICAST> mtu 1500
          ether 0a:00:27:00:00:01
```

```
        inet 172.29.253.1 netmask 0xffffff00 broadcast 172.29.253.255
vboxnet2: flags=8843<UP,BROADCAST,RUNNING,SIMPLEX,MULTICAST> mtu 1500
        ether 0a:00:27:00:00:02
        inet 192.168.77.1 netmask 0xffffff00 broadcast 192.168.77.255
```

Your host has three interfaces assigned to the following IPs:

```
vboxnet0   -   10.20.30.1       (Guest's IP 10.20.30.40)
vboxnet1   -   172.29.253.1     (Guest's IP 172.29.253.190)
vboxnet2   -   192.168.77.1     (Guest's IP 192.168.77.88)
```

It might be surprising, but these interfaces are not removed, even if you shut down the VMs. If you use the $ vagrant destroy command to remove all three guests, it won't affect the interfaces vboxnet0, vboxnet1, and vboxnet2. To remove the interfaces from the host, use the following commands:

```
# Host OS
$ VBoxManage hostonlyif remove vboxnet0
$ VBoxManage hostonlyif remove vboxnet1
$ VBoxManage hostonlyif remove vboxnet2
```

■ **Note** On Windows, VBoxManage.exe is not in the path, so you need to prepend the full path. Here is an example:

```
# Host OS
$ /c/Program\ Files/Oracle/VirtualBox/VBoxManage.exe hostonlyif remove vboxnet0
```

How does the DHCP configuration work? When you use DHCP to configure private networks, be aware that the DHCP server is managed by VirtualBox; it is not the server available on your network. Even if your host is configured with the DHCP server on your network, guests are configured only with the DHCP server managed by VirtualBox. When you boot the machine defined in Listing 8-19, Vagrant starts a new DHCP server managed by VirtualBox. You can verify it with:

```
# Host OS
$ VBoxManage list dhcpservers
```

The output of the preceding command should include at least one DHCP server:

```
NetworkName:    HostInterfaceNetworking-vboxnet0
IP:             172.28.128.2
NetworkMask:    255.255.255.0
lowerIPAddress: 172.28.128.3
upperIPAddress: 172.28.128.254
Enabled:        Yes
```

The DHCP server can be identified by HostInterfaceNetworking-vboxnet0. Its IP is 172.28.128.2, and it assigns IPs starting at 172.28.128.3. When the DHCP server is running, Vagrant uses it to create and configure a new interface. When the booting is finished, the output of the following command:

```
# Host OS
$ ifconfig
```

will include the interface bound to the network IP 172.28.128.1 (depending on your previous actions, the interface may be named vboxnet5, vboxnet8, and so on):

```
vboxnet0: flags=8843<UP,BROADCAST,RUNNING,SIMPLEX,MULTICAST> mtu 1500
          ether 0a:00:27:00:00:00
          inet 172.28.128.1 netmask 0xffffff00 broadcast 172.28.128.255
```

If you now open the SSH session to your guest and run the following:

```
# Guest OS
$ ifconfig
```

you will see that your guest is assigned the lowest IP address offered by DHCP, which is 172.28.128.3:

```
eth1      Link encap:Ethernet  HWaddr 08:00:27:22:75:88
          inet addr:172.28.128.3  Bcast:172.28.128.255  Mask:255.255.255.0
          inet6 addr: fe80::a00:27ff:fe22:7588/64 Scope:Link
          UP BROADCAST RUNNING MULTICAST  MTU:1500  Metric:1
          RX packets:8 errors:0 dropped:0 overruns:0 frame:0
          TX packets:10 errors:0 dropped:0 overruns:0 carrier:0
          collisions:0 txqueuelen:1000
          RX bytes:1732 (1.7 KB)  TX bytes:1332 (1.3 KB)
```

Similar to vboxnet interfaces, the DHCP server managed by VirtualBox is not removed when you destroy the guest. From time to time, it can result in strange behavior in which Vagrant announces that the DHCP server is already in use. When that happens, you can manually remove the stale DHCP server with this:

```
# Host OS
$ VBoxManage dhcpserver remove --netname HostInterfaceNetworking-vboxnet0
```

Everything should work just fine.

Public Networks

If you configure your guest with public networks, it becomes available for remote access. Before doing this, make sure that you understand the security risks explained in Chapter 4.

To configure a public network, use the Vagrantfile shown in Listing 8-20.

Listing 8-20. Public Network

```
Vagrant.configure(2) do |config|
  config.vm.box = "ubuntu/trusty32"
config.vm.network "public_network"
end
```

The configuration shown in Listing 8-20 starts a VM and uses the DHCP server on your network to set up networking. If your host contains multiple interfaces, you have to choose one of them. For public networks, Vagrant doesn't create any new interfaces; it uses an existing one (it does not start a DHCP network managed by VirtualBox).

To avoid questions about which interface to use, you can use the `bridge` parameter like this:

```
config.vm.network "public_network", bridge: 'en1: Wi-Fi (AirPort)'
```

And if you don't want to use DHCP, you can provide an IP:

```
config.vm.network "public_network", ip: "192.168.0.17"
```

Running the `$ ifconfig` command inside the guest will prove that the IP assigned to one of the interfaces was retrieved from the DHCP server on your network.

Synced Folders

Vagrant synchronizes the host's directory containing the Vagrantfile with the guest's /vagrant directory, which is a default Vagrant behavior that doesn't require any Vagrantfile entries. If you want, you may be more verbose using the code shown in Listing 8-21.

Listing 8-21. Public Network

```
Vagrant.configure(2) do |config|
  config.vm.box = "ubuntu/trusty32"
  config.vm.synced_folder ".", "/vagrant"
end
```

When the system is brought up, Vagrant informs you about synchronized folders with this message:

```
==> default: Mounting shared folders...
    default: /vagrant => /some/path/on/host
```

The first path passed to `synced_folder` is the host's path, which can be absolute or relative to the project's root directory. The second path, which is the guest's path, it is absolute (it can't be relative). The guest path is always created if it does not exist. Although the host's path is not created by default, this behavior can be changed with the `create` parameter.

When using an absolute path as a first parameter, remember the differences between platforms. Depending on your host OS, you have to use one of these solutions:

```
# Host OS: Windows
config.vm.synced_folder "c:\\some\\path", "/vagrant"
# Host OS: u*ix
config.vm.synced_folder "/some/path", "/vagrant"
```

One Vagrantfile may contain an arbitrary number of `synced_folder` entries, like in Listing 8-22.

Listing 8-22. Synchronizing Multiple Folders

```
Vagrant.configure(2) do |config|
  config.vm.box = "ubuntu/trusty32"
  config.vm.synced_folder "./some/dir/first", "/first", create: true
  config.vm.synced_folder "./some/dir/second", "/second", create: true
end
```

The sync_folder has the following parameters:

- create: If the host's directory doesn't exist it will be created (defaults to false)

- disabled: Should the synchronization be turned on? (defaults to true)

- group: Group of the guest's directory (defaults to ssh user)

- owner: Owner of the guest's directory (defaults to ssh user)

- type and mount_options: Define the method of synchronization

Synchronization Types

Vagrant offers four types of synchronization:

- Default synchronization supported by the provider (bidirectional, slowest performance)

- NFS (bidirectional, best performance)

- rsync (one-way host-to-guest)

- SMB (bidirectional, performance comparable with NFS)

Before you start using the various synchronization types, let's first measure the performance of disk operations within the guest OS.

Benchmarking Disk Operations

To measure the efficiency of filesystem I/O operations in the guest, you will use the Linux dd command. It copies some amount of data from one place to another and asserts the speed of this operation. The parameters if and of set the name of input and output files. The amount of data to be copied is defined with bs and count: bs sets the block size, and count sets the number of blocks. The total number of bytes to be copied is equal to this:

```
bs * count
```

You can use dd to test both read and write efficiency.

The command shown in Listing 8-23 copies 10,000 blocks, each block of 1 K bytes from /dev/zero to /vagrant/abc. Thus, this command benchmarks writing to a shared directory.

Listing 8-23. Efficiency of Writing to a Shared Directory

```
# Guest OS - shared dir write benchmark
$ dd if=/dev/zero of=/vagrant/abc bs=1k count=10k
```

Another command to test efficiency is shown in Listing 8-24. It copies the contents of /vagrant/abc to /tmp/def. Thus, it benchmarks reading from a shared directory.

Listing 8-24. Efficiency of Reading /vagrant/abc file

```
# Guest OS - shared dir read benchmark
$ dd if=/vagrant/abc of=/tmp/def bs=1k count=10k
```

To measure native I/O operations within the guest, you can use the commands shown in Listings 8-25 and 8-26.

Listing 8-25. Efficiency of Writing to a Native Filesystem

```
# Guest OS - native filesystem write benchmark
$ dd if=/dev/zero of=/tmp/native-abc bs=1k count=10k
```

Listing 8-26. Efficiency of Reading from a Native Filesystem

```
# Guest OS - native filesystem read benchmark
$ dd if=/tmp/native-abc of=/tmp/native-def bs=1k count=10k
```

Boot the machine shown in Listing 8-21 and run the test shown in Listing 8-23 (writing to the shared directory). Repeat the command a couple of times and record the best results (I got about 11 MB/s):

```
10240+0 records in
10240+0 records out
10485760 bytes (10 MB) copied, 0.945521 s, 11.1 MB/s
```

Next, run the test shown in Listing 8-24 (reading from the shared directory). My results were these:

```
10240+0 records in
10240+0 records out
10485760 bytes (10 MB) copied, 0.970321 s, 10.8 MB/s
```

▓ **Note**   Read/write operations on a shared drive run at about 11 MB/s.

Now use the tests shown in Listings 8-25 and 8-26 to assert the efficiency of the native filesystem in the guest. You will get much better results. Mine were the following:

```
10240+0 records in
10240+0 records out
10485760 bytes (10 MB) copied, 0.0244637 s, 429 MB/s
```

▓ **Note**   Read/write operations on a guest's native filesystem run at about 400 MB/s.

Remember that there is an enormous discrepancy in performance between the shared folder and the guest's native filesystem. It can be summarized as follows:

```
Shared folder: 10 MB/s   vs.    Native filesystem: 400 GB/s
```

The shared directory is about 40 times slower than native I/O operations in the guest OS.

■ **Note** The results you achieve depend on many different factors, such as amount of data and block size. The following commands produce different results:

```
$ dd if=/dev/zero of=/tmp/native-abc bs=100k count=1k
$ dd if=/dev/zero of=/tmp/native-abc bs=1k count=100k
```

The main purpose of the tests is to show you the differences between the efficiency of various solutions.

VirtualBox Shared Folders

CHARACTERISTICS: BIDIRECTIONAL; READ: 10 MB/s; WRITE: 10 MB/s

If you don't provide any value for this parameter, Vagrant will use the default solutions supported by the provider you use. Thus, when working with VirtualBox, the Vagrantfile shown in Listing 8-27 implies using the native VirtualBox synchronization method.

Listing 8-27. Default Synchronization

```
Vagrant.configure(2) do |config|
  config.vm.box = "ubuntu/trusty32"
end
```

This is very easy to use, but offers the worst efficiency.

■ **Note** Keep in mind that if a project's directory resides somewhere different from the hard drive, the performance will be below any reasonable level. Do not run your Vagrant–driven virtual environments residing on removable USB memory or network-mapped drives.

NFS

CHARACTERISTICS: BIDIRECTIONAL; WRITE: 20 MB/s; READ: 400 MB/s

The configuration for using NFS shared folders is shown in Listing 8-28.

Listing 8-28. Using NFS for Synchronization

```
Vagrant.configure(2) do |config|
  config.vm.box = "ubuntu/trusty32"
  config.vm.network "private_network", type: "dhcp"
  config.vm.synced_folder ".", "/vagrant", type: "nfs"
end
```

You will get unbelievable speedup when you use NFS. Notice that for NFS to work, you need private networking. Also, NFS is not available by default on Windows. On hosts running Windows, Vagrant ignores type: nfs. You can circumvent this restriction by using the https://github.com/GM-Alex/vagrant-winnfsd plug-in (discussed in Chapter 10).

■ **Note** If your host runs Linux, you might have to install NFS.

■ **Tip** When you boot the VM configured with NFS, Vagrant will ask for the root's password at some point. You can avoid it by following the "Root Privilege Requirement" hint in Vagrant's documentation: https://docs.vagrantup.com/v2/synced-folders/nfs.html.

---

rsync

CHARACTERISTICS: ONE-TIME, ONE-WAY HOST-TO-GUEST

The rsync type performs one-way synchronization from host to guest and is purposed mainly for situations in which both the default mechanism and NFS fail. An example configuration for rsync synchronization is shown in Listing 8-29.

Listing 8-29. rsync Synchronization

```
Vagrant.configure(2) do |config|
  config.vm.box = "ubuntu/trusty32"
  config.vm.synced_folder ".", "/vagrant", type: "rsync",
    rsync__exclude: ".git/"
end
```

Keep in mind that rsync synchronization is performed only once: during $ vagrant up. When you boot the VM, Vagrant copies the contents of the synchronized folder from host to guest using the rsync utility. Vagrant does not monitor the folder on the host for any changes. To change this behavior, use the rsync_auto parameter set to true.

Remember that this is a one-way communication only. If you change the files in your guest, those changes are not reflected in your host.

What's the purpose of this strange method of synchronization? It allows you to take advantage of the native filesystem efficiency of your guest. Imagine the following workflow:

1. You work with your code in the project's root directly with your tools running on host.

2. The HTTP server serves the application saved in the native filesystem (for example, in the /app folder in the guest).

3. To run the application, you synchronize the files: the contents of the project's root is sent to the /app folder in the guest.

4. You visit the application with your browser; the HTTP server serves the application using only the native filesystem.

The advantage of this workflow is that you can use the full speed of the native filesystem; the disadvantage is that it can be more difficult to set up.

USING GIT FOR HOST => GUEST SYNCHRONIZATION

Yet another solution for a host->guest one-way synchronization is to use git with a post-update hook. To perform a push operation, git needs SSH. But Vagrant configures the SSH that you can use to access your host. So if you have a git repository somewhere on the host and somewhere on the guest, you can easily perform a push from host to guest. The workflow and the advantages are exactly the same as in case of rsync.

■ **Tip** To use the rsync type, you need the rsync application in your path. On Windows hosts, you can install rsync.exe the same way you installed make.exe in Chapter 7.

Server Message Block (SMB)

CHARACTERISTICS: BIDIRECTIONAL

The SMB shared folder is available on Windows hosts. It is purposed to replace native VirtualBox synchronization to achieve better efficiency. The example configuration is shown in Listing 8-30.

Listing 8-30. SMB Synchronization

```
Vagrant.configure(2) do |config|
  config.vm.box = "ubuntu/trusty32"
  config.vm.synced_folder ".", "/vagrant", type: "smb"
end
```

To use this SMB type, you need administrator privileges.

Platform-Related Configuration

You might need to use a different configuration, depending on your host OS. To do so, use the ffi library and if instruction, as shown in Listing 8-31.

Listing 8-31. Host-Dependent Configuration

```
Vagrant.configure(VAGRANTFILE_API_VERSION) do |config|
    config.vm.box = "ubuntu/trusty32 "

    require 'ffi'
    if FFI::Platform::IS_WINDOWS
        print "\n\n ===> win\n\n"
        config.vm.synced_folder ".", "/vagrant", :nfs => false
        config.vm.network :forwarded_port, guest: 80, host: 8880
    else
        print "\n\n ===> not win\n\n"
        config.vm.network :private_network, ip: "192.168.0.100"
        config.vm.synced_folder ".", "/vagrant", :nfs => true
    end
end
```

Summary

This chapter acted as a comprehensive compendium of various configuration options. Instead of memorizing the syntax of all the configuration options, I advise you to concentrate on these essentials:

- When can setting the VM name or guest hostname be important?

- How can you pin down the problems with $ vagrant up?

- How much memory and how many processors should you allocate for a VM?

- What are the basic characteristics of the three approaches to networking: forwarded ports, private networks, and public networks?

- What are the basic characteristics of the four ways to set up shared directories: the default VirtualBox shared filesystem, NFS, rsync, and SMB?

One thing is certain: before proceeding to the next chapters, you have to understand the way networking works and how Vagrant handles shared folders. As to the rest, you can return here if necessary.

In this chapter, you used some commands that are not strictly related to Vagrant. It often happens that you have to use additional tools to find out the more subtle aspects of various options. The investigation concerning memory relied on the commands to inspect the guest's RAM; eatmemory program; and to turn on swap: dd, mkswap, and swapon:

```
# Guest OS
$ free m
$ cat /proc/meminfo
$ sudo lshw
```

The analysis of the network-related aspects of using Vagrant was possible thanks to the hostname and ifconfig commands, together with the VBoxManage utility, which is shipped with VirtualBox. And the performance of filesystem was measured with dd.

In the Next Chapter, You Will Learn . . .

Well, you are done. You know all the basic facts about Vagrant, and it is time to use them. In the next chapter, I will share my experience of using Vagrant in practice.

Reading List

The most important resources for Vagrant configuration are, of course, the documentation:

- http://docs.vagrantup.com/v2/vagrantfile/machine_settings.html

- http://docs.vagrantup.com/v2/vagrantfile/ssh_settings.html

- http://docs.vagrantup.com/v2/networking/index.html

- http://docs.vagrantup.com/v2/synced-folders/index.html

The list of low-level configuration options offered by VirtualBox is available here:

- www.virtualbox.org/manual/ch08.html#vboxmanage-modifyvm

For a guide to private networks, refer to Wikipedia:

- `http://en.wikipedia.org/wiki/Private_network#Private_IPv4_address_spaces`

I found a solution to deal with stale DHCP among Vagrant issues here:

- `https://github.com/mitchellh/vagrant/issues/3083`

The dd command to benchmark I/O operations is described at askubuntu.com:

- `http://askubuntu.com/questions/87035/how-to-check-hard-disk-performance`

The commands to turn on swapping come from getcomposer.org:

- `https://getcomposer.org/doc/articles/troubleshooting.md`

For a general introduction to virtual memory, read these Wikipedia articles:

- `http://en.wikipedia.org/wiki/Virtual_memory`
- `http://en.wikipedia.org/wiki/Paging`

Finally, to resolve the problems I met during the configuration of X11 forwarding, I found the following article helpful:

- `https://coderwall.com/p/ozhfva/run-graphical-programs-within-vagrantboxes`

Test Yourself

1. How do you set the VM name?

2. When do you have to use the VM name?

3. Why would you need to use the GUI console?

4. How do you debug the problems that cause $ `vagrant` up to hang?

5. How much RAM should you allocate to your VM?

6. How can you find out the amount of RAM and the size of the swap file in Ubuntu Linux?

7. How and why would you configure the guest hostname?

8. What is the purpose of defining the post-up message? How do you do it?

9. What SSH properties can you define within the Vagrantfile?

10. How do you run an X11 application inside a VM with the window displayed on the host?

11. Which values can be assigned to the `config.vm.box` configuration variable?

12. What is the purpose of using checksums for boxes?

13. What are the basic characteristics of port forwarding?

14. What are the basic characteristics of private networks?

15. What are the basic characteristics of public networks?

16. What are the similarities and differences between forwarded ports, private networks, and public networks?

17. What are the similarities and differences between all types of shared folders?

18. Is it possible to define some options within the Vagrantfile to be applied only if the host runs one specific OS (Windows, for example)? How do you do it?

Exercises

1. Boot the machine configured with the code shown in each of the listings included in this chapter. Watch the output of $ vagrant up to find the message produced by the config options included in a given example.

CHAPTER 9

■ ■ ■

One True Workflow

There is no such thing as the one true workflow that all Vagrant users can apply. Your requirements and settings may be completely different from mine, and solutions that work for me may be unsuitable for you. This chapter focuses on the importance of the workflow. To get satisfactory results when working with Vagrant, you should follow certain procedures; otherwise, you will end up wasting lots of precious time.

Here are the most crucial tips for using Vagrant most efficiently:

- Use git and semantic versioning for your boxes.

- Keep your application code and your box in separate repositories.

- Generate base boxes with Packer (don't ever do it manually).

- Generate your customized boxes with Packer or a `build.sh` script.

- Use modularized definitions for provisioning.

- Store every submodule in a new repository; it can be Puppet module, Chef cookbook, or Ansible playbook.

- Use git and semantic versioning for submodules.

- Bake everything that developers may need inside the box.

Most Common Antipattern

When I started my adventure with Vagrant in 2012, I made the error of misusing provisioners. Do you remember how you proceeded in Chapter 6? There were two roles: the system engineer's role and the developer's role. The key point is that time-consuming provisioners (such as compilation of Ruby, for example) should be applied only when you work as an engineer (when you prepare the base box for developers).

To help you understand the problem, I prepared a new version of the "Songs for kids" application written in Ruby. It is available at `https://github.com/pro-vagrant/songs-app-rails-antipattern.git`.

Open the command line and run the example:

```
# Host OS
$ cd folder/with/examples
$ git clone https://github.com/pro-vagrant/songs-app-rails-antipattern.git
$ cd songs-app-rails-antipattern
$ vagrant up
```

In this example, the $ vagrant up command might need more than 30 minutes to finish. The Vagrantfile configuration for this antipattern is shown in Listing 9-1.

Listing 9-1. Antipattern: Developer's Vagrantfile with Time-Consuming Provisioners

```
Vagrant.configure(2) do |config|

  config.vm.box = "ubuntu/trusty32"

  config.vm.network :forwarded_port, guest: 3000, host: 3333, host_ip: "127.0.0.1"

  config.vm.provision "shell", path: "install-puppet-modules.sh"

  config.vm.provision :puppet do |puppet|
    puppet.manifests_path = "puppet/manifests"
    puppet.manifest_file  = "default.pp"
    puppet.options = ['--verbose']
  end

$script = <<SCRIPT

cd /vagrant
rails server -b 0.0.0.0 -d

SCRIPT

  config.vm.provision "shell", inline: $script, run: "always"

  config.vm.post_up_message = "The application is available at http://127.0.0.1:3333"

end
```

The VM created by the configuration shown in Listing 9-1 will be exactly the same as the configuration in the "Songs for kids" example discussed in Chapter 2, in which you used a base box that contained all the software baked inside the guest. The guest used by the antipattern example, on the other hand, downloads the source code of Ruby and Ruby on Rails and then recompiles them. This compilation is a time-consuming process; developers just waste their time. Usually, there is no rational justification for using this approach; certainly not during training or classes.

Puppet provisioners perform downloading and compiling. First use the shell provisioner to install the Puppet modules:

```
config.vm.provision "shell", path: "install-puppet-modules.sh"
```

then run the Puppet manifest to download, compile, and install Ruby and Ruby on Rails:

```
config.vm.provision :puppet do |puppet|
  puppet.manifests_path = "puppet/manifests"
  puppet.manifest_file  = "default.pp"
  puppet.options = ['--verbose']
end
```

Is it an Antipattern?

Is the solution shown in Listing 9-1 really useless? As I mentioned, during training this approach is a pure waste of clients' time, but it might be unavoidable or even appealing in some situations. Why? Because it relies on a well-known base box produced by Ubuntu. It has benefits for both the person who published (me, of course) and the person who downloaded (you, of course) the `https://github.com/pro-vagrant/songs-app-rails-antipattern.git` example.

The solution shown in Listing 9-1 might be appealing because of the following reasons:

- You don't have to host a binary box. They are large; what will happen if a few thousand people try to run the examples at the same time? Nothing funny, for sure.

- You're not responsible for the contents of the box (you won't be blamed if the box causes any trouble).

If you want to run the application shown in Listing 9-1, you might be less reluctant to run the binary box produced by Ubuntu than by someone else. And because `ubuntu/trusty32` is just a bare-bones Ubuntu, you can use your own homemade version of Ubuntu.

As you can see, the solution labeled as an antipattern can be useful in some scenarios. In fact, I used this very solution once when I was applying for a job. I solved the examination assignment and created a Vagrant-driven environment that relied on a bare Ubuntu base box.

To summarize:

- If you prepare the application that is supposed to be used by someone else, you may find the approach shown in Listing 9-1 interesting.

- If you prepare a box for your coworkers or students, you should bake everything inside the box.

■ **Note** While I was working on this book, I was undecided about whether I should rely on bare–bones base boxes such as `ubuntu/trusty32` or prepare my own boxes. If I worked with the `ubuntu/trusty32` base box, I wouldn't have to worry about hosting boxes or be responsible for the boxes. Users would be much more at ease using well-known boxes (such as `ubuntu/trusty32`).

But the time needed to run the examples in Chapter 2 would be much longer. Because I consider Chapter 2 the most essential and important part of the book, I decided to use my own boxes. To increase security, I used checksums to validate the contents of the downloaded boxes. And for those who are still reluctant to try my boxes, I prepared instructions to generate the underlying boxes. This may also turn out useful if the number of downloads of my boxes exceeds a reasonable level.

Generating Base Boxes

I described the antipattern only to convince you that developers in your company should not work with bare–bones base boxes that waste their time. Instead, you should generate the boxes to contain all the necessary software within them. In my opinion, the best ways to do this are as follows (and described in the following sections):

- Generate bare–bones base boxes with Packer

- Customize bare–bones boxes with provisioners

Generating Base Boxes with Packer

The sooner you start generating your own boxes with Packer, the better. Here are the most obvious advantages of using Packer:

- You don't have to use binary boxes downloaded from the network. As you remember from Chapter 4, that may be an important security concern.

- With Packer, you can generate base boxes automatically.

- When you generate the box, the version of guest additions will be updated.

- When you generate the box, the software installed in your base box is also updated.

What are the alternatives to using Packer? You can rely on publicly available base boxes, such as ubuntu/trusty32, or you can generate a base box manually using the procedure described in Chapter 7. Both solutions are much worse than using Packer.

When I work with Packer definitions, I don't embed everything that I might need into the base box; I prefer to get them lean. The only component that I include in base boxes is the latest version of the Puppet provisioner. Depending on your requirements, you may find it useful to install some additional software packages, or change the default user and well-known SSH keys.

I use the boxcutter templates available at https://github.com/boxcutter. The procedure to generate the Ubuntu 14.04 base box is shown in Listing 9-2.

Listing 9-2. Generating the Ubuntu 14.04 Base Box with Puppet

```
# Host OS
$ cd folder/with/examples
$ git clone https://github.com/pro-vagrant/ubuntu.git
$ cd ubuntu
$ echo "CM := puppet" > Makefile.local
$ echo "UPDATE := true" >> Makefile.local
$ make virtualbox/ubuntu1404-i386
```

If you finish running the commands shown in Listing 9-2, the box will be created in the file:

```
box/virtualbox/ubuntu1404-i386-puppetlatest-1.0.16.box
```

Of course, the numbers in the filename might be different:

```
1.0.16
```

This is the version number and it evolves in time. To use this box, you need to install it in your system by using the following:

```
$ Host OS
$ cd box/virtualbox/ubuntu
$ vagrant box add ubuntu1404-i386-puppetlatest-1.0.16 ubuntu1404-i386-puppetlatest-1.0.16.box
```

When it is finished, the box is ready to be used. You can verify it with this:

```
$ Host OS
$ vagrant box list | grep  ubuntu1404
```

The preceding command should print the complete name of the box:

```
ubuntu1404-i386-puppetlatest-1.0.16
```

The base box that you have generated is ready to be used, so you can proceed with customization.

Generating Customized Boxes

■ **Note** Before proceeding with the commands presented in this section, you have to install the base box `ubuntu-1404-i386-puppetlatest-1.0.16.box`, as described in the previous section.

When the bare-bones Ubuntu base box is ready, you can generate the customized boxes that I used in Chapter 2. The box for the "Songs for kids" application written in AngularJS is available at https://github.com/pro-vagrant/vagrant-box-factory-apache.

To build the box, run these commands:

```
# Host OS
$ cd folder/with/examples
$ git clone https://github.com/pro-vagrant/vagrant-box-factory-apache.git
$ cd vagrant-box-factory-apache
$ ./build.sh
```

The `./build.sh` script generates the box file by running two commands:

```
$ vagrant up
$ vagrant package --vagrantfile VagrantfileToInclude --output "${name}-${version}.box"
```

The first command boots the VM; the second generates a box file using two variables: `name` and `version`. After running the `./build.sh` script, you should find a file similar to the following in the current directory (the numbers `5.6.7` will be replaced by the latest version):

```
apache-v5.6.7.box
```

There are two important things to note from the `vagrant-box-factory-apache` example:

- File provisioner
- Two levels of Vagrantfile configuration

Let's first take a look at the Vagrantfile used in the `vagrant-box-factory-apache` example, which is shown in Listing 9-3.

Listing 9-3. Vagrantfile in the vagrant-box-factory-apache Example

```
Vagrant.configure(2) do |config|

  config.vm.box = "ubuntu1404-i386-puppetlatest-1.0.16"

  config.ssh.insert_key = false
```

```
# Copy all box-*.txt files into /home/vagrant/ in Guest OS
config.vm.provision "file", source: "box-version.txt", destination: "box-version.txt"
config.vm.provision "file", source: "box-name.txt", destination: "box-name.txt"
config.vm.provision "file", source: "box-author.txt", destination: "box-author.txt"
config.vm.provision "file", source: "box-date.txt", destination: "box-date.txt"

# Create /usr/bin/guestvm script in Guest OS
config.vm.provision "file", source: "guestvm", destination: "/home/vagrant/guestvm"
config.vm.provision "shell", inline: "mv /home/vagrant/guestvm /usr/bin && chmod 755
/usr/bin/guestvm"

config.vm.provision "shell", path: "install-puppet-modules.sh"
config.vm.provision "puppet"
```

end

The configuration shown in Listing 9-3 starts with the name of the base box:

```
config.vm.box = "ubuntu1404-i386-puppetlatest-1.0.16"
```

The box named ubuntu14-04-i386-puppetlatest-1.0.16 is generated in the section titled "Generating Base Boxes with Puppet". Thanks to the following, the generated box will use well-known SSH keys:

```
config.ssh.insert_key = false
```

Then comes the new part that makes use of file provisioners:

```
config.vm.provision "file", source: "box-version.txt", destination: "box-version.txt"
```

The file provisioner is useful if you want to copy the file from host to guest. The preceding instruction copies the file named box-version.txt from project's root directory on the host into the guest. The newly created file will be stored as /home/vagrant/box-version.txt.

In the same manner, copy three other files named box-name.txt, box-author.txt and box-date.txt:

```
config.vm.provision "file", source: "box-name.txt", destination: "box-name.txt"
config.vm.provision "file", source: "box-author.txt", destination: "box-author.txt"
config.vm.provision "file", source: "box-date.txt", destination: "box-date.txt"
```

All these files are used in the guest to find additional information about the VM, which is useful if you run multiple guests at the same time or release different versions of the box. Thanks to these files, you can easily print some information about the box within the guest OS by using this:

```
# Guest OS
$ guestvm
```

The guestvm command is a bash script that you copy into the guest and then move to the /usr/bin directory with the file provisioner and inline shell provisioner:

```
config.vm.provision "file", source: "guestvm", destination: "/home/vagrant/guestvm"
config.vm.provision "shell", inline: "mv /home/vagrant/guestvm /usr/bin && chmod 755
/usr/bin/guestvm"
```

Finally we install Puppet modules:

```
config.vm.provision "shell", path: "install-puppet-modules.sh"
```

and run Puppet provisioners:

```
config.vm.provision "puppet"
```

The command to package the box uses a new parameter: --vagrantfile:

```
$ vagrant package --vagrantfile VagrantfileToInclude --output "${name}-${version}.box"
```

This parameter sets the name of the Vagrantfile that should be packed within the box. The name VagrantfileToInclude is the name of the file in the project's root directory. Its contents are shown in Listing 9-4.

Listing 9-4. VagrantfileToInclude Configuration File

```
Vagrant.configure(2) do |config|
    currentDirectory = Dir.pwd.strip
    config.vm.provision "shell", inline: "echo -n #{currentDirectory} > box-directory.txt"
end
```

The code in Listing 9-4 creates a new file within the /home/vagrant/box-directory.txt guest OS. This file contains the full path leading to the project on the host system. The script creates a variable named currentDirectory with the following Ruby code:

```
currentDirectory = Dir.pwd.strip
```

Then the script prints the value of this variable to the /home/vagrant/box-directory.txt file using the inline shell provisioner:

```
config.vm.provision "shell", inline: "echo -n #{currentDirectory} > box-directory.txt"
```

I use this embedded Vagrantfile configuration that is baked into the box for the purpose of the guestvm script. If you use any of my boxes, you can run the following command within the guest OS:

```
# Guest VM
$ guestvm
```

It will provide you with the basic information about the guest VM, such as the following:

- Box name
- Box version
- Date when the box was generated
- Guest Additions version
- Project root directory (most important)

All this facts are very handy when you work with multiple projects and many guest versions. Please remember that you can embed the following types of configuration into the `VagrantfileToInclude` file:

- Network configuration
- Shared directory configuration
- Provisioners
- Other options discussed in Chapter 8

■ **Note** Customized boxes can be created using three different approaches:

- You can use packer and chef/bento or boxcutter projects, as described in Chapter 7
- You can use Packer with OVF files, as described in Chapter 7
- You can use a bash script similar to `build.sh` discussed in this example

The results are similar: to create a box, you need to run a single command on your host. Because you can't create a guest OS within the guest OS, this command has to be run on your host.

One final note about the `vagrant-box-factory-apache` example: the box configuration is stored in a git repository. You can display the project history with this:

```
# Host OS
$ cd folder/with/examples
$ cd vagrant-box-factory-apache
$ git log --oneline --decorate
```

The output of this command contains tags such as `v0.4.3`, `v0.4.2`, and so on:

```
06173d1 (HEAD, tag: v0.4.3, origin/master, master) Version 0.4.3
91d3ff3 Move Puppet manifest to manifests/
c7d4ff3 (tag: v0.4.2) Version 0.4.2
5090d2e Verbose explanation for file provisioners and guestvm
37de9c5 Simplify puppet provisioners
2aeeb56 Fix CS
2e65fea Fix CS
2cc9798 (tag: v0.4.1) Version 0.4.1
```

To generate the version of the box, for example `v0.4.3`, use the following commands:

```
# Host OS
$ cd folder/with/examples
$ cd vagrant-box-factory-apache
$ git checkout v0.4.3
$ ./build.sh
$ checkout master
```

You have the following advantages when you use git:

- All box versions are located in one repository.

- Each version is easily accessible (you need only the $ git checkout command).

- If you use semantic versioning, the project moves forward in a predictable manner.

I strongly advise you to do the following:

- Use git to manage the customized box

- Tag releases by using git tags

- Use semantic versioning strategy

To find out the latest version of the project, you can use this:

```
# Host OS
$ cd folder/with/examples
$ cd vagrant-box-factory-apache
$ git checkout master
$ git describe
```

The $ git describe command prints the unique name of the latest revision that you can use as the box filename, which is exactly what I did in the ./build.sh script. The following variable:

```
version=`git describe`
```

is used within the command:

```
$ vagrant package --vagrantfile VagrantfileToInclude --output "${name}-${version}.box"
```

Modularize Boxes with Provisioner Modules

When you're comfortable with the provisioning basics, consider using modularized definitions. No matter which provisioner you prefer, each supports modularization.

With Puppet, you work with *modules*; in Chef terminology, they are called *cookbooks*; and Ansible uses the term *playbook*. You will find more information here:

- Puppet modules: https://forge.puppetlabs.com

- Chef cookbooks: https://supermarket.chef.io

- Ansible playbooks: https://galaxy.ansible.com

I chose Puppet, but you can use any solution. The key point is that for each task that you need to perform in your boxes, such as configuring Apache virtual hosts, you should use modules (either existing ones or your own implementations).

Take a look at Listing 9-3. First, Puppet modules are installed with the shell provisioner:

```
config.vm.provision "shell", path: "install-puppet-modules.sh"
```

The Puppet manifest that will use the modules runs as follows:

```
config.vm.provision "puppet"
```

The install-puppet-modules.sh script is shown in Listing 9-5, which is a bash script that installs the modules needed for this box. The first three modules are produced by Puppetlabs, and the other three are my own creations.

Listing 9-5. Script install-puppet-modules.sh from vagrant-box-factory-apache

```
#!/usr/bin/env bash

echo "Install Puppet modules..."

sudo puppet module install puppetlabs-apache --version 1.4.0 --force
sudo puppet module install puppetlabs-concat --version 1.2.0 --force
sudo puppet module install puppetlabs-stdlib --version 4.6.0 --force

sudo puppet module install gajdaw-ubuntu --version 0.1.13 --force
sudo puppet module install gajdaw-diverse_functions --version 0.1.1 --force

sudo puppet module install gajdaw-environment --version 0.1.4 --force
```

The following command installs version 1.4.0 of the puppetlabs-apache module:

```
sudo puppet module install puppetlabs-apache --version 1.4.0 --force
```

You can find the documentation for this module at https://forge.puppetlabs.com/puppetlabs/apache.

The puppetlabs/apache module simplifies the tasks of installing and configuring the Apache web server. The two other modules by Puppetlabs contain various functions used by Apache module:

```
sudo puppet module install puppetlabs-concat --version 1.2.0 --force
sudo puppet module install puppetlabs-stdlib --version 4.6.0 --force
```

The following three modules are available at https://forge.puppetlabs.com/gajdaw:

```
gajdaw-ubuntu
gajdaw-environment
gajdaw-diverse_function
```

- The first module, gajdaw-ubuntu, updates Ubuntu:

  ```
  $ sudo apt-get update
  ```

- The second module, gajdaw-environment, installs packages such as git, mc, lynx, and apache2-utils. It also removes the mesg n command from the /root/.profile file[1] and adds cd /vagrant to the /home/vagrant/.profile file.

- The last module, gajdaw-diverse_functions, contains some utility functions used within the modules.

---

[1]That's how I get rid of stdin: is not a tty message (discussed in Chapter 6).

The point of modularization is that the same actions performed by one of the modules, for example the actions done by gajdaw-environment module, can be easily repeated in every box that you generate.

The manifest to apply modules installed with install-puppet-modules.sh is shown in Listing 9-6.

Listing 9-6. Script manifests/default.pp from vagrant-box-factory-apache

```
include stdlib
include environment

class { ubuntu: stage => setup }

class {
    'apache': default_vhost => false;
}

apache::vhost { 'app.lh':
    port          => '80',
    docroot       => '/vagrant/web',
    docroot_owner => 'vagrant',
    docroot_group => 'vagrant',
}
```

First we include two modules: stdlib and environment (their full names are puppetlabs-stdlib and gajdaw-environment):

```
include stdlib
include environment
```

Next there are instructions to include the ubuntu module (full name gajdaw-ubuntu) with the stage parameter set to setup:

```
class { ubuntu: stage => setup }
```

Then we use the apache module (full name puppetlabs-apache) with default_vhost set to false:

```
class {
    'apache': default_vhost => false;
}
```

Finally, we use the apache::vhost-defined resource that is shipped with the apache module to create a virtual host:

```
apache::vhost { 'app.lh':
    port          => '80',
    docroot       => '/vagrant/web',
    docroot_owner => 'vagrant',
    docroot_group => 'vagrant',
}
```

Of course, this is not a complete course on writing Puppet modules; you have to consult other sources for an introduction to Puppet or other provisioning solutions. But I want you to be aware of gains when working with modularized provisioning scripts. Using the apache Puppet module, you don't have to struggle with `httpd.conf` files, directives, and so on. The apache module and its configuration are governed by simple entries that rely on the `puppetlabs-apache` module. It makes the whole task of defining virtual hosts much simpler.

For Puppet, exactly the same manifest can be applied on arbitrary platforms. You can use it on Ubuntu, CentOS, and FreeBSD, to name a few. For your own modules, the gain is that you have a single place in which you define given behavior, and the same behavior can be applied in many different boxes. For example, I used the `gajdaw-environment` module in each of the box examples in Chapter 2.

Embedding Submodules

Remember that submodules live on their own; each submodule becomes a new project. To avoid confusion, use git and the semantic versioning strategy for each submodule. This leads to another problem, however: how can you embed a submodule in a box?

Puppet has two approaches:

- git submodules
- shell provisioner with the `$ puppet module install` command

I prefer to use the second approach, which is exactly what I did in Listing 9-5. The advantage of this solution is that Puppet modules are stored in just one place: in their own repo; they are not embedded in every project that uses them. For example, the files of the `gajdaw-environment` module are included only in the `https://github.com/puppet-by-examples/puppet-environment` repository.

You can't find them inside `vagrant-box-factory-apache/` directory, even though this project uses the module. How does it happen? The following command is executed inside the guest VM:

```
$ sudo puppet module install gajdaw-environment --version 0.1.4 --force
```

The module gets installed inside the guest within the `/etc/puppet/modules/environment` directory.

I prefer it this way to avoid problems with submodule synchronization. It comes at a price, however: each time you build the box, the module gets downloaded from the Internet. It could be an antipattern (the following sidebar discusses this in more detail).

EFFICIENCY OF GIT SUBMODULES

Using git submodules is more efficient than installing Puppet submodules with `$ puppet module install` because you don't have to download submodules when building the box; they are on the hard drive within the project's directory. Depending on your settings, this may be important. If you often build the box, and it downloads tens and hundreds of submodules, there is no point in using the shell provisioner and `$ puppet module install` command. In that case, you can even call using `$ puppet module install` with shell provisioners an antipattern. There is no doubt that git submodules are a much more efficient solution. I have chosen the shell provisioner with `$ puppet module apply` because I strongly prefer to have just one place in which I work on my modules. If you work with git submodules, remember that your module is stored in many different places.

Another problem is the version of the submodule. With Puppet, you have two choices:

- `$ sudo puppet module install gajdaw-environment --version 0.1.4 --force`
- `$ sudo puppet module install gajdaw-environment`

The first command installs version 0.1.4 of the gajdaw-environment submodule (just this module and nothing else). The second command installs the latest version of the submodule with all the dependent modules. I prefer to stick with a hard-coded version such as the following because it is more predictable:

```
$ sudo puppet module install gajdaw-ubuntu --version 0.1.13 --force
```

When you give the concrete version number, such as 0.1.13, you are guaranteed that Puppet will use this version. In case the newer version is not backward-compatible, doing so helps to avoid errors. Remember that when you use hard-coded version numbers, you have to explicitly include all the dependent submodules. That's the reason why Listing 9-5 contains the following:

```
sudo puppet module install puppetlabs-concat --version 1.2.0 --force
sudo puppet module install puppetlabs-stdlib --version 4.6.0 --force
```

If you used the $ puppet module install command without a hard-coded version for Apache, Puppet would install the latest version of the apache module together with the latest versions of all dependent modules, such as puppetlabs-concat and puppetlabs-stdlib.

Although the code presented in Listing 9-5 is Puppet-related, you should be aware of the strategy:

- Using external submodules

- Using git and semantic versioning for submodules

- Using hard-coded versions for submodules

This strategy will help you manage dependencies between different functionalities in your modules. And hard-coded versioning will provide predictable results.

If you use git submodules to work with Puppet modules, you will find puppet.module_path useful (it is used to point to the directory that contains the Puppet modules):

```
Vagrant.configure("2") do |config|
  config.vm.provision "puppet" do |puppet|
    puppet.module_path = "modules"
  end
end
```

If you want to see the git submodules in action, try to build the box available at https://github.com/pro-vagrant/vagrant-box-factory-apache-git-submodules.git.

Here are the commands that you need to execute:

```
# Host OS
$ cd folder/with/examples
$ git clone --recursive https://github.com/pro-vagrant/vagrant-box-factory-apache-git-submodules.git
$ cd vagrant-box-factory-apache-git-submodules
$ ./build.sh
```

The --recursive parameter that is used in the $ git clone command turns on the recursive mode, in which git clones the main repo together with all the submodules.

Puppet Submodule Antipattern

Thanks to the following, you can use Puppet modules as a part of your project:

```
Vagrant.configure("2") do |config|
  config.vm.provision "puppet" do |puppet|
    puppet.module_path = "modules"
  end
end
```

Putting your Puppet modules inside modules without referring to git submodules is a common pitfall. Working this way the Puppet submodule is not versioned on its own, so it is very difficult to share among the boxes. If you work with just one box that uses this particular module, you will be fine. But when you start using the submodule in different boxes, you will encounter severe difficulties. So remember that if a submodule is to be used by two or more boxes, it should be stored in a separate git repository with its own versioning and tagging strategy.

Bake Everything in the Customized Box

After the discussion and analysis included in the section titled "Most Common Antipattern," the concept of baking everything inside the box should be clear now. I just want to underline a more subtle aspect of it. When you work with an application that uses a package manager (for example, a project written in Ruby on Rails), you may want to include the dependencies inside the box. That's what was done in the rails-vX.Y.Z. box used in the "Songs for kids" applications discussed in Chapter 2.

The box available at https://github.com/pro-vagrant/vagrant-box-factory-rails uses the gajdaw-bundle_install module:

```
class { 'bundle_install':
  repo => 'https://github.com/pro-vagrant/songs-app-rails.git',
  require => Class['ruby', 'rails', 'nodejs']
}
```

The box is generated with the following command:

```
$ ./build.sh
```

During this process, the code of the gajdaw-bundle_install module runs the following command for the project "Songs for kids":

```
$ bundle install
```

Thanks to this trick, when you use the box for the "Songs for kids" application, you don't have to run bundle install. I use this trick for boxes prepared for Ruby on Rails applications as well as for boxes for PHP Symfony applications, which helps me to minimize the time necessary to run the application. This is very important during classes and trainings. With all the components embedded in the box, and the box already downloaded and installed in the system, the new project can be started in a minute. I do not waste the time during classes nor during trainings.

Summary

To avoid problems, I recommend following these practices:

- Use git and semantic versioning for your boxes.

- Use two levels of boxing: bare-bones boxes (such as `ubuntu1404-i386-puppetlatest-X.Y.Z`) and customized boxes (such as `apache-vX.Y.Z`).

- For bare-bone boxes, use Packer and JSON definitions. You can use the `chef/bento` or `boxcutter` project for them. (I consider doing this manually a complete disaster, not just an antipattern.)

- Build your customized boxes on the basis of bare-bone boxes (i.e., `apache-vX.Y.Z` is built on the basis of `ubuntu1404-i386-puppetlatest-X.Y.Z`).

- Create build scripts for customized boxes (such as `build.sh`) or use Packer definitions and the OVF format of bare-bones boxes.

- Use the provisioner to customize your boxes (e.g., for `apache-vX.Y.Z`, you can use the Puppet provisioner).

- Use modularized provisioners (e.g., for `apache-vX.Y.Z`, use the `puppetlabs-apache` and `gajdaw-environment` modules, among others; the same modules can be used in many boxes).

- Every submodule should be stored as a new independent project.

- Use git and semantic versioning for your submodules (e.g., module `gajdaw-environment` is a new git project with its own history and versioning strategy).

- Use git submodules or shell provisioners with the `$ puppet module install` command to embed your module in your project (e.g., in `apache-vX.Y.Z` you use the shell provisioner with the `$ puppet module install` command).

- Use hard-coded versions of your submodules (e.g., in the `apache-vX.Y.Z` box configuration, use `gajdaw-environment vX.Y.Z`).

- Bake everything inside the boxes (e.g., in the `rails-vX.Y.Z` box, you run `bundle install` to include the gems that are used by the example application).

Remember the following:

- If you prepare the application to be used by people you don't know (such as an open-source project available for everyone), you may want to rely on some well-known and publicly trusted base boxes, such as `ubuntu/trusty32`.

- If you work on a closed project available only to your colleagues and coworkers, you will get the best Vagrant experience by creating a new binary box that includes all the software; you will be responsible for hosting and distributing the box.

In the Next Chapter, You Will Learn . . .

The basic course of Vagrant is now finished. In the next chapter, I will show you more-advanced concepts of using Vagrant.

Reading List

Modularization is a very important aspect of using SCM tools. Every provisioner uses a slightly different approach and terminology, but they all serve the same purpose: to extract the pieces that can be reused. For a list of available modules that can be used with Puppet, Chef, and Ansible, see the following web sites:

- Puppet modules: `https://forge.puppetlabs.com`
- Chef cookbooks: `https://supermarket.chef.io`
- Ansible playbooks: `https://galaxy.ansible.com`

Git submodules are explained at `http://git-scm.com/book/be/v2/Git-Tools-Submodules`.

Test Yourself

1. How can you configure the box to maximize the time necessary to run the application? Discuss it using the "Songs for kids" application written in Ruby on Rails.

2. How can you configure the box to minimize the time necessary to run the application? Discuss it using the "Songs for kids" application written in Ruby on Rails.

3. Why is it useful to run the application using the bare-bones base box and provisioners? Discuss it using the `songs-app-rails-antipattern.git` example.

4. What are the advantages of modularized provisioning scripts?

5. What are the three ways to generate customized boxes?

Exercises

1. Run the application `https://github.com/pro-vagrant/songs-app-rails-antipattern`.

2. Generate the base box named `ubuntu1404-i386-puppetlatest-X.Y.Z.box`. Use the commands shown in Listing 9-2.

3. Install the `ubuntu1404-i386-puppetlatest-X.Y.Z` box in your system.

4. Generate the box named `apache-vX.Y.Z`. Use the `https://github.com/pro-vagrant/vagrant-box-factory-apache` repository and the base box that you generated and installed in Exercises 2 and 3.

5. Install the `apache-vX.Y.Z` box in your system under the name `my-apache`.

6. Run the `https://github.com/pro-vagrant/songs-app-angularjs` application using the `my-apache` box that you installed in your system in Exercise 5.

7. Generate the box named `django-vX.Y.Z`. Use the `https://github.com/pro-vagrant/vagrant-box-factory-django` repository and the base box that you generated and installed in Exercises 2 and 3.

8. Install the `django-vX.Y.Z` box in your system under the name `my-django`.

9. Run the application `https://github.com/pro-vagrant/songs-app-django` using the `my-django` box that you installed in your system in Exercise 8.

10. Generate the box named `rails-vX.Y.Z`. Use the `https://github.com/pro-vagrant/vagrant-box-factory-rails` repository and the base box that you generated and installed in Exercises 2 and 3.

11. Install the `rails-vX.Y.Z` box in your system under the name `my-rails`.

12. Run the `https://github.com/pro-vagrant/songs-app-rails` application using the `my-rails` box that you installed in your system in Exercise 11.

13. Generate the box named `symfony-vX.Y.Z`. Use the `https://github.com/pro-vagrant/vagrant-box-factory-symfony` repository and the base box that you generated and installed in Exercises 2 and 3.

14. Install the `symfony-vX.Y.Z` box in your system under the name `my-symfony`.

15. Run the application `https://github.com/pro-vagrant/songs-app-symfony` using the `my-symfony` box that you installed in your system in Exercise 14.

16. Generate the box that uses git submodules: `https://github.com/pro-vagrant/vagrant-box-factory-apache-git-submodules`.

CHAPTER 10

■ ■ ■

Going Pro

Now that you have mastered the contents of the first nine chapters, you should be ready to use Vagrant-driven development environments created by other system engineers effectively and with ease. I hope that I have convinced you that it is a simple process and that there is nothing to worry about. You should also be able to create your own base boxes.

But to advance your knowledge to the next level (the pro level), you have to practice introducing Vagrant-driven workflows for others. I prefer to associate the *pro* adjective with real-life achievements. In other words, you need a challenge: for example, the task of preparing the box and the workflow for the next web application produced by your company.

For me, the challenge was to reorganize the way I taught various web development-related courses, which was the playground that provided the necessary feedback to evaluate Vagrant in real-life settings. And the result is astonishing. I can truly say that Vagrant has changed the way I work.

In this chapter, I will help you plan your strategy of going pro with Vagrant. I will also discuss some Vagrant features that weren't discussed in previous chapters:

- Using multimachine settings

- Debugging

- Using Vagrant plug-ins

- Using Atlas

- Versioning boxes

- Sharing the development environment

The Challenge

Find a project with which you can use Vagrant in practice. If you work alone, it might be the next web site that you build. If you are one of the team, try to persuade your colleagues or boss to give Vagrant a try (it won't be too easy, but it might work). Remember that to convince anybody about Vagrant's virtues, you have to demonstrate its best features. So far, I haven't found any better solutions than the four "Songs for kids" examples from Chapter 2. Four frameworks in four minutes. (And in my case, it means literally four minutes because I have all the boxes installed and ready at hand).

Your colleagues might be more demanding, however. If so, you can do the following:

- Create a much more elaborate example than "Songs for kids."

- Use Vagrant-driven VMs to demonstrate existing web applications such as GitLab or Redmine.

- Create the examples and VMs that run in different operating systems.

To avoid disappointment, at least try to build all the boxes discussed in this book. You should also run the "Songs for kids" examples on all kinds of platforms and hardware used by your colleagues. You will experience how time-consuming and difficult boxing can be and how efficient (or inefficient, for that matter) the virtualized development environment can be. It is good to know it right from the beginning. You will also need an HTTP server capable of serving large files. Using your local infrastructure to distribute base boxes can drastically reduce the download time and improve the overall Vagrant experience.

SCM Tools

As discussed in Chapter 6, software installation within the guest is done with SCM tools. (If you don't know any of them, this should be the next topic for you to master, especially if you will be responsible for creating base boxes used by others).

As of now, the most popular solutions are these:

- Puppet (project started in 2005)

- Chef (project started in 2009)

- Salt (project started in 2011)

- Ansible (project started in 2012)

I chose Puppet, but you may prefer something else. Instead of advising you which SCM is the one and only, I prefer to emphasize the role of modularization. No matter which SCM you use or plan to master, you should know how to use modules authored by others and how to write your own modules.

For example, if you need to install Apache, start by investigating these:

- Puppet modules: `https://forge.puppetlabs.com/puppetlabs/apache`

- Chef cookbooks: `https://supermarket.chef.io/cookbooks/apache2`

- Ansible roles: `https://galaxy.ansible.com/list#/roles/428`

■ **Note**   Remember that learning SCM can be another stumbling block. Mastering Puppet, Chef, or Ansible is a task of its own, and you may need some extra time to do so.

Keep in mind that having a basic knowledge of bash scripting and Ruby is handy when working with advanced Vagrantfiles and script provisioners.

Development/Production Mapping

How do you create 1:1 production-development mapping? One solution is to use the same SCM modules that are used to configure the production server to create base boxes for developers. If your organization already uses SCM to configure production servers, your task is really easy: all you have to do is create a base box for the OS used by the production servers and use the existing SCM solutions to configure the VM.

If your organization doesn't use SCM solutions, you have to adopt one of them, master it, and create modules that will be used by the production and development environments.

Multimachine Settings

If the infrastructure required to run your application is more complicated and runs different services on different machines, you might be interested in multimachine settings. Vagrant supports multimachine configurations, and Listing 10-1 shows how to configure two virtual machines: one for a web server and one for a database server within a single Vagrantfile.

Listing 10-1. Vagrantfile for a Two-Machine Environment

```
Vagrant.configure(2) do |config|

  config.vm.define "web" do |web|
    web.vm.box = "chef/centos-6.5-i386"
  end

  config.vm.define "db" do |db|
    db.vm.box = "ubuntu/trusty32"
  end

end
```

When you run $ vagrant up for the configuration shown in Listing 10-1, the output will include the following messages:

```
Bringing machine 'web' up with 'virtualbox' provider...
Bringing machine 'db' up with 'virtualbox' provider...
==> web: Importing base box 'chef/centos-6.5-i386'...
==> web: Matching MAC address for NAT networking...
...
==> web: Mounting shared folders...

==> db: Importing base box 'ubuntu/trusty32'...
==> db: Matching MAC address for NAT networking...
...
==> db: Mounting shared folders...
```

The machine configured with config.vm.define "web" do |web| is labeled as ==>web, like this:

```
==> web: Importing base box 'chef/centos-6.5-i386'...
==> web: Matching MAC address for NAT networking...
...
```

The second machine, the one configured with config.vm.define "db" do |db|, is announced with messages that begin with ==>db:

```
==> db: Importing base box 'ubuntu/trusty32'...
==> db: Matching MAC address for NAT networking...
```

■ **Note** If the Vagrantfile configures only one machine, it is labeled as `==>` `default`. (You can find this level in Listing 3-2 in Chapter 3, for example).

Each machine can use an arbitrary base box. For the web machine, I used CentOS:

```
web.vm.box = "chef/centos-6.5-i386"
```

The db machine runs a bare-bones Ubuntu:

```
db.vm.box = "ubuntu/trusty32"
```

For each machine, you can use all the configuration options discussed in Chapter 8. The following code snippet explains how to use the `ssh.insert_key` and `memory` options for a web VM:

```
config.vm.define "web" do |web|
  web.vm.box = "chef/centos-6.5-i386"
  web.ssh.insert_key = false
  web.vm.provider "virtualbox" do |v|
    v.memory = 1024
  end
end
```

When you boot a multimachine environment, labels assigned to VMs (web and db in the previous examples) are used to identify the machines. The `$ vagrant status` command reports the status like this:

```
Current machine states:

web                     running (virtualbox)
db                      running (virtualbox)
```

The web and db machines can be managed independently. To open the SSH session, you should use `$ vagrant ssh db`. In a similar manner, you can use other commands, such as these:

```
$ vagrant halt web
$ vagrant destroy web
$ vagrant up web
```

If you don't provide a name, the command will be executed for every machine or for the primary machine only:

```
$ vagrant halt
$ vagrant destroy
$ vagrant up
```

To set the primary machine, use the `:primary` parameter in the Vagrantfile:

```
config.vm.define "web", primary: true do |web|
...
end
```

Debugging

When you encounter problems during booting, and the guest system hangs on, the --debug flag may help you to resolve the issue. The $ vagrant up -debug command produces verbose output with precise information about executed commands. Together with the GUI window (for details, refer to Listing 8-2 in Chapter 8), the flag can help to diagnose the problem.

Using Vagrant Plug-ins

The Wiki page available at https://github.com/mitchellh/vagrant/wiki/Available-Vagrant-Plugins contains an official collection of Vagrant plug-ins that enhance Vagrant's functionality. The following sections describe some plug-ins that you may find useful. For precise instructions on how to use them, see their individual documentation.

Vagrant-cachier Plug-in

This plug-in, which is available at http://fgrehm.viewdocs.io/vagrant-cachier, manages the cache folder of various applications (such as apt, gem, npm, and composer) on a per-base box basis. The cache is not stored within a guest; it is moved to the host and accessed through a shared directory. So if you run multiple VMs that use the same base box, or boot and destroy the same VM many times (each time provisioning it), commands such as the following download the packages from the network and store them locally in the host:

```
# Guest OS
$ sudo apt-get install
$ bundle install
$ composer install
```

In other words, the cache is shared by all the base box instances. Each package is downloaded just once per base box and reused in every VM that uses the same base box. This process can radically reduce the time necessary to run the $ vagrant up command.

For example, if you use this plug-in and run the following command in one of the VMs, the packages downloaded by apt-get are stored within the host:

```
# Guest OS
$ sudo apt-get update
```

If you switch to another VM and run the following, the packages updated in the second VM are not downloaded from the network; they come from cache that is stored on the host:

```
# Guest OS
$ apt-get update
```

Vagrant-winnfsd Plug-in

This plug-in, which is available at https://github.com/GM-Alex/vagrant-winnfsd, turns on the NFS type for shared folders on hosts running Windows. As you remember, this process can improve the efficiency of HDD read/write operations.

Vagrant-puppet-install Plug-in

This plug-in, which is available at `https://github.com/petems/vagrant-puppet-install`, installs the Puppet provisioner in the guest OS. If you embed Puppet in the base box build with Packer (as with the boxcutter project in Chapter 7), this plug-in not necessary. But if you use bare bones boxes devoid of SCM, you may find it useful.

Vagrant-omnibus Plug-in

This plug-in, which is available at `https://github.com/chef/vagrant-omnibus`, installs the Chef provisioner in the guest OS. It is handy if you work with bare base boxes and need to install Chef.

Vagrant-hostupdater Plug-in

This plug-in, which is available at `https://github.com/cogitatio/vagrant-hostsupdater`, helps manage the hosts file on the host.

Vagrant-vbguest Plug-in

This plug-in, which is available at `https://github.com/dotless-de/vagrant-vbguest`, updates VirtualBox Guest Additions within the guest to match the VirtualBox version installed on the host.

Working with Atlas.Hashicorp.com

The Atlas service, available at `https://atlas.hashicorp.com`, was originally intended to be a hosting platform and catalog for Vagrant boxes. It can serve also as the following:

- A platform to build boxes with Packer
- The solution to deploy the application
- The platform to share the development environment with others

To try it, visit `https://atlas.hashicorp.com`, register, and then log in. I will guide you how to use Atlas for your own box that is served by your own HTTP server. I assume that the box is saved in the file named `lorem-v0.4.3.box` and is already uploaded to the HTTP server and available under `http://example.net/lorem/lorem-v0.4.3.box`.

If you host the `*.box` files on your own HTTP server, you can use Atlas free of charge. For boxes hosted in the Atlas, you will be charged for transfers that your boxes generate.

After logging in to your Atlas account, you will see the dashboard, which will resemble Figure 10-1. To create the first box, press the Begin button that corresponds with the Create a Vagrant Box option.

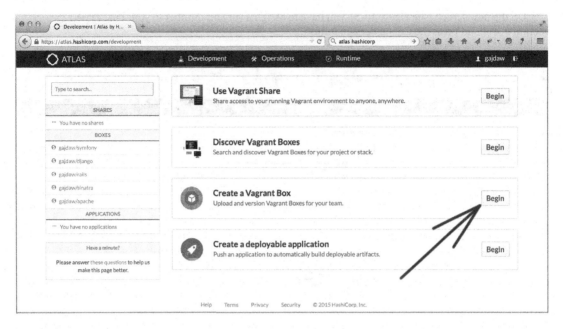

Figure 10-1. *Atlas user's main window*

The procedure starts with a dialog box to fill in some basic information about the new box. The most important thing is the name. Type the name lorem and press the Create Box button, as shown in Figure 10-2.

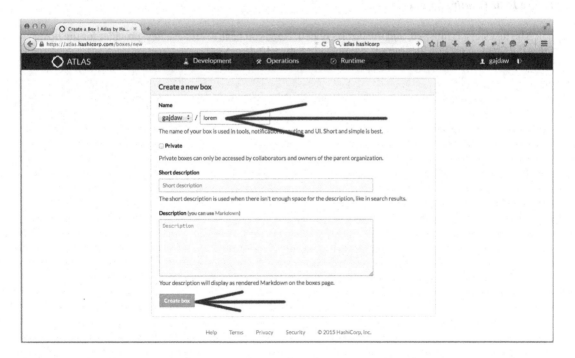

Figure 10-2. *Setting up the box name*

On the next screen (see Figure 10-3), you have to assign a version number to your box. Type version 0.4.3 and press the Create Version button.

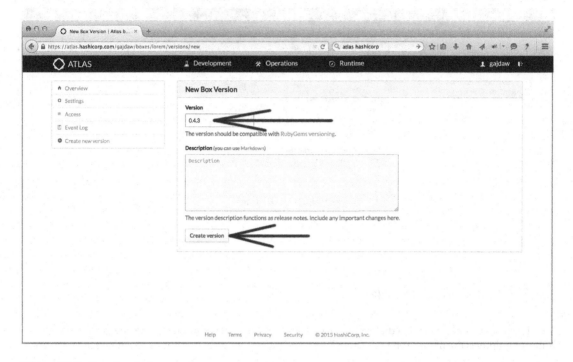

Figure 10-3. *Creating the box version*

The first stage is finished, and the box is created. Now, you have to create a new provider for the box. Press the Create New Provider button, as shown in Figure 10-4.

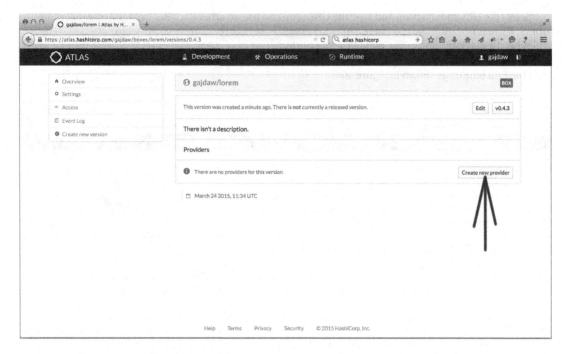

Figure 10-4. *Creating a new box provider*

Now you are in the next dialog box, shown in Figure 10-5. Type the name of the provider: `virtualbox`.

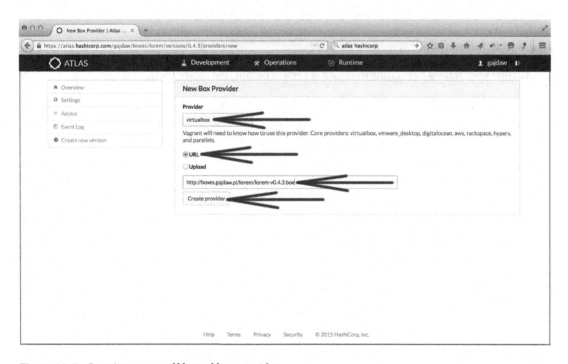

Figure 10-5. *Creating a new self-hosted box provider*

Select the URL radio button and type the URL (you can use an arbitrary URL, even the one that is not correct; there is no URL validation here): http://example.net/lorem/lorem-v0.4.3.box.

When this is done, press the Create Provider button.

When this phase is finished, there is just one more thing to do: you have to release the box. To do so, press the Edit button, as shown in Figure 10-6.

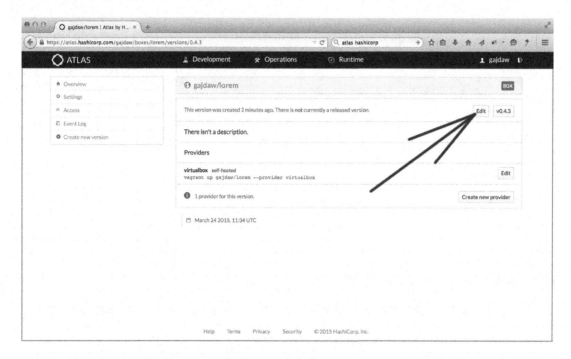

Figure 10-6. *Releasing a box by pressing the Edit button*

Finalize your actions by pressing the Release Version button (see Figure 10-7).

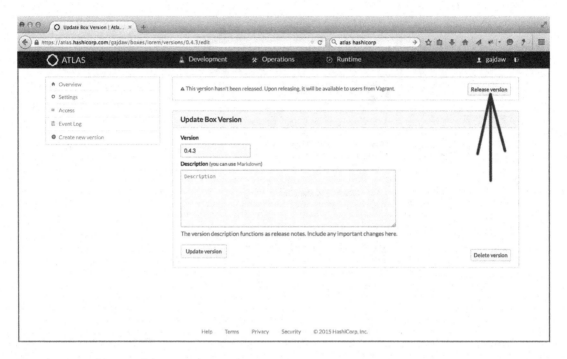

Figure 10-7. *Releasing a box*

The box is available in the panel displayed on the left side of the window. Figure 10-8 shows where to find the box you created.

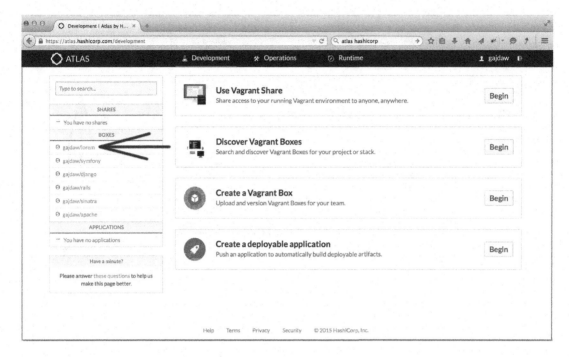

Figure 10-8. *Newly created box is available in the left panel*

If your Atlas service username is johnny, the box you created will be available as johnny/lorem. Use this name in the Vagrantfile:

```
Vagrant.configure(2) do |config|
  config.vm.box = "johny/lorem"
end
```

Boot the VM. Vagrant will resolve the name johnny/lorem into the URL you provided in the dialog box shown in Figure 10-5 and download the box from the server.

To verify the way the box named vendor/box is resolved into the URL, create the Vagrantfile shown in Listing 10-2.

Listing 10-2. Vagrantfile for ubuntu/precise32

```
Vagrant.configure(2) do |config|
  config.vm.box = "ubuntu/precise32 "
end
```

The $ vagrant up command executed for the VM shown in Listing 10-2 will produce the output that begins with the messages shown in Listing 10-3.

Listing 10-3. Output of $ vagrant up for the VM in Listing 10-2

```
Bringing machine 'default' up with 'virtualbox' provider...
==> default: Box 'ubuntu/precise32' could not be found. Attempting to find and
install...
    default: Box Provider: virtualbox
```

```
    default: Box Version: >= 0
==> default: Loading metadata for box 'ubuntu/precise32'
    default: URL: https://atlas.hashicorp.com/ubuntu/precise32
==> default: Adding box 'ubuntu/precise32' (v12.04.4) for provider: virtualbox
    default: Downloading: https://atlas.hashicorp.com/ubuntu/boxes/precise32/
                          versions/12.04.4/providers/virtualbox.box
```

This is a single machine configuration, so the machine is labeled as ==> default.
Take a look at the URLs included in the output:

```
https://atlas.hashicorp.com/ubuntu/precise32
https://atlas.hashicorp.com/ubuntu/boxes/precise32/versions/12.04.4/providers/virtualbox.box
```

When you use the ubuntu/precise32 name, Vagrant resolves it into https://atlas.hashicorp.com/
ubuntu/precise32. This URL serves as a gate for all providers and for all versions.

You use VirtualBox and the default version 12.04.4, which is reflected in the next URL:

```
https://atlas.hashicorp.com/ubuntu/boxes/precise32/versions/12.04.4/providers/virtualbox.box
```

Finally, if you use curl, as follows:

```
# Host OS
$ curl https://atlas.hashicorp.com/ubuntu/boxes/precise32/versions/12.04.4/providers/
virtualbox.box
```

you will see that the following is just a redirect to https://cloud-images.ubuntu.com/vagrant/precise/
current/precise-server-cloudimg-i386-vagrant-disk1.box:

```
<html>
  <body>
    You are being
      <a href="https://cloud-images.ubuntu.com/vagrant/precise/current/precise-server-
      cloudimg-i386-vagrant-disk1.box">redirected</a>.
  </body>
</html>
```

The procedure of resolving the URL to download the box using the name is depicted in Figure 10-9.

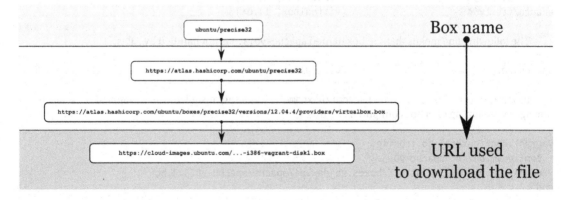

Figure 10-9. *Resolving the URL using the name*

Versioning Boxes

The concept of versioning boxes loosens the ties that bind developers (who use boxes) and system engineers (who create boxes). System engineers can upload new versions of boxes without influencing developers in any way. Developers update the boxes they use when they consider it appropriate.

For example, consider the scenario in which a system engineer working at the example.net company publishes version 1.0.0 of the box named rails:

```
example-net/rails    (virtualbox, 1.0.0)
```

Developers start using this box. Then a system engineer uploads a new version:

```
example-net/rails    (virtualbox, 2.0.0)
```

Developers may continue to use version 1.0.0 or can upgrade to version 2.0.0. They make the decision and perform the update when they consider it appropriate. Nothing is imposed on them.

Here is how it is done in practice. Each box available through the vendor/box name in the Atlas catalog, such as ubuntu/precise32, is versioned. The dialog box shown in Figure 10-3 requires you to type the version of the box. You can't skip or avoid denoting the version in Atlas. For each name, you can upload any number of versions.

When you use vendor/box name, one of the first things that Vagrant does during $ vagrant up is to check whether the version you have installed in your system is up to date. It is announced with this:

```
==> default: Checking if box 'ubuntu/precise32' is up to date...
```

If your box is stale, you will see a message about it.

When you run the $ vagrant box list command, the output contains the name of each box, together with the name of the provider and box version:

```
apache-v0.3.3                     (virtualbox, 0)
apache-v0.4.0                     (virtualbox, 0)
apache-v0.4.3                     (virtualbox, 0)
django-v0.2.4                     (virtualbox, 0)
gajdaw/apache                     (virtualbox, 0.1.0)
gajdaw/apache                     (virtualbox, 0.3.2)
ubuntu/precise32                  (virtualbox, 12.04.4)
ubuntu/trusty32                   (virtualbox, 14.04)
ubuntu/trusty64                   (virtualbox, 14.04)
```

The following line means that the box named apache-v0.3.3 is not handled by Atlas:

```
apache-v0.3.3                     (virtualbox, 0)
```

Its name doesn't have the form of vendor/boxname. It was either installed with $ vagrant box add or during $ vagrant up for a box configured like this:

```
Vagrant.configure(2) do |config|
  config.vm.box = "apache-v0.3.3"
  config.vm.box_url = "http://boxes.gajdaw.pl/apache/apache-v0.3.3.box"
end
```

The apache-v0.3.3 box has just one version, denoted as 0.

The following line informs you about the box named ubuntu/precise32:

```
ubuntu/precise32                    (virtualbox, 12.04.4)
```

The name of the box comes from the Atlas catalog. The version of the box is 12.04.4.

And the following two lines mean that you have installed two versions of the gajdaw/apache box on your system:

```
gajdaw/apache                       (virtualbox, 0.1.0)
gajdaw/apache                       (virtualbox, 0.3.2)
```

One of the lines is denoted as 0.1.0; the second as 0.3.2. Because the name of the box matches vendor/boxname pattern, you know that the name is resolved through the Atlas.

If you want to update the box used in your project to the latest version, run the $ vagrant box update command. If there is nothing to update, you will see this message:

```
==> default: Checking for updates to 'ubuntu/precise32'
    default: Latest installed version: 12.04.4
    default: Version constraints:
    default: Provider: virtualbox
==> default: Box 'ubuntu/precise32' (v12.04.4) is running the latest version.
```

Otherwise, your box will be updated.

Vagrant allows you to ask for a specific version of the box with the vm.box_version configuration entry, as shown in Listing 10-4.

Listing 10-4. VM Running a Concrete Version of a Box

```
Vagrant.configure(2) do |config|
  config.vm.box = "gajdaw/apache "
  config.vm.box_version = "1.2.3"
end
```

The value you assign to vm.box_version can use multiple constraints separated with commas, as follows:

```
  config.vm.box_version = ">0.1,<0.3"
  config.vm.box_version = "<2.0,>=1.0"
```

When you ask for a version that does not exist, as in Listing 10-4, $ vagrant up fails with this message:

```
The box you're attempting to add has no available version that
matches the constraints you requested. Please double-check your
settings. Also verify that if you specified version constraints,
that the provider you wish to use is available for these constraints.

Box: gajdaw/apache
Address: https://atlas.hashicorp.com/gajdaw/apache
Constraints: 1.2.3
Available versions: 0.1.0, 0.3.1, 0.3.2
```

The final part of the message informs you about the available versions:

```
Available versions: 0.1.0, 0.3.1, 0.3.2
```

If the version you ask for with vm.box_version exists and is not installed on your system, Vagrant will install it. When you have multiple versions of a box, some Vagrant commands may need additional parameters. To remove version 0.3.2 of the gajdaw/apache, box, use $ vagrant box remove gajdaw/apache --box-version 0.3.2.

During my classes and training, I prefer to use the exact box version numbers of my boxes, such as 0.1.2. You can achieve this effect by using this configuration:

```
Vagrant.configure(2) do |config|
  config.vm.box = "apache-v0.3.3"
  config.vm.box_url = "http://boxes.gajdaw.pl/apache/apache-v0.3.3.box"
end
```

You can also use this configuration:

```
Vagrant.configure(2) do |config|
  config.vm.box = "gajdaw/apache"
  config.vm.box_version = "0.3.3"
end
```

If you work this way, you don't have to remind anyone about updates.

Sharing Your Environment

The Atlas service allows you to share the development environment running on your machine with your colleagues. Anyone can gain remote access to your application. The first step of using shares is to register with the Atlas service.

HTTP Shares

The HTTP share allows others to access the web application running within your VM with a web browser. To allow others to visit your app, go to the directory with one of the examples (it might be "Songs for kids" written in AngularJS)[1]:

```
$ cd folder/with/examples
$ cd songs-app-angularjs
```

Boot the application with $ vagrant up and then run $ vagrant login. You will be asked to type your Atlas credentials. When this is done, you can start sharing your application by running $ vagrant share. You will see output containing the following:

```
==> default: Your Vagrant Share is running! Name: exquisite-hare-7519
==> default: URL: http://exquisite-hare-7519.vagrantshare.com
==> default:
```

---

[1]This example was discussed in Chapter 2.

```
==> default: You're sharing your Vagrant machine in "restricted" mode. This
==> default: means that only the ports listed above will be accessible by
==> default: other users (either via the web URL or using 'vagrant connect').
```

Your application is available to anyone through http://exquisite-hare-7519.vagrantshare.com. And because everyone who knows this URL can access your application, you have to be careful not to reveal any sensitive data. Notice that the persons who use the preceding URL do not need to install Vagrant on their machines.

To stop the share, press Ctrl+C on your keyboard; to log out from Atlas, run $ vagrant login -logout.

SSH Shares

Use SSH shares if you want to allow other developers to SSH into your VM. First, go to one of your projects and boot the VM:

```
$ cd folder/with/examples
$ cd songs-app-django
$ vagrant up
```

Log in to your Atlas account with $ vagrant login and start the share with $ vagrant share -ssh. You will be asked to invent a new password that will protect your share:

```
==> default: Generating new SSH key...
    default: Please enter a password to encrypt the key:
    default: Repeat the password to confirm:
```

After typing the new password twice, Vagrant will start the share and print the following message:

```
==> default: Your Vagrant Share is running! Name: fast-boar-5405
==> default: URL: http://fast-boar-5405.vagrantshare.com
==> default:
==> default: You're sharing your Vagrant machine in "restricted" mode. This
==> default: means that only the ports listed above will be accessible by
==> default: other users (either via the web URL or using 'vagrant connect').
==> default:
==> default: You're sharing with SSH access. This means that another user
==> default: simply has to run 'vagrant connect --ssh fast-boar-5405'
==> default: to SSH to your Vagrant machine.
==> default:
==> default: Because you encrypted your SSH private key with a password,
==> default: the other user will be prompted for this password when they
==> default: run 'vagrant connect --ssh'. Please share this password with them
==> default: in some secure way.
```

Your application now has the HTTP share accessible through http://fast-boar-5405.vagrantshare.com. The SSH share that can be used to open SSH session to your guest is $ vagrant connect --ssh fast-boar-5405.

When you run the $ vagrant connect command, Vagrant will ask for the password that you typed and retyped previously.

To stop the SSH share, do the following:

1. Press Ctrl+C.

2. Log out with $ vagrant login -logout.

3. Destroy the VM with $ vagrant destroy -f.

If you want to start the SSH share without running the HTTP share at the same time, use the --disable-http flag: $ vagrant share --ssh --disable-http.

Summary

The details described in this chapter made your journey complete. You began with an introduction that may help you to get your Vagrant-related competencies to a Pro level. Then a number of technical details were discussed that will become useful at some point:

- Using multimachine settings

- Debugging

- Using Vagrant plug-ins

- Using Atlas

- Versioning boxes

- Sharing the development environment

Reading List

For documentation concerning Atlas, go to https://atlas.hashicorp.com/help. Keep in mind that this is a new project that is evolving. The section titled "Current and future integrations" at https://atlas.hashicorp.com should give you a hint about the huge plans that Mr. Mitchell Hashimoto and his company have. It looks like a final solution that will help you to integrate all aspects of your workflow.

To learn more about Vagrant plug-ins (especially about developing them), refer to the documentation at https://docs.vagrantup.com/v2/plugins/index.html.

If you are interested in versioning self-hosted boxes without using Atlas, refer to the "Tutorial about versioning self-hosted boxes" at https://github.com/hollodotme/Helpers/blob/master/Tutorials/vagrant/self-hosted-vagrant-boxes-with-versioning.md.

Test Yourself

1. How do you configure a multimachine development environment?

2. How do you boot and halt different guests when working with multimachine settings?

3. How can you debug the $ vagrant up command?

4. Which Vagrant plug-ins are you familiar with? What is their purpose?

5. Why would you want to use Atlas?

6. What is the concept of Vagrant box versioning?

7. How can you define a required version of a base box within the Vagrantfile?

8. How can you update the box used in a project?

9. How can you install an arbitrary version of a box on your system?

10. How can you uninstall an arbitrary version of a box on your system?

Exercises

1. Create a Vagrantfile for a multimachine development environment. Boot the environment and analyze the messages produced by Vagrant. Finally, destroy all the guest VMs.

2. Register and log in to the Atlas.hashicorp.com service.

3. Generate a box shown in this book (the box discussed in Chapter 9, for example) and publish it on Atlas.

4. Find out which versions of gajdaw/apache are available?

5. Install the gajdaw/apache version 0.1.0 box on your system.

6. Install the gajdaw/apache version 0.3.3 box on your system.

7. Update the gajdaw/apache box to the latest version.

8. Remove all versions of the gajdaw/apache box from your system.

9. Boot one of the examples from Chapter 2 and start the HTTP share for it.

10. Boot one of the examples from Chapter 2 and start both the SSH and HTTP shares for it.

11. Boot one of the examples from Chapter 2 and start only the SSH share for it, not the HTTP share.

Index

Get the eBook for only $5!

Why limit yourself?

Now you can take the weightless companion with you wherever you go and access your content on your PC, phone, tablet, or reader.

Since you've purchased this print book, we're happy to offer you the eBook in all 3 formats for just $5.

Convenient and fully searchable, the PDF version enables you to easily find and copy code—or perform examples by quickly toggling between instructions and applications. The MOBI format is ideal for your Kindle, while the ePUB can be utilized on a variety of mobile devices.

To learn more, go to www.apress.com/companion or contact support@apress.com.

All Apress eBooks are subject to copyright. All rights are reserved by the Publisher, whether the whole or part of the material is concerned, specifically the rights of translation, reprinting, reuse of illustrations, recitation, broadcasting, reproduction on microfilms or in any other physical way, and transmission or information storage and retrieval, electronic adaptation, computer software, or by similar or dissimilar methodology now known or hereafter developed. Exempted from this legal reservation are brief excerpts in connection with reviews or scholarly analysis or material supplied specifically for the purpose of being entered and executed on a computer system, for exclusive use by the purchaser of the work. Duplication of this publication or parts thereof is permitted only under the provisions of the Copyright Law of the Publisher's location, in its current version, and permission for use must always be obtained from Springer. Permissions for use may be obtained through RightsLink at the Copyright Clearance Center. Violations are liable to prosecution under the respective Copyright Law.

Get the eBook for only $5!

Printed in the United States
By Bookmasters